The
Cluster
College

Jerry G. Gaff
and Associates

BAUM

THE CLUSTER COLLEGE

Jossey-Bass Inc., Publishers
615 Montgomery Street · San Francisco · 1970

THE CLUSTER COLLEGE
by *Jerry G. Gaff and Associates*

Jossey-Bass, Inc., Publishers
615 Montgomery Street
San Francisco, California 94111

Library of Congress Catalog Card Number 77–110641

International Standard Book Number ISBN 0–87589–062–8

Manufactured in the United States of America
Composed and printed by York Composition Company, Inc.
Bound by Chas. H. Bohn & Co., Inc.

JACKET DESIGN BY WILLI BAUM, SAN FRANCISCO

FIRST EDITION

Code 7012

The Jossey-Bass Series in Higher Education

General Editors

JOSEPH AXELROD, *San Francisco State College*

MERVIN B. FREEDMAN, *San Francisco State College
and Wright Institute, Berkeley*

Preface

Several convictions form the assumptive base of *The Cluster College*. First, I believe that American colleges and universities need major reshaping. At first blush this statement may sound trivial; of course something must be done about campus problems. However, most solutions to campus unrest that have been proposed are essentially political; the loud right-wing calls to crack down on students or the equally loud left-wing demands to crack the educational-military-industrial complex are more political slogans than educational policies. The required reshaping is primarily educational and has to do with the way colleges and universities honor their primary commitments to educate the youth of the nation. *The Cluster College* examines the educational plight of American institutions of higher learning.

        Second, and more optimistically, I believe efforts are under way to perform the required reconstruction. The most significant innovations are not new facilities or practices but new ideas and concepts; not hardware but head-ware. As Martin (1968, p. 47) has declared,

> The most significant development in higher education over the
> last twenty years is not the introduction of computer-assisted

instruction, nor the expansion of federal funding and federal influence, nor the rise of institutional consortia, nor growth in numbers, facilities, and other things of this sort. The development of greatest consequence has been in the realm of the mind and the spirit and has to do with ideas and personalities.

This book is concerned about some of these new ideas and efforts to translate them into practice.

Third, I believe that many serious problems in undergraduate education emanate from what sociologists term structural matters; that is, they result from the ways institutions organize interactions among students, faculty, and administrators. Much of the literature dealing with the problem of undergraduate education assumes that difficulties arise primarily from individual traits and moral defects. For example, students have been assailed for being rebellious and disrespectful on the one hand or for being conventional and uninvolved on the other; faculty are condemned either for leading students in demonstrations or for having ignored their students in favor of more lucrative research and publication activities; administrators are criticized for being lenient by the establishment press and for being pawns of the establishment by the underground press. While no segment of mankind is immune to perversity, I prefer to assume that most academics are men of good will. However, they are restricted by the very structures under which they work and study. As Clark (1968, p. 5), in the aftermath of the campus disturbances at the country's greatest universities, says, "If we did not know it before, we know it now— good scholars and good students can make a bad educational system. *Everything depends on how they are put together.*" This book examines a variety of new ways to put students, faculty, and administrators together.

A fourth conviction underlying this book is that ideas have consequences. To an educational researcher this conviction constitutes a mandate to study, systematically and empirically, such consequences of an idea system—in this case, of the cluster college concept. To this end I have tried to assemble reports of the best research that has been conducted to date on the outcomes of cluster colleges. The five data-based research reports that constitute the bulk of the second part of the book provide impressive objective evidence of the value of cluster colleges and their assorted structural innovations. These studies and my own experiences have led me to conclude that there is considerable merit to cluster colleges; however, I have also learned that these new ideas and practices are no panacea. Indeed, they create several special problems and unleash unanticipated consequences, some of them antithetical to their consciously stated purposes. This book examines both kinds of consequences.

My interest in the cluster college originated when I joined the faculty of Raymond College as an assistant professor of social science. I assumed that position in the fall of 1964, the school's third year of operation, participated actively in the life of the school, and resigned in 1967 to join the staff at the Center for Research and Development in Higher Education at the University of California, Berkeley. I was attracted to Raymond because I thought this cluster college would provide a supportive environment for the kind of teaching I wanted to do. I thought it would offer me an opportunity to be closer to students, for me to know them and for them to know me more intimately, and to have a greater impact upon their thought processes and personal development than might be the case in other settings. My expectations were more than fulfilled. During my stay at Raymond I was able to encounter several students personally, to listen to their joys and sorrows, to help them cope with their problems, and to observe several young persons grow toward maturity. These experiences caused me to grow intellectually and personally far more than I had originally expected. Upon further reflection and with greater familiarity with other cluster colleges I decided that my experiences, though not unique, might contain some transfer value for other schools and other educators. That is how I came to coordinate the contents of this book.

In trying to conceptualize my experiences with cluster colleges, I have come to develop something of an educational philosophy, especially concerning what loosely has been called "liberal education." Although that philosophy is far from being either final or exhaustive, I wish to expose some fragments so that the reader may perceive when and how they color what follows. I have come to believe that a liberal education should free a student from the necessarily parochial ideas a late adolescent inevitably brings with him to college; that it should liberate his mind by introducing him to new and more profound knowledge about the cultural, social, and physical world surrounding him; that this knowledge should enhance and illuminate his private inner world; and that his encounter with this knowledge should lead to a personal transformation from an immature person with confining attitudes, beliefs, and opinions into a more mature and expansive young man or woman with a personality consonant with his greater understanding. Such an education involves, I believe, both negative and positive aspects; it often means precipitating intellectual, value, and even emotional crises in the lives of students and simultaneously helping them to resolve their crises in ways that are more personally satisfying and socially useful than their earlier patterns. I would like to think that by cultivating the minds and personalities of their students, institutions of higher learning might act as catalysts to constantly renew their society.

But these are enough confessions. The reader has now been adequately warned of my biases, and it is up to him to ascertain when and how they enter into the pages that follow.

Berkeley, California
February, 1970

JERRY G. GAFF

Contents

The Authors

John Bilorusky is research assistant at the Center for Research and Development in Higher Education, University of California, Berkeley

Donald R. Brown is professor of psychology, resident psychologist at the Center for Research on Learning and Teaching, and fellow at the Residential College, University of Michigan

Jerry G. Gaff is assistant research psychologist at the Center for Research and Development in Higher Education, University of California, Berkeley

Paul Heist is professor of higher education and research psychologist at the Center for Research and Development in Higher Education, University of California, Berkeley

H. R. Kells is associate provost at Rutgers, The State University of New Jersey

James A. Kulik is lecturer in psychology and research associate at the Center for Research on Learning and Teaching, University of Michigan

Warren Bryan Martin is coordinator of development at the Center for Research and Development in Higher Education, University of California, Berkeley

Theodore M. Newcomb is professor of psychology and sociology and associate director of the Residential College, University of Michigan

David J. Reimer is research assistant at the Center for Research on Learning and Teaching, University of Michigan

William R. Revelle is research assistant at the Center for Research on Learning and Teaching, University of Michigan

Clifford T. Stewart is director of the Office of Institutional Research, The Claremont Colleges

Judith K. Wilkinson is research assistant at the Center for Research and Development in Higher Education, University of California, Berkeley

Harris Wofford, Jr., is president of the State University of New York College at Old Westbury and president-elect of Bryn Mawr College

The
Cluster
College

Part One

INNOVATIONS

The improvement of undergraduate instruction in the university . . . will require the solution of many sub-problems: how to give adequate recognition to the teaching skill as well as to the research performance of the faculty; how to create a curriculum that serves the needs of the student as well as the research interests of the teacher; how to prepare the generalist as well as the specialist in an age of specialization looking for better generalizations; how to treat the individual student as a unique human being in the mass student body; how to make the university seem smaller even as it grows larger; how to establish a range of contact between faculty and students broader than the one-way route across the lectern or through the television screen; how to raise educational policy again to the forefront of faculty concerns [pp. 118–119].

CLARK KERR
The Uses of the University

Chapter 1

The Cluster College Concept

Jerry G. Gaff

~~~~~~

The idea of a cluster college is quite simple; it is merely a semi-autonomous school on the campus of a larger institution which shares, to a significant extent, facilities and services with the other schools. The idea of a cluster college is not new; it dates back at least to 1249 in England and to the founding of Oxford University (Radcliffe-Maud, 1967). The idea of a university composed of a federation of several closely linked colleges is not new even in the United States; this is the basic organization employed by the Claremont Colleges and the Atlanta University Center since the 1920s. What *is* new is the fact that American educators have rediscovered the collegiate model of university organization

3

and are increasingly using it in an attempt to improve undergraduate education. This rediscovered model represents one of the most promising innovations affecting undergraduate liberal education during the 1960s, a time when fresh ideas and novel practices swept the land.

The cluster college concept offers an organizational plan that can relieve some of the serious problems facing the nation's two common types of institutions of higher learning, the large university and the small liberal arts college. The American university has grown almost unmanageably large and has acquired a number of functions that detract from undergraduate education. The cluster college concept provides a mechanism whereby the monolithic university can decentralize and specialize its operations; that is, it can create a number of undergraduate subcolleges, each of which may feature a closer community, warmer student-faculty relations, and more personalized instruction than is possible under the monolithic structure. The small liberal arts college has always been plagued by scarce resources. For this type of school the cluster college concept offers a plan whereby two or more colleges can form a federation and combine their intellectual, economic, and cultural resources; while each school may retain its essential autonomy, each federated college can benefit from an enriched multi-college environment. In either event the cluster college is an organizational device that is being used to capture the special values of both the small college and the large university without their inherent limitations.

Cluster colleges are a significant innovation not only because they offer a useful model for organizing colleges within a university center, but also because collectively they are adopting new ways to structure students' educational experiences within the college. Often starting with a blank slate, these new schools are critically examining traditional academic customs; not infrequently they reject conventional curricula, grading practices, instructional techniques, and student-faculty relationships. Yet their rejection of the past is not merely a negative act, for the cluster colleges are attempting to forge creative new academic practices as functional alternatives to the traditional ones. They are starting with new assumptions that are consonant with modern times and with current knowledge about the educational process, and they are attempting to build institutions with more vital curricula, improved grading procedures, more individualized instruction, and closer student-faculty relationships.

Considering the entire sweep of colleges and universities throughout the United States, the cluster college movement is a small but growing phenomenon. To date about fifty universities have taken some steps toward a collegiate pattern of organization, and several others are studying the possibility. During 1969 in California alone Johnston College at the University of Redlands, Robert Maynard Hutchins School of Liberal Studies at Sonoma State College, and College Number Five at the University of California at Santa Cruz admitted their charter classes; planning was under way for future cluster colleges at Chabot Junior College, San Jose State College, University of California at San Diego, and the Claremont Colleges—representing all segments of the California system. Schools located literally from Maine to California and Washington to Florida; public and private; Protestant, Catholic, and independent; multiversities, predominantly undergraduate colleges, and junior colleges—schools of every type have been attracted to the cluster college concept. The broad base and accelerating growth rate of cluster colleges suggest that this form of academic organization may become even more widespread in the future.

Although the cluster college concept is not new, it came into prominence in the United States only during the decade of the 1960s. There are a number of reasons why the cluster idea became popular then, but perhaps the most general reason is that conventional practices were assailed on all fronts. Student activists were most vocal critics of academic customs, but quieter critics emerged from the ranks of professors, administrators, trustees, politicians, researchers, and the general public. Faced with increasing evidence that existing practices were breaking down, educators sought new ideas. Indeed, there were so many new ideas in the air and so many new ideas being tried that the 1960s may be regarded as the decade of innovation in higher education. Miller (1967, p. 138) expressed the mood of the nation well:

Innovation is the new "in" word. Conferences meet to advance it, legislation is written to entice it, educational laboratories are conceived to guarantee it, journals propose to spread it, and assemblies are sponsored to understand it. Are we innovative or not? That is the new query of the educational world.

In this ferment the cluster college idea was considered and seized upon as a way to solve the problems of many different kinds of schools. Perhaps these problems and the cluster college solution can best be seen by examining two types of cluster colleges: the subcollege and the federated college.

The primary concern of the university is knowledge, and Kerr (1963, p. 88) reflects the radically changed attitude toward it in contemporary America:

> Knowledge has certainly never in history been so central to the conduct of an entire society. What the railroads did for the second half of the last century and the automobile for the first half of this century may be done for the second half of this century by the knowledge industry: that is, to serve as the focal point for national growth.

No longer is knowledge regarded as a useless luxury for the elite few; rather, it is increasingly viewed as indispensable for the smooth, efficient operation of the technologically complex society, as the precondition for solving pressing social problems ranging from national defense to disease, from poverty to pollution.

The university has responded to the nation's need. It has played a major role in triggering and sustaining the much-touted knowledge expansion, which according to Bell (1966, p. 74) has caused its shock waves to reverberate in four different directions; it has led to "the 'exponential growth' of knowledge, the 'branching' of new fields of knowledge, the rise of a new intellectual technology, and the rapid expansion of research and development as an organized activity of government." The university has helped to transmit this fund of knowledge to more students at every level of higher education and has helped to diffuse it throughout the social fabric more widely than ever before in the country's history. The university, to use Kerr's (1963, p. 87) phraseology "has become a prime instrument of national purpose."

The university has had to make severe internal changes in

order to yield to the national calling, and perhaps they have been summarized best by Bell (1966, p. 88):

> In less than seventy-five years, the modern university, with the graduate school at the center rather than the college (despite its overwhelmingly larger number of students), has come to dominate American higher education. The graduate school arose in response to several needs: the increase in knowledge, the emphasis on scholarship as against teaching, the corollary emphasis on research as a coequal function of the university professor, and the need to train teachers for the burgeoning number of colleges in the country. These needs remain, and, in fact, are multiplied by the proliferation of new fields of knowledge and the extraordinary increase in college attendance in the country.
>
> What is new today, and constitutes the further transformation of the American universities, is the predominant concern with research, the creation of new research institutes, centers, and laboratories, as the major organizational feature of the university, and the role of the federal government in underwriting the costs of this development. The university today, whether private or state, has come to be a quasi-public institution in which the needs of public service, as defined by the role of the research endeavor (whether initiated by the government or by the faculties), becomes paramount in the university.

To Bell's general description of the modern university may be added Kerr's 1963 (pp. 7–8) statement of the size and influence of a single institution (which has grown from seven to nine campuses since then):

> The University of California last year had operating expenditures from all sources of nearly half a billion dollars, with almost another 100 million for construction; a total employment of over 40,000 people, more than IBM and in far greater variety of endeavors; operations in over a hundred locations, counting campuses, experiment stations, agricultural and urban extension centers, and projects abroad involving more than fifty countries; nearly 10,000 courses in its catalogues; some form of contact with nearly every industry, nearly every level of government, nearly every person in its region. Vast amounts of expensive equipment were serviced and maintained. Over 4,000 babies were born in its hospitals. It is the world's largest purveyor of white mice. It will soon have the world's largest primate colony.

It will soon also have 100,000 students—30,000 of them at the graduate level; yet much less than one-third of its expenditures are directly related to teaching.

In their general and specific statements, these two students of American higher education contend that the great gains in knowledge production, graduate training, and service to the society have been correlated with the decline of the college and the relative neglect of teaching. As research develops, teaching lags; as professors spend more time consulting with government and business, they have less time to spend consulting with students; as teachers devote more time and energy to graduate education, they have less to devote to undergraduate education. In short, the transformation of the university into an instrument of national purpose has been made in part at the expense of undergraduate liberal arts education. And this at a time when record numbers of undergraduates populate nearly every university in the country.

Though the problem of providing a vital undergraduate liberal education is serious, it is a limited one considering the total functioning of the university. The basic question is this: How is it possible to have a university which is dedicated to serving society by creating new knowledge, by diffusing knowledge widely, by applying knowledge to the solution of social problems, and *still* provide an effective liberal education?

The problem is aggravated by the increased numbers of students who seek a college education. During recent years the system of higher education has greatly expanded. United States Office of Education surveys indicate that the total college student population leaped from 3,610,007 in 1960–61 to 7,571,636 in 1968–69, more than doubling the enrollment during the first eight years of the decade. This numerical growth is found at every level of higher education, junior colleges, four-year schools, and graduate centers. Much of this increase in enrollment can be attributed to the important demographic fact that the post-World War II baby boom has hit the campuses; part of it also reflects an increase in the proportion of high school graduates who seek some college education. The total of first-time college enrollments in fall 1960 represented 50 per cent of all high school graduates that spring; the comparable figure for 1968 was 54 per cent (ACE, 1969).

This increased enrollment has been accommodated in two ways. First, several new colleges have been constructed. The number of colleges and universities identified by the Office of Education surveys increased from 2,028 to 2,483 during an eight-year period, a jump of 22 per cent. While their number is impressive, the addition of new institutions has not been sufficient to handle the deluge of students. Enrollment has increased far more rapidly than the rate at which new colleges have been constructed; this fact indicates that higher education has responded to the numerical growth of students primarily by enlarging existing institutions. The average number of students enrolled in an institution of higher learning increased from 1,828 in 1960 to 3,049 in 1968. The number of institutions enrolling over 30,000 students increased from four to twenty-five in a decade (Grant, 1969). In the wake of this rapid expansion, most students are attending colleges that are truly massive organizations; one observer noted with scorn that this growth has transformed most public colleges and universities into "large state preserves."

In considering how to provide effective liberal education to larger numbers of students in today's large and complex universities, some schools have turned to the cluster college concept. They have rediscovered the college structure of the venerable Oxford and Cambridge Universities. These British universities are composed of many colleges, each one having corporate independence, its own faculty, and its special academic program. Because they are located on the same campus, the colleges of each university are functionally interdependent; that is, they cooperate and share their resources to a considerable extent. Several American schools have adopted a modification of this structure to provide more institutional support for undergraduate education. Some universities that have maintained but a single large liberal arts college have established one or more small semiautonomous cluster colleges on their periphery. Some newer universities plan to populate the entire campus with clusters of undergraduate colleges. But unlike their British counterparts, these small, usually liberal arts colleges are not legal entities. They are subcolleges, semiautonomous structural subunits of the larger university whole. Like the colleges of the Oxford-Cambridge system, the colleges of the cluster cooperate a great deal and share their facilities and services.

Variously called residential colleges, living-learning centers, inner colleges, or satellite colleges, subcolleges are said to offer a number of advantages over contemporary universities. Because the cluster college is by definition small, it can create a closer community, offer more personalized instruction, and foster warmer student-faculty relations than can a large centralized university. The problem of impersonality may not be so much a function of the absolute size of universities as of the way that size is organized; if the large university can be structured so that students are placed within a smaller group, they may feel the environment is more supportive, experience less alienation, and become more involved in their education. Educators in college after college have come to the conclusion that they must organize the campus so that it will seem smaller as it grows larger. The subcollege is one way some schools have responded to this challenge.

A second advantage of the collegiate pattern is its diversity; a university composed of separate undergraduate colleges each with a different program offers the structured diversity and the alternative programs which are consonant with the wide range of individual differences of an ever-increasing number of students. McConnell and Heist (1962) have documented that students vary strikingly on a number of intellectual and personality characteristics between colleges, and the diversity of students within a single large university has been stressed by Trow (1966). A university featuring a variety of subcolleges each with a different philosophy and program can offer a greater variety of educational experiences than can a single college with all students in the same college, all subject to the same admission requirements, academic requirements, and social regulations. Such an institution, it is argued, serves the needs of a diverse student body better than the more monolithic structure of the conventional university.

A third advantage frequently cited as a reason for developing a cluster college is that the new school may experiment with new philosophies or methods of education. Given the present climate of innovation and change throughout the United States, the cluster college offers a mechanism whereby experimentation can be carried out on a limited scale, which can be afforded by most universities.

Furthermore, Hatch (1960) has argued that the problems facing higher education are so massive that piecemeal reform, such as modifying the grading system here and tinkering with the curriculum there, is not sufficient to their magnitude; radical reform of the basic structures is required. A university can effect this kind of holistic reform by establishing a semiautonomous college within the larger university. There are several pragmatic advantages to instigating innovation by placing a subcollege outside the conventional structure. Most obvious is the relative ease of effecting change when the traditional restraints and inertia of an established order are removed. Also, the values of quality traditional programs within the larger unit need not be sacrificed for some untried promises of a revised system. The subcollege scheme allows the regular programs to persist even while radical experimentation is carried on at the periphery of the institution.

As a by-product of experimentation in a structurally separate unit, the rest of the university may be provoked into making educational reforms. Some innovators believe that just as the university has served as the critical conscience of the society, so may the cluster college serve as the critical conscience of the university as it becomes an "instrument of national purpose." Not only can the subcollege serve as a reminder of the institution's commitment to liberal arts undergraduate education, but it can try out some specific innovations which may be useful in other parts of the university. Because it permits experimenting with new philosophies and educational practices in a modest way, a peripheral unit is sometimes used as a proving ground for new ideas. In this sense the subcollege represents the risk capital of the university, a place where educators may be boldly innovative, where successful innovations may be transferred to other sections of the institution, and where even total failure could cause little damage to the university.

Finally, the subcollege can share the facilities and the services of that larger unit. This arrangement makes it possible for a cluster college to be established at a substantial savings when compared to the costs of creating a comparable totally independent college. At the same time, the subcollege can enjoy the rich intellectual and cultural resources of the university, resources that simply are not available to even the best small independent colleges.

Perhaps the subcollege form of cluster college could be understood better if it were distinguished from some other efforts to decentralize a large center of learning. A cluster college is not to be confused with an academic department or a school (for example, a school of engineering) within the conventionally structured university, although these are both ways of decentralizing the institution. Unlike the department, which has a limited responsibility for advancing and communicating knowledge within a particular field of investigation, the subcollege has the larger responsibility of providing for the entire education of its students. And contrasted with a school of engineering, for example, which is an integral part of the university, the subcollege enjoys greater autonomy; it has its own institutional identity and program autonomy, as symbolized by its own name and as signified by its own total educational program, including its own curriculum, faculty, and possibly residence halls. If the subcollege is added to a previously existing enterprise, it may gain autonomy by being placed outside the ongoing university hierarchy replete with deans, departmental chairmen, and faculty committees; often it is directly responsible to a few of the highest ranking university administrators. This arrangement frees it from the restraints of the established power structure, allows it to develop its own and perhaps innovative program, and protects those innovations from the usual academic establishment and its vested conventional interests.

As the subcollege must be differentiated from the traditional department or school, so must it be distinguished from several other interesting and imaginative contemporary attempts to decentralize the large university, to make it more responsive to the educational needs of undergraduates. One of these innovative efforts is a residential clustering program, examples of which can be seen in the "living-and-learning" dormitories at Michigan State University, the "college-within-the-college" development at the University of Kansas, the "arts experiment" at Ohio State University, the "Foster project" at Indiana University, the "clustering program" at Florida State University, the "house plan" at Cypress Junior College, and the "college plan" at the State University of New York at Stony Brook. Taking their cue from the Harvard "house plan" (Jencks and Riesman, 1962), these are innovations that attempt primarily to restructure the non-classroom environments of students. More specifically, they attempt to provide a haven from the impersonality of the larger university, to structure opportunities for meaningful peer-group interaction, and to channel the peer-group influence toward academic values. The programs try to achieve these purposes in a number of ways, such as, by housing students together in relatively small living units, by having a few faculty live in the dormitories, by locating some faculty offices within the living units, and by holding a few classes, especially the introductory classes commonly offered to freshmen and sophomores, in small sections within the living units. However useful these innovations may be, they are conceptually different from the subcollege: none of them have curricular autonomy, a separate faculty, or a fully developed academic program. While they cannot be considered to be colleges at all, in the strict sense of the term, these programs remain interesting innovations designed to enhance the existing undergraduate program through restructured living group arrangements.

Another type of decentralization effort has emerged in recent years, a special lower division academic program within universities. Relying on the historic model of Alexander Meiklejohn's Experimental College at the University of Wisconsin, experimental colleges have been established at such places as the University of California, Berkeley, and at San Jose State College. At Berkeley (Tussman, 1969), for example, 150 students, six faculty, and five graduate teaching assistants focus their studies on a limited number of key intellectual issues in the history of Western thought; they examine these issues from several disciplinary vantage points in a few significant periods of history, such as ancient Greece, seventeenth-century England, and contemporary America. Operating without the usual course structure, without the conventional A–F grading system, and within a closely knit group, students may satisfy their "distribution" requirements in this program and go on to upper division work to pursue an academic major elsewhere in the university. While this two-year arrangement is a useful innovation and provides a significantly different educational experience for students, the Experimental College is not, strictly speaking, a college at all. It does not provide a full four-year educational program, although it is a different way to structure lower division undergraduate education, a novel way to satisfy some of the general education requirements of the College of Letters and Science.

While the clustering program and the lower division program are aimed at correcting deficiencies in the large university by decentralizing and by regrouping segments of academia, while each represents promising innovations, and while each in its own way attempts to achieve many of the same purposes as the subcollege, these programs are conceptually different from the cluster college. Accordingly, they lie outside the main focus of the present work.

While all subcolleges attempt to foster the atmosphere of the small college within the context of a large school, no two are exactly alike. Some of the most important organizational variations which have been adopted by the clustering universities are examined in the following pages. The institutions listed in Table 1 are all of those that could be identified as operating subcolleges in 1969; they are the basis for the following discussion of the ways universities have accommodated subcolleges.

Universities differ in terms of the size of their subcolleges. Although cluster colleges are by definition small, *small* is a relative term. At Rutgers a "small" school has 3,500 students, at Michigan State 1,200, at Fordham 100. Exactly how planners decided upon the specific size of schools and what educational rationale underlies these decisions is not easy to determine. Perhaps the most cogent reasoning behind the determination of a particular size is provided by McHenry (1964, p. 32), Chancellor of the University of California, Santa Cruz. Referring to the work of Theodore Newcomb, he wrote:

> Mr. Newcomb's discussion of size and homogeneity is especially apt. He considers that Oxford, Cambridge, Harvard and Yale, and several small colleges, have succeeded in arousing effective group loyalties through groupings of a few hundred. He urges that formal membership be kept moderate in size and homogeneous, but large enough for a range of selectivity for companion choosing. One test he suggests is that most students should be able to recognize one another. He says that 300 to 400 is a reasonable guess as to optimal size.

Such a rationale seems to underlie the determination of

the approximate size of each subcollege. However, there are vary-
ing estimates among reasonable men as to how strong "effective
group loyalties" should be to foster optimum learning and how
many peers a student needs for a reasonable "range of selectivity"
in choosing companions. An educator whose experience is primarily
in a university with 20,000 students may in all good conscience
assign different numbers to these guidelines than will one whose
experience is in a college of 2,000.

Decisions within universities are made not only on the basis
of educational rationale but also within certain practical constraints.
The size of the subcolleges is determined in part by the social resources available to the institution and the proportion of these
resources it is willing to commit to the cluster college. Small subcollege size in some instances may reflect the poverty or timidity of
the university, as well as its commitment to the educational benefits
of small size.

The number of subcolleges established on different campuses shows considerable variation. Several schools have spawned
but a single cluster college, while other institutions plan to have a
campus made up wholly of them. The number of colleges—
twenty—projected at Santa Cruz is the largest number yet planned
at any American university. Here again it is difficult to ascertain
why any given number of subcolleges has been chosen. There
appear to be two general kinds of rationales. Some schools, like
Wayne State or Hofstra, seem to conceive of the subcollege as a
kind of experimental school (or perhaps more accurately as a
demonstration project) in which innovations are implemented in
a modest fashion on the periphery of the existing school. The subcollege is seen by other schools, such as Santa Cruz and San
Diego, as a way to structure the entire university so as to provide
program diversity for groups of students with quite different interests. It seems likely that the almost universal lack of an articulated rationale underlying the choice of the number of colleges indicates that such decisions may have been made largely on the
basis of extra-educational factors.

There is variation in the location of subcolleges within the
administrative structure of the university. Most subcolleges are
typically headed by a provost or dean who is directly responsible

Table 1

SAMPLE OF COLLEGES AND UNIVERSITIES WITH SUBCOLLEGES

		Subcollege
		Approximate ceiling
	Date of	*population*
Institution	*establishment*	*enrollment*
1. Wayne State University		
Monteith College	1959	1200
2. Wesleyan University		
College of Social Studies	1960	100
College of Letters	1960	100
3. University of the Pacific		
Raymond College	1962	250
Elbert Covell College	1963	250
Callison College	1967	250
4. University of California		
Santa Cruz		
Cowell College	1965	600
Stevenson College	1966	600
Crown College	1967	600
Merrill College	1968	600
College Number Five	1969	600
5. Goddard College		
Greatwood		200
Northwood	1965	200
6. Hofstra University		
New College	1965	150
7. Michigan State University		
Justin Morrill College	1965	1200
Lyman Briggs College	1967	1200
James Madison College	1967	1200
8. Nasson College		
New Division[a]	1965	
9. Oakland University		
Charter College	1965	350
New College	1967	350
Allport College	1969	350
10. University of California San Diego		
Revelle College	1958	2500
Muir College	1967	1500

[a] Reassimilated into Nasson College in 1969.

Table 1 (*Cont'd*)

SAMPLE OF COLLEGES AND UNIVERSITIES WITH SUBCOLLEGES

11. Fordham University		
Bensalem College	1967	100
12. University of Michigan		
The Residential College	1967	1200
13. Western Washington State College		
Fairhaven College	1967	600
14. City University of New York,		
Kingsborough Community College		
Brighton	1968	750
Darwin	1968	750
15. Rutgers - The State University of		
New Jersey		
Livingston College	1968	3500
16. Colby College		
Program in Human Development	1969	400
Program in Intensive Studies in		
Western Civilization	1969	400
Program in Bilingual and		
Bi-cultural Studies	1969	400
17. Grand Valley State College		
Thomas Jefferson College	1969	600
18. University of Nebraska		
Centennial Education Program	1969	600
19. State University of New York,		
College at Old Westbury		
Urban Studies College	1969	500
Disciplines College	1969	500
General Program	1969	500
20. Redlands University		
Johnston College	1969	600
21. St. Edwards University		
Holy Cross College	1967	
Maryhill College	1967	
22. St. Olaf College		
The Paracollege	1969	500
23. Sonoma State College		
Hutchins School of Liberal		
Studies	1969	750
24. University of Vermont		
Experimental Program	1969	400

to the academic dean of the university. Yet clustering universities have created an essential tension between the interests of the college and the interests of the university. In schools where subcolleges have been added to existing programs, some subcolleges may be said to be placed "outside" the existing structure and others "inside" it. In the former pattern the new school is allowed considerable freedom to design an academic program, to devise a social program, to establish courses, and to set graduation requirements. Subcolleges of this type, exemplified by those at St. Olaf and Pacific, may proceed fairly independently of established university traditions, the academic senate and its committees, the dean of students office, and other university powers. This arrangement frees the new school from the constraints of the past and provides it with autonomy to fashion new ways in education, ways that might not be sanctioned by the rest of the university.

A somewhat different pattern is found in subcolleges that are placed "inside" the existing structure of the university. In these schools, such as the ones at Michigan State and Michigan, the subcollege may be unable to deviate from the all-university regulations concerning the admission requirements or graduation requirements, must clear courses through the faculty curriculum committee, must abide by university-wide social regulations, must borrow faculty from the all-university departments. While such schools do have freedom in devising their internal programs, they have more constraints placed upon them at the outset, constraints which impose limits upon their range of choice.

In new universities intended to be composed wholly of subcolleges, a different pattern has developed. There the subcollege is placed in essential tension with university-wide academic departments to which all faculty belong. Here the colleges have the responsibility for providing for the total education of their students, and the departments have the responsibility of advancing and teaching knowledge within their disciplines. These competing powers have joint responsibility for formulating the academic program for the university.

Universities vary in terms of the proportion of work a student can do in one of their subcolleges. Most subcolleges provide at least half of the courses a student takes, and all allow students to take some work in other colleges. But there is considerable variation in terms of the relative proportion of work students normally take within their college.

In some universities which have added subcolleges, Western Washington, for example, students are expected to obtain a major in an academic discipline by taking most of their specialization work on the main campus. In other places, students take most of their work within their subcollege because it does not require a major, because it offers advanced work in an area of their major concentration, or because it is large enough to offer a fairly wide range of advanced courses itself.

The resources, facilities, and services of the entire university are available to the subcollege, but there is variation in patterns of cooperation. Four general areas of cooperation are academic, social, student personnel services, and administrative and financial services.

In the academic realm one of the most obvious areas of sharing involves course offerings. The university as a whole offers a greater number of specialized courses in a wider variety of fields than does any single subcollege. Accordingly, there are typically provisions for students at one college to take courses, especially at advanced levels, given by another; some subcolleges even expect students to take most of their specialized work outside their own college.

Faculty resources also are shared among the colleges. Within a subcollege there are likely to be only a few persons with any one academic specialization, but because they are part of a larger university, faculty have access to colleagues with similar specialties. By associating with these like-minded colleagues, the faculty of a subcollege may gain intellectual stimulation, keep up with developments within their field of specialization, and share research interests or efforts. Three different techniques have emerged to achieve these advantages. At some universities that have grafted subcolleges onto existing schools, faculty members are hired by the subcollege, perform most of their work within the context of that school, and make any contact they may desire to make with their colleagues in other schools informally; Hofstra and Pacific have staffed their subcolleges primarily in this fashion. In other older universities, Michigan and Michigan State, for example, the academic departments "lend" faculty to the subcollege for a short period of time; at the end of that time, usually three years, faculty are expected to return to the departments whence they came. Yet another approach has been used largely at new universities which are to be composed entirely of subcolleges. At San Diego and Santa Cruz, for instance, each faculty member has a dual appointment in one of the colleges and in one of the university-wide academic departments; he is hired and promoted upon recommendation of both the provost of the college and the chairman of the academic discipline. He is responsible to both administrators, and he lives with this dual loyalty as long as he remains at the institution. Of course, whatever arrangement is adopted has serious consequences for the autonomy of the subcollege and the extent to which faculty assign their primary loyalty to the college.

Several academic facilities are usually shared. Two examples may illustrate. The central library is regarded as a common university resource, an arrangement which allows the subcollege to have access to a large collection of books and periodicals. A number of different patterns of placing the library holdings throughout the campus are emerging. Often a subcollege will supplement this central library with a small general library for the use of its undergraduate students. In addition, sophisticated and expensive modern laboratory facilities are shared among faculty and students at several colleges. Occasionally each subcollege will have its own rather simple laboratory for use with lower-level teaching but use the more specialized equipment for advanced instruction and research.

A second area of cooperation is in the financial and administrative realm. Cooperation here is an economy not only in terms of dollars but also in terms of time. If the college is freed from the burden of providing supportive administration, such as running a business office, engaging in development activities, conducting public relations, doing record-keeping, providing maintenance services, effecting security, and recruiting students, its personnel can devote a greater portion of their time directly to the task of educating its students. While most subcolleges rely on the central administration to conduct most of these supportive services, they usually find it necessary to maintain close ties with the central offices; a liaison person, usually an administrator of the college, often attempts to bridge these gaps.

A third general area of sharing is social and extracurricular activities. Students at subcolleges are typically allowed to participate in the social and extracurricular activities available on the university campus. Here again the subcollege has access to a more varied program than it could mount on its own.

A fourth area of cooperation is what may be called student personnel services, that is, health services, psychological and vocational counseling, dormitory supervision, student discipline, financial aid, and similar matters. While most of these services are usually centralized, some subcolleges, especially those that want to develop a distinctive or innovative social as well as academic style, may administer their own dormitory and social program.

Universities vary in terms of the major focus and concern of their subcolleges. While subcolleges typically offer a general liberal arts education, a school may attempt to create its own distinctive tone or orientation which colors the whole academic and social program. The orientations thus far adopted by the schools are generally of two sorts. First are those emphasizing an entire academic division, for example, the humanities at Justin Morrill, social sciences at James Madison, and natural sciences at Lyman Briggs. The emphasis upon one of these three classical divisions of knowledge serves to indicate its commitment to undergraduate education appropriate to that area and reflects its concern for the interrelatedness of knowledge within that division. A second kind of orientation reflects a concern for an important social problem; the most frequently adopted foci are urban problems examined by the Urban Studies College at Old Westbury and international problems attacked by Callison. Typically a school offers interdisciplinary courses within its major focus, encourages students to pursue their interests in these areas through independent study, or provides some related off-campus field experience which supplements students' more conventional academic work.

What, one may ask, does a university do for an encore? What kind of orientations do subcolleges have after they use up the three major divisions of knowledge and the more pressing or fashionable social problems? Since Santa Cruz has projected nine colleges, it may provide an answer to this question. For this purpose some rather simplistic tags indicate the orientation planned for each school: humanities; social sciences; natural sciences; international relations; performing arts; the historical and social context of modern physical sciences; the city; historical inquiry and classical thought; and man's natural environment. The overarching concern of each college is a blend of the concerns of the various academic departments and several contemporary social problems. Of course, the possible combinations and permutations of the disciplines and social problems are numerous; apparently the human imagination is not at a loss for thinking of new directions for new colleges, directions which are consonant with both academic tradition and social necessity.

In this regard Spurr (1968, p. 18) has noted:

> One real contribution of the subcollege concept has been that it offers the possibility of making available multiple curriculums in the liberal arts side by side. If one is thought to be too restrictive and another too permissive, a third can be developed in parallel so that time and usage can point to an improved vision.

Spurr's comments highlight an important fact—the clustering universities have asked a different question than the more conventional ones. Rather than asking about *the* liberal arts curriculum, the clustering institutions are asking about *alternative* liberal arts curricula. In asking this new question, these schools are implicitly rejecting the notion that there is a single best plan for all students; rather, they assume that the diversity of students requires a diversity in curricula. By developing subcolleges with a number of different foci, they are attempting to bend the institutional structures to the needs of the students; they are using their resources to enlarge the range of choice available to the undergraduate.

These alternative organizational provisions represent different ways in which universities have attempted to incorporate subcolleges within their structures. It may be expected that these different arrangements will produce quite different kinds of subcolleges and learning environments. Like universities, small colleges have problems that can be met by the cluster concept.

One might want to quibble with Putnam (1968, p. 41) concerning the following diagnosis of "the basic problem," or even with the assumption that there is a single fundamental problem facing American higher education, but he cannot sidestep the larger issue raised:

> The basic problem in American higher education today is its fractionation into some 2,000 diverse collegiate institutions varying in size from minicollege to multiversity, in quality from superficial to superlative, in purpose from bibliolatry to universality. Each prides itself on its identity, independence, and individuality.

The fractionation described in this excerpt is the outcome of a long history of a lack of national policy, or perhaps more accurately, a laissez-faire policy, toward higher education. This approach was the natural one for a society with a capitalistic economy. The results of this hands-off policy toward higher education have paralleled those of a free economy. Colleges and universities have grown wherever and whenever a religious body, legislature, community, or benefactor took a fancy to plant them. Schools have competed openly for faculty, students, and the support of philanthropists—practices indicative of the struggle of the marketplace. Rugged individualism, America's response to the challenges of the frontier, has become a fundamental stance of the colleges and universities which have been scattered through the countryside. In higher education, as in business, when competition is unregulated, the strong get stronger and the weak get weaker. Accordingly, this system has produced its own robber barons as well as its struggling small businessmen, its great universities and elite colleges as well as pockets of collegiate poverty.

While this system may have been adequate for an earlier era, it is increasingly viewed as an anachronism. Pattillo and Mackenzie (1965, p. 56), in a report of research on institutions affiliated with religious bodies, decry the lack of cooperation existing even within similar religious denominations:

> No one can justify the operation of four Presbyterian colleges in Iowa, three Methodist colleges in Indiana, five United Presbyterian institutions in Missouri, nine Methodist colleges in North

Carolina '(including two brand new ones), and three Roman
Catholic colleges for women in the city of Milwaukee.

Unregulated competition is a waste of the country's resources, and
it is not even to the self-interest of individual institutions, save for
the most prestigious. Today pressures are mounting for colleges
and universities to coordinate their efforts, to substitute cooperation for competition, and to place their individualism within a
broader context of interdependence.

While these pressures emanate from several sources, perhaps the two most significant are the increased importance of
higher education to the nation and the increased cost of providing
quality education. Because they provide the educated citizenry
necessary to operate our complex society, colleges and universities
are coming to be seen as social assets too valuable to be buffeted
about by the winds of chance; they are increasingly recognized as
important intellectual resources which must be used wisely for the
common good. The lack of coordination of efforts, the duplication
of services, the lack of full utilization of intellectual talent, and
the existence of weak and or even impotent institutions become
serious problems not only to the institutions directly involved but
also to the whole of the society.

A second general force that challenges institutional isola-
tionism is the economic squeeze that faces even the most affluent
schools. As colleges and universities have come to play a larger
part in the conduct of national life, their stock has risen, and they
are suffering from an educational inflation. As knowledge has increased, schools have added specialized courses; as faculty members
have become more sought after, their salaries have increased; as
schools have expanded their academic offerings, the cost of supporting services and facilities has also risen. At the same time, the
"productivity" of professors seems not to have shown any significant increase; a faculty member can still educate about the same
number of students now that he could years ago. Few schools can
afford the luxury of duplication and lack of coordination at today's
prices.

While the pressures of academic expansion and financial
cost are felt by all institutions, they weigh most heavily upon the

small colleges. McCoy (1968, p. 39) has summed up the plight of
the small college:

> The liberal arts college, while enjoying the sense of community
> due to the relative smallness in size, must reach for vital re-
> sources and for scope in curriculum through cooperation with
> other colleges, universities, government, and other agencies.
> Economic facts and human limitations dictate that a college
> community of 1,000 to 2,500 students can afford to offer only a
> limited number of majors, specialized facilities, and expert per-
> sonnel.

Largely private, often with ties to religious bodies, occasionally
serving a special clientele, and typically having only a local sphere
of influence, small colleges as a group are more vulnerable to these
academic demands and economic pressures than are larger schools.

The number of schools that fall into this category is impressive. The Office of Education (Grant, 1969) reported that in
1968 there were a total of 1166 colleges which enrolled fewer than
1,000 students. Pattillo and Mackenzie (1965) studied 817 institutions affiliated with religious bodies in 1962–63 and reported
that they had an average of only 1,098 students each. In 1966,
the 1,446 private institutions enrolled 33 per cent of all students
but had an average enrollment of 1,374 per institution. A report
(Howard, 1967) of 100 predominantly Negro institutions showed
that in 1965 they had a combined enrollment of 125,092, or 60
per cent of all Negro students in the United States; they had an
average student body of 1,250. Although some small colleges
possess greater educational resources than some large ones, and
while many denominational, private, or Negro schools are neither
small, academically impoverished, nor financially weak, McCoy's
contention about the inherent limitations of small colleges applies
in the main to these types of schools.

In the face of the restriction of academic and economic resources, McCoy (1968, p. 40) has proclaimed the old era of institutional independence, individualism, and competition dead:
"Given the task before us, a sense of self-sufficiency is as obsolete
for the isolated college as it is, and always has been, for the solitary
individual." And a new era—one which accepts the fact of institutional interdependence, affirms the values of cooperation, and

recognizes the need for coordination in higher education—has been celebrated by Johnson (1968, p. 87):

> Interinstitutional cooperation is here to stay and grow, despite its inherent limitations. When to use it, where to channel it, what machinery to run it, and how to balance its independence and accountability will be the tests of educational statesmanship in the future.

It is significant that hundreds of colleges have seized the initiative and sought out advantages offered by the new age of interdependence. Moore's (1967) survey of interinstitutional cooperation uncovered 1,131 different colleges and universities which have entered into 1,017 voluntary cooperative arrangements with other institutions, arrangements designed to strengthen all parties.

One particular kind of consortium, an extreme form of cooperation, is a federation of colleges. A federation is a close association of two or more colleges which are geographically contiguous and which share, to a significant extent, their educational resources. While each college of the cluster maintains its corporate independence, the several schools are educationally interdependent. Such a federation is conceptually different from other forms of consortium; it characteristically is wider in scope, serves more functions, is assisted by closer geographical ties, and is united by a tighter bond than other consortia. By establishing a federation, the schools may create an institution that is larger, more diverse, and richer in resources than any of the individual colleges. In this way the cluster college concept offers promise for alleviating some of the small college's most serious problems.

Applying the Oxford-Cambridge model of the collegiate university, the Claremont Colleges were the first to adopt this form of organization in the United States. James Blaisdell, then president of Pomona College, engineered the first cluster college effort in the United States in 1925. Claremont Colleges have used a federation as a structural mechanism with which to expand their educational range and at the same time effect operating economies. Specifically, by combining their intellectual resources the several colleges offer a broader curriculum, have more and more varied intellectual expertise, attract larger numbers and different types of students, and generate more social and intellectual stimulation through such diversity than any single school could hope to do. In addition, the federation allows the larger institution to become more than an exclusively teaching-oriented group of colleges; it provides an organizational base for some faculty to secure support for their research, and it allows the group to mount a modest but quite respectable graduate program. Central services can be shared, thus eliminating the inefficient practice of maintaining separate business offices, admissions offices, and other supporting services. Academic savings can also be achieved at the same time quality is improved because costly advanced courses can serve a greater number of students, and the central library can grow while avoiding needless duplication of volumes.

If the academic demands and economic pressures on colleges are much greater now than they were in the 1920s, one might reason that cluster college federations would have been adopted with increasing frequency during subsequent years. However, such is not the case. Up to 1967 there was only one other federation of colleges—the Atlanta University Center of Higher Education, established in 1929. Despite the rapid growth of consortia, only a few schools have yet been willing to take steps to effect such close ties as federation would require. Their reluctance is understandable, for the barriers to close cooperation are many and great. Putnam (1968, p. 41) has summarized the main reasons as "geography, rivalry, inertia, preoccupation, mission, system of control, and uncertainty of purpose or outcome." These largely practical objections have doubtless been major reasons why schools have not cooperated in the past. Moore's (1967, p. 306) study of interinstitutional cooperation found that about 500 schools totally rejected the idea of cooperation, and according to the author, "generally speaking, these were the institutions which needed cooperation the most."

If there have been few federations formed, a number of colleges and universities such as Carnegie-Mellon and Case Western Reserve Universities have merged their facilities and resources. A merger combines two or more existing schools into one; it has one board of trustees, one administration, one faculty, and one set of academic structures. In a merger each school loses its individual identity and becomes a part of the new unit, although the identity of each school may be retained in the new name. A merger may be quite valuable, but it is outside the focus of this work. Suffice it to say that the cluster concept offers an alternative to a merger. A cluster college federation can effect the economies and increase academic resources of the member schools while allowing each to retain its earlier identity and distinctive institutional features.

Cluster college federations have not been popular in the last four decades, but there is some evidence that there is new interest in that organizational form. For example, Kirkland College opened its doors in 1968 adjacent to Hamilton College, and they form the nucleus of what is expected to become a series of colleges on the same site in Clinton, New York. Although not a true cluster because of the distance between them, Amherst, Mount Holyoke, Smith and the University of Massachusetts have effected a close working relationship and founded Hampshire College in their midst in 1969. A number of other schools are actively planning for future federations. While college federations never have been popular in the United States, these few examples suggest that the cluster college concept may be increasingly used as a practical educational structure which allows primarily small colleges to keep abreast of the knowledge expansion, to honor the growing social demand for higher quality and more diverse education, and to effect much-needed economies.

It may be significant that of all these college federations only the Atlanta University Center was formed from existing schools and required some geographical movement to effect the union. All others have made federations by starting whole new colleges contiguous to existing schools. As the subcollege has been used largely as a mechanism for large universities to accommodate growth, so the college federation has been used by small colleges primarily as a way to grow larger while retaining the values associated with small size.

There are many alternative routes to federation and to the advantages it holds; the following pages describe some of the basic variations among three cluster college federations. Those federations and the member schools are contained in Table 2.

Various numbers of colleges can be members of a cluster college federation. These federations vary from two to five under-

Table 2

SAMPLE OF FEDERATED COLLEGES AND UNIVERSITIES

Institution	Date of establishment
1. Claremont Colleges	
Pomona College	1887
Claremont Graduate School and University Center	1925
Scripps College	1926
Claremont Men's College	1946
Harvey Mudd College	1955
Pitzer College	1963
2. Atlanta University Center of Higher Education	
Atlanta University	1929[a]
Morehouse College	1929[a]
Spelman College	1929[a]
Morris Brown College	1932[a]
Clark College	1941[a]
Interdenominational Theological Center	1958
3. Hamilton College	1793
Kirkland College	1968

[a] Date when cooperation began.

graduate colleges. The coordinate college pattern in which two schools in geographical proximity form a close alliance is an old form of cooperation; the "marriages" between Harvard and Radcliffe, Columbia and Barnard, Hobart and William Smith are historical examples. Such institutional liaisons typically have been confined to male and female schools, as though it would constitute a public indiscretion to make any other match. The Claremont Colleges and the Atlanta University Center provide historical examples, and the only current examples, of the multiple college pattern. Each of these complexes has five undergraduate colleges and one graduate school. There is no theoretical limit as to the number of colleges which might compose a federation; the upper limit would probably be determined by the economic principle of diminishing returns, that is, whenever the addition of another unit promises to detract more than it would add to the collective.

There is some variation in the size of the federation and

size of each federated college. Usually the individual schools enroll from 500 to 1,200 students, and the size of the entire federation is not expected to exceed that of a small university, say 5,000 students. Since the member schools typically are committed to the values of the small college, they seek to preserve themselves from the two threats of isolation and large size. The particular size of both individual colleges and entire federations seems to be determined by what the several schools believe to be the appropriate balance between the size necessary to maintain a varied program and the size which is likely to destroy the community of the small college. Of course, a number of practical considerations enter into the decision as well, perhaps the most important being the realistic opportunities to form alliances with other schools or the sufficient resources to found a new college in the group.

The federations vary in terms of the kind and extent of sharing that occurs among the several schools. Generally, all the areas of cooperation that have been described for the subcollege may be found in the federated college, along with two additional areas of sharing. First, two or more colleges may combine forces to offer a modest graduate program. By careful and coordinated selection of faculty, by searching out special needs that the larger and more conventional graduate schools have been unwilling to satisfy, and by aggressively seeking external funds for these specific purposes, federated colleges may establish a distinctive graduate program of limited proportions. Second, the federation may provide faculty scholars with an organizational base to support some of their own research. In these ways, the functions of predominantly teaching-oriented colleges can be expanded, and faculty may be encouraged to engage in some of the activities of their counterparts in the larger universities. Some believe that involvement of a portion of the faculty in research and graduate teaching might enhance the quality of instruction in the predominantly undergraduate colleges of the federation.

There are a number of different ways by which the separate colleges can be joined together and their common interests administered. One device used is to have an interlocking board of trustees, some persons serving on the boards of all participating colleges. Another mechanism is to superimpose a central administration upon the separate administrations of each college; at Claremont, for example, the presidents of the several colleges compose a coordinating council for determining policy of the federation. This council then appoints a president and other administrative officers who are charged with the responsibility for administering most of the cooperative endeavors of the schools. A third linking device is a federation-wide graduate school which attempts to coordinate courses and faculty among the various schools. Of course, all of these formal structures are supplemented with a host of informal ties between individuals and groups on the campus.

Despite these various formal and informal structures to effect collaboration, the essential autonomy of the separate colleges is left intact. Even at Claremont, where there is perhaps the highest level of centralization, most of the authority still resides in the member colleges. Benezet (1965, p. 200), former president of Claremont Graduate School and University Center, has commented on former president Blaisdell's comparison of the Claremont plan with the federation of the United States:

> Dr. Blaisdell would have been closer if he had said that we emulate the U.N. with a limited secretariat. It might be presumptuous even to suggest such a comparison; but I assure you the president of Claremont Graduate School and University Center feels not at all like Lyndon B. Johnson, even in miniature, and considerably more akin to Mr. U Thant.

The proponents of the cluster college concept, whether the subcollege or federated college type, are challenging the utility of the conventional models of institutional organization, the large monolithic university and the small limited-resource college. At the same time they are advancing an alternative organization scheme. The cluster college concept, they argue, offers a model for both the small college and the large university, a model which allows each to serve the purposes they have traditionally espoused and to alleviate the inherent limitations of each kind of institution. The ideal of the cluster college adherents is not simply the university, but the clustering university, not simply the small college, but the small college within a center of learning. The small college model assumes that students profit from community and intimacy; the large university model assumes that students thrive in diversity and stimulation. Several educators have come to believe that the cluster college model, calling for the creation of small centers of community within large centers of diversity, offers a viable device for preserving the best features of both the small college and the large university at a time when each of these traditional American institutions is increasingly suffering from its own peculiar problems.

Chapter 2

Organizing Learning Experiences

Jerry G. Gaff

~~~~~~

The collegiate pattern of organization by itself is but a form; it has no content. Nothing in its logic prescribes any particular goals or any set of practices. In fact, cluster colleges may be science-engineering schools such as Harvey Mudd in the Claremont complex, vocational-technical schools such as are planned at a few junior colleges, or professional schools such as the teacher education college being considered at one university. However, almost all of the cluster colleges established to date are liberal arts colleges.

It is the liberal arts tradition that to date has provided the educational content for the collegiate form.

Again, nothing in the logic of a liberal arts college either prescribes or proscribes any given set of academic procedures. Liberal arts colleges are a very diverse group of schools; they encompass a wide variety of curricula, grading systems, residential patterns, and student rules. However, cluster colleges as a group are in the tradition of experimental liberal arts colleges, and their programs are aligned to such other liberal arts colleges as Antioch, Reed, and Sarah Lawrence.

If there is nothing in the logic of cluster colleges to define their programs, there is a great deal in their psycho-logic. Because cluster colleges are typically new schools, educators in cluster colleges have enjoyed the rare opportunity to design a complete college program, largely free from the restraints of the past. Before marking on their clean institutional tablets, the architects of these new schools have given serious thought to the purposes to be served by their schools, to traditional academic customs, and to alternative routes to their avowed purposes. Such critical examination has led most planners to reject many traditional practices and to choose a number of innovative procedures. Their general mood can be observed in this statement by Neville (1967, pp. 2–3):

> I think the problem of preserving the identity of the individual on a large campus and of offering him the maximum opportunity to develop his individual talents and to acquire a sense of his potential worth to society will not be solved to any large degree by decentralizing student services, including instruction. . . . The problem can be solved only by effecting some very basic changes in the nature and organization of the learning experiences offered to undergraduates.

It is largely the process of creating a new college that has led cluster college planners to join with the experimental college tradition. The cluster college concept provides the form and the experimental liberal arts college tradition provides the content; together they define the character of most existing cluster colleges.

This chapter will survey the internal structures of cluster colleges, focusing on the many innovations they have incorporated within their programs. While this chapter focuses on internal innovations of cluster colleges, it is important to note that it is *not* assumed that every cluster college is innovative, that each school is like all other cluster colleges, that only cluster colleges are innovative, or that all members of a college actively support all of its innovations. In fact, a few cluster colleges appear to be quite traditionally structured, sometimes because the established school of which they are a part has granted them relatively little autonomy, sometimes because founders lacked either imagination or boldness, and sometimes because the founders felt that established ways were the best ways. Also, it should be obvious that each college, like each human being, is unique; there is considerable variation among these schools in the kinds of innovations which they adopt. In addition, cluster colleges certainly are not alone in criticizing traditional educational practices and in devising creative alternatives to them; as was suggested in Chapter One, many colleges —public and private, small and large, new and old—increasingly criticize old ways and seek new ways to educate the youth. Finally, there may be fundamental disagreement within any given college over its new practices. With these delimitations in mind, the internal structure of the cluster colleges can be examined.

In terms of their professed goals the cluster colleges tend to be quite traditional, perhaps even reactionary. At a time when colleges and universities are gearing up to create new knowledge, to provide graduate and professional training, and to assist social organizations to utilize the latest knowledge, cluster colleges are reaffirming age-old commitments to teach undergraduate students. In taking this institutional stance they are not blind to the values of scholarship, advanced training, or direct social service. They are merely reasserting that whatever other obligations a university assumes, it has a primary duty to teach undergraduate students. When that mission is compromised by other competing obligations, then special institutional supports, such as subcolleges, are needed to assure that undergraduate students receive the quality of education to which they are entitled.

Further, the colleges are typically committed to the traditional values of what they loosely call liberal education. This term has always been filled with different, often conflicting, meanings; its various definitions have been vague, ill-defined, and hopelessly idealistic. And yet down through the years the term *liberal educa-tion* has managed to function as a guiding ideal for a particular kind of college education. None of the cluster colleges have made any conceptual breakthrough to clarify the meaning of this term; their literature, just like that of the most crusty catalogue of the most conventional college, refers to a liberal education as one that fosters a host of "good" outcomes in students, such as acquiring knowledge, developing thinking skills, broadening awareness, ele-vating esthetic tastes, nurturing creativity, stimulating curiosity, fostering social responsibility, and the like.

Yet when they use the term *liberal education,* the cluster colleges usually mean several things. First, they mean that they are not primarily vocational training schools. Their literature states that professional schools and preprofessional programs typically have been based upon narrowly conceived purposes, dominated by a utilitarian view of knowledge, and functioned to produce techni-cally competent but personally limited graduates. Cluster colleges typically reject specific vocational preparation as one of their pur-poses; rather, they declare themselves for a nonvocational, or better, a multivocational preparation. That is, they anticipate that a broad nonutilitarian education will provide students with a basic intel-lectual background that in the long run will be useful in many different vocations or professions.

In addition, cluster colleges declare that a liberal education means far more than simply having students take some specific courses, accumulate a certain number of credits, or maintain a minimal grade-point average. Their literature asserts that these conventional requirements for a liberal arts degree are not the true ends of a liberal education. At best they are merely the means, and at worst a hindrance, to the human ends implied by the term *liberal education.*

Finally, cluster colleges usually reject the assumption that there is any such entity as *the* liberal arts program. The very fact that there are different liberal education programs on the same campus indicates that cluster colleges reject the common ideas that all students must master the same body of knowledge or acquire the same intellectual methods or that certain courses in the liberal arts will necessarily broaden the minds or transform the values of students. Cluster colleges tend to use the term in a more active sense, to use it as a verb rather than as a noun, as it were. That is, they talk of an education which liberates students from cultural stereotypes, generates new thoughts, informs their personal values, and in general expands what Lazarsfeld and Thielens (1958) have called their "effective scope." In the thinking of the cluster college innovators, any experiences that help students to broaden their range of ideas, values, or skills, whether classroom or not, whether on or off campus, whether cognitive or emotional, may be part of a liberating education.

If cluster colleges have accepted the ancient task of liberally educating young men and women, the ways by which they propose to accomplish this task are quite contemporary. Most cluster college spokesmen argue that several conventional academic customs that may have been appropriate for an earlier time currently militate against the very goals of a liberal education they have been assumed to serve. The discipline-based curriculum, classroom-centered study, the elective principle, the lecture method of instruction, the A–F grading system, the credit unit system of accounting for a student's educational growth, the separation between the curriculum and the extracurriculum, the preponderance of typically collegiate extracurricular activities, the hierarchical structure of administration, the separation of students from faculty and administrators, the four-year college career, and the separation of the campus from life in the surrounding community—these are some of the major customs being challenged by cluster colleges. Some cluster colleges hold that all of these customs are vestigial organs, operating against the values of a liberating educational experience. Further, these schools are trying to create contemporary alternatives to these traditional forms, alternatives that more effectively assist student growth. The remainder of this chapter contains a discussion of each of these practices—both criticisms of them and some alternatives cluster colleges have put into practice.

The chief function of the college curriculum is to foster the intellectual development of students. The academic disciplines, through which knowledge traditionally has been gathered, stored, and transmitted, have long been assumed to be the building blocks of the curriculum, but several cluster colleges have questioned the usefulness of that assumption. One document circulated to members of a clustering university (Office of the Academic Vice-President, 1967) is critical of the "ideas of the academic discipline" on three different grounds—philosophical, pedagogical, and administrative.

Philosophically, cluster collegians acknowledge that the knowledge expansion has destroyed the notion that each discipline is a coherent integrated body of knowledge; as knowledge has expanded, old disciplines have become so splintered that they no longer constitute a meaningful whole. Also it is argued that no discipline is an island unto itself. The boundaries of academic disciplines are not logical boundaries; indeed, in recent years they have tended to become blurred and indistinct as disciplinary cross-fertilization has been a significant feature of the knowledge expansion. A final philosophical criticism of the idea of the academic discipline is that a discipline is not an entity; it is not an actual division of the "real world." On the contrary, it is a concept, an invention of the human mind, which has been used to order knowledge about the world. However, several academics treat the disciplines as though they were actual entities; they have committed the fallacy of reifying concepts. It is pointed out that a glance beyond the walls of academe reveals that the world of mind and matter, of ideas and institutions does not obey the arbitrary disciplinary categories that scholars use to study it.

The academic disciplines are not epistemological units, yet because some persons have thought of them as though they were, they have led to a number of undesirable educational consequences. First, scholars, teachers, and students too often halt their inquiries at the imagined boundaries of their disciplines. In addition, at a time when some of the most exciting intellectual activity is occurring in the interstices between the disciplines, there is little commerce between scholars working on similar problems from within the traditions of different disciplines. A third consequence of the division of labor along disciplinary lines is that some thinkers see their colleagues in other disciplines as rivals. Rather than contributing to a community of scholars where intellectuals offer mutual support as they perform the difficult tasks of creating knowledge and helping students to gain familiarity with it, some academics have experienced a hardening of the categories. This fact has served to create a climate of competition, disrespect, and distrust among men who choose simply to examine different parts of the elephant.

In addition to these philosophical criticisms, the cluster colleges have leveled pedagogical criticisms at academic disciplines. Traditionally, liberal arts colleges have attempted to help students acquire an education that permits them to learn something of the scope of human knowledge and to know some portion of that knowledge in some detail. In curricula that rest upon the base of academic disciplines, these intellectual purposes have been immediately translated to mean that the student should have an acquaintance with several disciplines and considerable knowledge about one discipline. These purposes have been traditionally implemented by distribution requirements, which state that a student must take some portion of his courses in a variety of disciplines, by major requirements, which state that he must take a portion of his courses in some particular discipline, and by electives, which permit him to choose the remaining courses as he desires. Cluster colleges challenge the utility of these practices, and they do so on several grounds.

It is asserted that disciplines are antithetical to the goal of offering a broad general education. This is so for several reasons. First, in the knowledge expansion disciplines have been multiplied and subdivided to such an extent that modern man's understanding of the world has become hopelessly fractured into more and more and smaller and smaller pieces. Naturally this increasingly specialized knowledge has made its way into the curriculum; the 1968 catalogue from the University of California lists a total of nearly 10,000 different courses. Given this situation the pedagogical problem is, as one cluster college professor (Wise, 1966) has put it, to provide an "integrated education in an intellectually disintegrated world"; that is, to help students develop a holistic world view which is based upon reliable knowledge of their world. When students take a total of thirty or forty courses, each focusing upon different fragments of knowledge contained within different disciplinary categories, that experience often does not allow them to develop a coherent view of the world. Also, in the structure of the modern university the task of educating the lower division, nonmajor student, the one who merely wants to acquire a broad general education, is typically neglected. The courses offered to meet the distribution requirements are typically survey courses, in which an effort is made to introduce the student to the several subdivisions of the field. Because of the expansion of the disciplines, these courses permit students to obtain little more than a guided tour of the intellectual terrain. Like the often caricatured American who "does Europe" in ten days, the student who "does a discipline" in one term with the help of a tour-guide teacher may have learned little of real value to him. In all of these ways the cluster colleges have declared that the disciplines have effectively hindered students from acquiring a broad intellectual education.

The pedagogical problems facing the colleges that attempt to provide students with a detailed understanding of some portion of knowledge by requiring a major are also severe. The major is criticized as being both too broad and too narrow an area of intellectual focus. It is too broad because an entire discipline today cannot be mastered by any one person; the most that can be expected is that he master some small segment and become generally familiar with the rest of the field. It is too narrow because almost every intellectual problem necessarily takes one into adjacent disciplines. In short, the cluster colleges assert that it is not enough for a student to complete the conventional distribution requirements and a major; these requirements do not adequately guarantee that he will have either a wide view of knowledge or an appreciation of a meaningful segment of it.

Because the efforts of faculty and students must be ordered and coordinated, every college requires some form of administrative structure. Given the disciplinary curriculum and the assumption that specialists in each field are the most competent persons to make decisions pertaining to that area, the departmental administrative structure has been the logical outcome. However, departments which have been consciously created to advance and promulgate knowledge within the disciplines often have served those ends only too well. One interoffice memo from an unnamed clustering institution has confronted this issue:

Rigidity and increased internecine struggle mark a university that seeks to grow through the proliferation of departments. The role of the departments as *political* units becomes more important than their role as *learning* units.

This departmental struggle to obtain a greater share of the resources, or perhaps to retain those it had last year, is a familiar theme on every campus, large or small. Such political struggles dissipate the energy and talents of the faculty; they are based upon the competitive principle that the strongest department wins the largest budget, controls the largest number of faculty positions, and offers the greatest number of courses. But to the extent that political concerns predominate, intellectual and educational concerns may suffer.

In addition, each department is charged with the limited responsibility of teaching the students in its courses the knowledge in its field; it has no formal responsibility for the students' intellectual education outside their field, for their emotional well-being, or for their social development. The departments' partial responsibility has led Martin (1965) to declare, only partly in jest,

> . . . Most faculty members assume responsibility for only a part of the student's mind, leaving the rest of the student's mind to other professors in other disciplines, and, finally, leaving what is left of the person to student personnel services.

However well the departmental administrative structure may serve the interests of the administration or the faculty, cluster college spokesmen claim that it often fails to serve the educational needs of the students.

If the cluster colleges have leveled these philosophical, pedagogical, and administrative arguments at the academic disciplines, what alternative curricular structures have they adopted? Basically, most cluster colleges have attempted to move beyond the academic disciplines; while few have gone so far as to eliminate disciplines, most have seen the need to supplement them. This supplementation occurs in several ways. The conventional disciplines have been placed within the context of larger areas of knowledge. Monteith, for example, organizes the curriculum around divisions of humanities, social science, and natural science; each division serves also as a basic administrative unit. The intention here is to encourage faculty and students to pursue their ideas and interests into adjacent fields of study and to make intellectual connections that might be ignored in a more fractured curriculum.

A somewhat more novel way to place disciplines in a larger context was developed at Nasson's New Division before that school was reassimilated into Nasson College. The curriculum was built around seven "provinces of knowledge"; Art and Letters, Mind and Spirit, Social Science, Behavioral Science, Physical Sciences, Biological Science, and Mathematics and Logic. The catalogue (1968–69, p. 89) has this to say about one of the provinces:

> The Province of Arts and Letters brings together various humanistic disciplines in a unified sequence of studies. Compartmentalization into art, aesthetics, literature, and music has been avoided, as have the usual organizations of study by general or national origin or historical period. Rather, the student participates in a program which encompasses and to that extent unifies the conventional divisions of the Province materials by focusing each year on a thematic issue or problem which seems universal in artistic expression.

This approach not only established new and broader categories around which to plan a curriculum, but in a radical departure from the rigid discipline concept it regards those categories as subjects of investigation. The passage continues:

> In rejecting the conventional ordering of materials as imposed, and perhaps as less meaningful than a more inherent order which may exist, the Province's approach is in a sense investigative: it tests the themes under study to ascertain if they are more than arbitrary choices by the faculty and students.

Because the themes studied in the province may change from year to year, Nasson's literature argues that the content of the curriculum is less likely to become stale and rigidified and is more likely to remain fresh and innovative.

A second procedure has been to place the disciplines within the context of social problems. At Old Westbury, for example, students have had one-third of their course load in fieldwork experience as early as their freshman year. This provision as well as their workshops which are held off-campus in community settings, are likely to be interdisciplinary because the field experience and the social problems to which it is directed know no disciplinary boundaries.

Whether because of their divisional structure or their field-work, cluster colleges feature curricula well sprinkled with inter-disciplinary courses, courses organized around intellectual themes, social problems, important men, or historical periods. Course titles like Values in Crisis (New College); Inquiry and Expression (Justin Morrill); History of the American Dream of Success (Stevenson); Atomism (Monteith); The Contemporary World (Residential College); and Alternative Futures (Old Westbury) are commonly found as integral parts of the curriculum. Often these nondisciplinary efforts are taught by two or more instructors with different educational backgrounds, disciplinary perspectives, and intellectual styles. It is expected that such cooperative teaching endeavors might provide a broader learning experience for students and at the same time constitute an enriching experience for the faculty.

Several schools attempt to promote an integrated educational experience for students by means of a prescribed core curriculum. This core curriculum generally is not defended on the grounds that it provides an overview of all knowledge, that the core represents any more valid or fundamental knowledge than that excluded from the core, or that it is the knowledge every proverbial educated man must have. The knowledge expansion has made each of these arguments sound like old rhetoric. There is simply too much knowledge for any one set of courses to survey it even in a superficial way, and there is not a consensus among reasonable men as to what knowledge is most fundamental or what that educated man must know. Rather, the idea of a core curriculum seems to be based more upon pragmatic and pedagogical grounds. Their small size places definite intellectual and economic constraints upon the cluster colleges; it is impossible for them to offer all of the valuable courses. But their locations in large universities make it unnecessary for them to do so. Typically, cluster colleges concentrate their resources in a limited area, such as urban studies, human ecology, or international relations. Then they typically emphasize those disciplines and courses most central to their concentration; often a portion of these courses is thought to be particularly relevant to the main purposes of the school, and these are required of all students. For instance, Madison requires students to complete a core sequence on policy planning prior to their concentrating on one of several policy areas. Core courses are usually both broader than most disciplinary survey courses in that they are interdisciplinary and narrower in that they are focused on a problem or theme. Occasionally core courses are arranged as integrated sequences of study with the earlier courses serving as a basis of the later ones. For example, Fairhaven offers a "Great Periods" historical sequence which features integrated courses on Greece, Caesar and Christ, Renaissance and Discovery, Reformation and Revolution, Nineteenth Century, and Twentieth Century. And Raymond has a math-science sequence in which each course —mathematics, physics, chemistry, and biology—builds upon the knowledge contained in the earlier courses.

A different way to bridge the disciplines has been instituted at New College Hofstra. There students and faculty attend a morning lecture in a core course; later in the day students meet in discussion sections with a faculty member from another discipline, and the group relates ideas of the core to the other field. This deliberate cross-disciplinary attempt assumes that professionals in a field may communicate basic ideas to amateurs (faculty in other specialties and students) and that the amateurs can conduct among themselves a meaningful intellectual discussion around these ideas.

Although cluster colleges appear to be primarily concerned with providing a broad general education, they are not at all blind to the values of specialization. However, most schools insist that specialized knowledge is not synonymous with the disciplinary major. Most schools allow students to plan a concentration program of study around intellectual problems of interest to them, whether they fall within a conventional discipline or not. Often a student together with a faculty advisor, or perhaps with an advisory committee, must work out the details of such individualized programs. It is important to note that even the most radical colleges make provision for students to acquire a conventional disciplinary major if they so desire; some of the more conventional even require students to obtain a major.

Specialization, whether interdisciplinary or not, is normally furthered through two main mechanisms: courses in other colleges of the university, and independent study. Concerning the first approach, every cluster college allows students to take courses in other schools of the university; one university even requires that each student take at least a third of his work outside his own college. Because the university is likely to offer a wide range of specialized courses in most fields, this extra-college instruction constitutes a rich resource for the cluster college student. Indeed, some cluster colleges argue that if the student can have the benefit of its own broad education and have access to the specialized instruction offered elsewhere on the campus, he has the best of both educational worlds.

The second device for broadening the limited curricular offerings of a college and for helping the student seeking specialized training is independent study. This mechanism allows a student to plan a course of reading, thinking, and writing in practically any area and to pursue it on his own initiative and on his own terms. The student may consult with his faculty sponsor frequently or infrequently; he may turn in regular assignments or may engage in a single term project; he may study on or off campus— all of these matters as well as the content of the course are open to negotiation. This technique of formalized self-study for credit allows students to specialize in nearly any subject matter they may desire, as long as it can be defended on intellectual grounds.

All of this discussion of a curriculum probably would be regarded as irrelevant by members of Bensalem, one of the most radical cluster colleges. There the faculty and students live together, and each person or group studies whatever he wants whenever he wants. Of course, students may take regular courses at Fordham, but the only kind of curriculum which can be identified at Bensalem is strictly ad hoc.

The problems of the departmental administrative structure have been attacked by some schools in the same way the problems of curricular fragmentation have been attacked, by enlarging the scope of faculty responsibility. Monteith, for example, organizes faculty around the divisions of natural science, social science, and the humanities. And at some schools which are quite small, faculty sit as a committee of the whole to conduct their business. It is thought that this procedure might make professors more mindful of their responsibilities to the whole student and encourage them to place educational considerations above political considerations.

In these several ways cluster colleges are attempting to achieve the time-honored purposes of helping students to gain an appreciation of both the expanding breadth and growing depth of knowledge and to use this knowledge in formulating their own world view. They argue that their innovations can more effectively achieve these goals than can the conventionally structured curriculum based on the sovereignty of the academic discipline with all of its philosophical, pedagogical, and administrative liabilities.

Most cluster colleges profess concern with the character and quality of conventional classroom instruction. Their criticism is centered chiefly upon the lecture method, more particularly upon what they see as its overuse; in fact, cluster college literature is replete with charges against lectures. It is said that lectures tend to reward students for becoming passive accepters of the opinions of others rather than active thinkers in their own right; to foster mistaken impressions about knowledge (that is, that it is absolute rather than tentative and static rather than dynamic); to be centered around the concerns of the teacher-expert rather than the interests of the student-learner; and to subject a large number of students to the same content and approach rather than individualizing and particularizing instruction to the needs of different students.

Obviously, no institution of higher learning legislates how faculty members must conduct their courses, and no cluster college attempts to do that. Indeed, all would doubtless endorse the statement from one catalogue (University of California, Santa Cruz, 1966–1967, p. 20): "Santa Cruz subscribes to no dogma about the process of teaching. Forms and methods of teaching vary widely, depending on the subject matter and purposes and on the particular instructor and students." But after making this disclaimer, the statement goes on to express a bias that pervades these schools, a strong preference for non-lecture methods of instruction:

Lectures are used where appropriate, as is television, to conserve teaching time for discussion in groups that are small enough to permit wide participation. Much teaching, at every level, is carried on in seminars. Particular emphasis is placed on independent study.

The reasoning behind the preference for non-lecture methods may have been summarized best by Taylor (in Select Committee on Education, 1965, pp. 445–54). Although not a cluster collegian, he has articulated a position concerning instructional approaches that appears to echo throughout these experimental colleges:

> There is nothing intrinsically wrong with the lecture as a mode of communication, provided it is given to those who want to hear it by people who have something fresh and original to say on a subject of interest to the listener. But it has to be used sparingly and for particular reasons. It should be a means of starting up some self-generating thought in the student, to start him thinking, imagining, and questioning. The reason for shifting the entire pedagogy away from lecturing toward discussion and independent study is that discussion and independent enquiry are the natural and most effective ways to learn. They do not require the continual presence of the teacher or any kind of educational authority to be effective. The students discuss all the time anyway; it is a question of how to get them discussing matters of significance to their education and of teaching them how to get the most out of discussion and enquiry. The real problem is to teach them how to teach others and how to learn from each other, from books, from experience, from their teachers, from anything.

While the cluster colleges have not abandoned the lecture, they tend to use it sparingly; and they tend to make greater use of other methods of teaching. The teaching techniques which seem to be preferred by the cluster colleges are the ancient methods of discussions, tutorials, and independent study, largely because they are individualized and personalized approaches.

Cluster colleges encourage the use of discussion teaching largely by scheduling small classes. While it is possible for a teacher to conduct a class of 100 or more students on a discussion basis and to lecture before a class of five, it is awkward to do so. Large classes tend to call for lecturing and small ones seem to call for discussing. In some schools, almost all classes are small enough that they can be conducted as seminars. Other schools, those at Santa Cruz for example, believe that to have all classes so small is both too costly and educationally unnecessary. As a result they have opted for a combination of a few large lecture classes and several small classes suitable for discussion.

An important by-product expected from discussion teaching techniques is the development of an intellectual community. Where students are taught "how to get the most out of discussion and enquiry" in their classes, their discussions outside of classes may be more rational and have more intellectual content; such outcomes would extend the range of their classes beyond the classrooms. Students who converse about serious intellectual issues in classroom are likely to continue such discussions in their rooms and in their dormitories. Of course, the reverse is also true. That is, when students are encouraged to discuss issues with their peers and teachers, they may be expected to bring some personal experiences into the classroom context and to direct academic discussions along lines which are personally relevant to them. In both these ways the often sharp division between the formal academic instruction of the classroom and the informal social life of the dormitory may be reduced. By "shifting the entire pedagogy away from lecturing toward discussion and independent study," cluster colleges expect to promote a more integrated and intellectual community.

Tutorials and independent study are encouraged generally by permitting students to design, with faculty members, courses that permit them to study areas of their interests. The opposite procedure is also promoted; that is, faculty members with special interests are encouraged to propose seminars they may be particularly interested in teaching. The rather flexible informal procedures that exist in most schools permit faculty and students to bring courses into existence with relative ease; such informality promotes the use of these more independent and individualized techniques. Self-study has been carried furthest, perhaps, by the Paracollege. Students are required to take only two courses, a freshman seminar and a senior seminar. All other work done by a student is independent study to prepare him for a general examination and a comprehensive examination. Some guidance is provided by syllabi and by biweekly tutorial meetings with a professor, but each student is expected to prepare himself for his examinations in his own way and at his own speed. If in the Paracollege the faculty member is primarily a resource person, this role is carried even further at Bensalem. Without a structured curriculum students pursue their own interests and frequently call upon the resident faculty for help—not just with intellectual matters, but with their personal and social concerns as well.

A common approach to learning, if not to teaching, is experiential. Asserting that people learn some things better by doing than by reading or talking, some schools encourage students to obtain some off-campus experience as an adjunct to their intellectual interests. For example, if a Merrill middle-class student is to learn about life in the Third World, part of that learning might involve living in a ghetto, working with a social agency, or traveling to a foreign country. Some schools offer academic credit for such experience; but if a student wants credit for an experiential course, he typically must present some evidence, either oral or written, that he has conceptualized some of his experience and gained cognitive understanding of the area under study. Experiences usually do not substitute for intellectual work; they are seen as a pedagogical device for stimulating intellectual understanding.

The academic cliché that the best way to learn a course is to teach it has been applied in some schools. New College Hofstra has proposed that students engage in "peer teaching" as another way to learn by experience. At Raymond several upperclassmen were selected to lead once-a-week discussion sections in connection with a first-term lecture course for freshmen. These student teachers attended a seminar dealing with both the content of the course and the issues involved in college-level teaching, were supervised and evaluated by a faculty member, and received academic credit for their experience.

Perhaps the most interesting thing about the instructional innovations attempted by the cluster colleges is that the highly publicized technological innovations are conspicuous by their absence. There is virtually no mention of programmed text, teaching machines, computerized instruction, instructional television, and the like. It appears that the cluster colleges are concerned to innovate more with human relationships than with technological equipment. Generally the preferred instructional procedures are those that are highly personalized; such procedures reinforce the driving ideas behind the whole of the cluster college movement.

Traditionally a student's educational progress is evaluated by means of letter grades and credit units. Usually he must accumulate approximately 120–125 units and compile an acceptable grade-point average in order to graduate. Several cluster colleges have been highly critical of this traditional procedure. One pamphlet (Raymond College, 1963, p. 9) states the general case against it:

> It is common knowledge that letter grades and testing programs have taken on dimensions all out of proportion to their worth in the attempt to evaluate an individual's academic, vocational and personal capabilities. These tabulations have been carried in recent times to such extremes that the person has often become the pawn of the system or, in other cases, the person has attempted to exploit the system for selfish advantage.

Because they believe the credit-unit, grade-point system to impede a student's education, several schools are searching for new ways to evaluate student achievement. Of course, the context of these schools is an important determinant of the kind of evaluation scheme they adopt. Because they are small and encourage personalized instruction, they actually embody a rather pervasive informal system of evaluation. In seminars or tutorials students get many opportunities to express their ideas; in these settings a student's intellect is engaged not in contrived testing sessions but in "natural" discussions throughout the term. Just as the student has opportunities to demonstrate his understanding, the professor has opportunities to evaluate what the student says and to communicate his judgments to the student in a host of ways, such as by clarifying a student comment, extending it, approving or rejecting it, asking for evidence to support it, ignoring it, and so on. Because faculty and students have many chances to meet outside of class, frequently they engage in conversation in non-classroom settings which provide other perspectives on student mental processes. In the give-and-take of discussions both in and out of class, student understanding or confusion is likely to become apparent and to evoke immediate feedback from professors.

Given this context, it is understandable that several schools have tried to minimize the importance of the traditional grade-point average. In one approach used at Kirkland and Callison, students are graded on the usual A–F basis, but the grades are not divulged to a student until he graduates, transfers, or otherwise severs his relationship with the college. By using conventional grades, school officials retain their administrative utility; by keeping them secret, they hope grades will not "take on dimensions out of all proportion to their worth." Other schools like Fairhaven have adopted a simple two-point system, pass or fail; unlike some schools which allow students to take a limited number of ungraded courses, all courses here are evaluated in this way. A variation on this theme is found at Santa Cruz and at Residential College, where pass-fail is used for most courses, but letter grades are used for large classes, where faculty have little chance to get well acquainted with their students, and for classes in a student's major field of study, where a grade-point average may be required for later graduate or professional school purposes. An even more radical nonpunitive grading system was adopted by Nasson's former New Division. There a two-point designation was used; the student either completed his work satisfactorily or his record read "Incomplete—No Prejudice." The rationale behind this scheme is that the college was more concerned with what students learned than with what they have failed to learn, and that students should be able to stop working on a course without sanction if they find that such work is not as valuable as they originally expected it to be.

Some schools which use these simplified evaluation schemes supplement these designations of pass, fail, or incomplete with descriptive statements. A teacher writes a paragraph or more to each of his students describing in some detail his reaction to the student's performance, perhaps making some candid suggestions of how the student might improve his achievement in subsequent courses. It is argued that this procedure, if faithfully followed, provides more educational feedback to a student than the usual letter grade. A variation of this procedure has been attempted at Old Westbury. There a few faculty members would meet individual students face to face for a frank discussion of their performance; this meeting permits students to talk back and to make student evaluation a two-way conversation.

Goddard and Bensalem have taken a very different approach to grading. Both places rely on students to evaluate themselves. It is the policy of each school for students to plan their own educational experience, and they believe that students who design their education to achieve their particular goals should evaluate their achievement in terms of those goals.

In addition to these attempts to free students from the restraints of the grade-point average, some schools have opted for comprehensive examinations. Residential College, for example, has adopted two sets of comprehensive examinations; one is at the end of the sophomore year, and successful completion of these tests is necessary for a student to remain in the program. A second set of comprehensives are administered during the senior year; a student's performance on those tests helps to determine his readiness to graduate. At Monteith a senior essay, rather than an examination, is required; the essay is seen as a capstone educational experience that allows a student to demonstrate what he has learned by writing a paper on a significant topic of his own choosing. Whichever of these procedures is used, the rationale behind comprehensive examinations or senior essays seems to be that they are a valuable educational experience to students, they free students from the tyranny of the grade, and yet they guarantee that the school will maintain its intellectual integrity.

The credit-unit system of reckoning a student's educational progress has also been criticized by some cluster colleges. One aspect of the attack has been aimed at the assumptive roots of that practice. In the credit-unit system, a student receives academic credit for a number of units equivalent to the number of hours he spends each week in classroom contact with a professor; the underlying assumption appears to be that students learn only from direct contact with the professor in class. This assumption is inappropriate for cluster colleges, where students are encouraged to pursue independent study projects, where they are urged to seek off-campus experiences, and where the whole college community is designed to stimulate learning.

The credit-unit system has been criticized also for pedagogical reasons. While most courses are assigned units ranging from two to five, the typical three-unit course predominates. Since convention decrees that the "normal" student load is fifteen to sixteen "hours" of course work, students take as a rule five or six separate courses at a time. This arrangement means that they have little time to study any course in depth; the competing time demands make it difficult for students to acquire more than a superficial understanding of all their courses. Also, in the press of time and facing the pressure of the grade-point average, students may resort to playing one course off against the others; often the course with the most assigned units gets most of the student's attention, often to the neglect of his less heavily weighted courses—regardless of their educational value.

To circumvent some of the problems associated with the credit-unit system, some cluster colleges have adopted a course system. In this system all courses are assigned an equal weight; a student registers for only a limited number of courses at a time; and a specified number of courses—not units—are required for graduation. At New Division, for example, all courses are regarded as equivalent in educational value; a student normally takes four courses each term; and a total of thirty-two courses is required for graduation. Raymond has carried this logic further by having students take only three courses per term, for three terms per year, for three years; successful completion of twenty-five of the twenty-seven courses is required for graduation.

Some schools have adopted programs that vary in duration from the traditional four years, the length of time the average student needs in order to accumulate the necessary credit units. New College (Hofstra), Bensalem, and Raymond all have implemented three-year programs. New College has performed this feat by extending the normal academic year to forty weeks and by tightly scheduling daily and weekly calendars. Thus a New College student may earn his 124 units required for graduation in three years. By shortening the time a student spends in college, these schools hope to take advantage of the better quality high school programs to speed the students into specialized graduate or professional schools or into the work force; or perhaps the "extra" year can be used as a break to extend formal schooling in order to broaden and enrich their personal lives. In the absence of firm knowledge to the contrary, these schools are hypothesizing that a student can become liberally educated in three years.

Other schools are encouraging some of their students to undertake programs that will extend their college careers beyond four years. Old Westbury and Merrill, for example, encourage students to gain some nonacademic fieldwork experience. While most students will be expected to graduate in four years, it is quite conceivable that the fieldwork may make it necessary for a student to extend his program beyond the normal four years.

A far more radical alternative to the credit-unit system is the contract system that Johnston College has adopted. In his freshman year a student plans a complete college program with the help of an advisor. This plan may involve regular courses, independent study, fieldwork experience, or almost anything that allows the student to realize his long-term objectives. This plan is then submitted to a larger faculty committee; once that committee approves it, it becomes a binding contract between the student and the college. The contract may be modified during the course of the student's career, but he is never without a contract with the school. As soon as he completes the contract to the satisfaction of his committee, the student graduates. Thus the length of time a student spends in college depends upon the nature of the contract he has negotiated and the speed with which he wants to complete his obligation.

In these ways, several cluster colleges have expressed their dissatisfaction with the traditional structures for evaluating the educational achievement of students and have attempted to originate new procedures with which to perform the tasks of judging and recording the educational development of their students.

Most definitions of the concept of community involve common experiences of members or common standards of judgments. By either criterion few contemporary institutions of higher learning can be called communities. The large size of many schools, the multiplicity of purposes, the separation of persons into formal categories of student, faculty, or administrator, the divisiveness between the departments—these attributes are deplored by cluster colleges. They prefer a college that more closely resembles a community; one in which members are bound by common experiences into a reasonably cohesive whole and in which they adhere to some common educational values.

Especially distasteful to cluster colleges is the frequently sharp distinction between the academic and social segments of student life. This separation can be seen in the distinction between the curriculum and the extracurriculum; it is found in college architecture where there are classroom buildings and student residences, each symbolizing a world unto itself; it can be seen in the administrative structure of the school, where there is an academic dean and a dean of students, each with a different set of responsibilities; it can be seen in the contrasting kinds of student discussions —the formal discussions about respectable academic subjects, which occur in class, and the "rap sessions" about the existential concerns of students, which take place outside of class. Cluster colleges say that where the intellectual issues of the classroom are separated from the rest of student life, a college program is not likely to provide a liberating education for students; where faculty have no more contact with students than in their formally structured class meetings, they cannot have much impact upon their students; and where students do not make connections between their academic work and the rest of their existence, their personal and social habits probably will not be informed by their intellect.

Several educational structures have been constructed in an attempt to unite the "living" and "learning" aspects of students' lives. In addition to their typically small size and residential character, they have created open and flexible academic structures which reduce the social distance between students and faculty in class. Discussion classes, independent study options, and off-campus experience are all flexible devices that may bring students into a more equalitarian relationship with faculty.

Some schools have chosen the core curriculum as a way to build a cohesive intellectual community. It is held that when all students take the same courses, they become acquainted with similar ideas, understand similar methods of investigation, and acquire a similar vocabulary, all of which provide a basis for them to engage each other in serious discussion outside of class. A brochure of the Residential College (1967–68, p. 4) has articulated this position:

> . . . the skills and content implicit in the core courses will constitute an intellectual capital shared by all students in a residential college "generation," a factor leading to a sense of close academic community. In addition, since these courses will be taught on the Residential College campus and will engage about three-quarters of an under-classman's time, they will, in a purely experimental way, reinforce this important sense of intellectual commonwealth.

When the core courses are taught as seminars, students may learn how to engage each other in dialogue, and they may continue such sophisticated discussions outside of class.

In addition, cluster colleges have devised non-classroom techniques of bringing students and faculty closer together. Some schools attempt to remedy the physical separation of the social and academic sides of life by scheduling classes and placing faculty offices in student dormitories. Several schools have a few faculty or administrators live in student residences or occasionally their administrators live on campus. At Santa Cruz, for example, the provost of each college lives in a university-owned home located on his college campus; at Bensalem the faculty live in the student residences. It is expected that these arrangements will likely stimulate personal interactions which can bridge the conventional divisions among members of the college.

Several colleges promote periodic formal gatherings of the entire community. Cowell, for instance, has instituted a "college night," in which all members of the college gather for an evening meal, announcements of interest to the group, and a special program. The program is typically intellectual and cultural—a lecture, panel discussion, musical program, modern dance, or avant-garde movie. Sometimes a discussion among interested participants follows the formal gathering. The idea of a college night symbolizes as well as anything the ideal of providing a common experience for all members of the community, the sharing of some common values, and the intellectual-cultural core of these values.

There are also several less formal or less regular gatherings among parts of the college. Lunch table conversations, chance meetings in dormitory hallways, mixed sporting events, meetings to discuss college problems, retreats to share reflections on the state of the school, off-campus forays to examine matters of interest in the local community, and because many of these new schools have become the object of national interest, meetings with frequent visitors to the school—these are a few of the informal activities among students, faculty, and administrators which are used to build a sense of community in some cluster colleges. These informal events are a kind of "planned spontaneity"; that is, these structures aim to maximize opportunities for students, faculty, and administrators to meet by "chance" and to encourage personal interactions among them.

Cluster colleges have been concerned about more conventional student activities. Most schools use to advantage their location within larger university settings by permitting their students to participate in any of the extracurricular activities offered by the collectivity. This approach allows students in each cluster college to gain access to the array of activities carried on by the entire campus.

However, some schools have taken firm stands against particular kinds of student activities. Sometimes students are not allowed to join social fraternities or sororities. It is said that these ancient campus organizations, with their overemphasis on social values, dating, and partying, have tended to cultivate a disrespect for the life of the mind. Since colleagueship and housing facilities are provided by the school, the primary functions served by the fraternity system have been appropriated by the college itself.

Also several schools make no provision for intercollegiate athletics. These most visible of college activities have grown in power all out of proportion to their educational value—they serve the physical needs of only a few students and frequently are costly drains on other educational programs. Cluster colleges appear to be more committed to the idea of intracollege athletics, programs which involve many students in regular exercise or which are designed to teach most students some enduring skills.

These are the primary alternatives devised by the cluster colleges in an attempt to create living and learning communities. They hope to bring students together within a community, to harness the power of the student peer group, and to direct it toward the educational purposes of the colleges.

Traditionally, the term *campus* has referred to a location removed from the hustle and bustle of daily life where men of ideas can engage in their scholarly pursuits. The metaphor of the ivory tower has long been used, sometimes with derision, to denote the gulf between the world of scholarly contemplation and the realm of practical action. During this period of social upheaval, some cluster colleges have questioned the idea of the isolated campus. One brochure (Livingston College, p. 3) declares, "Livingston College will have no ivory towers. . . . the gap between the campus and the community must be narrowed." What makes this statement more than a statement in a public relations document is that the publication goes on to specify the educational structures that will be adopted to support the claim:

> In part, this will be done by encouraging appropriate discussion inside and outside of class, by bringing nonacademic people to the campus, by case studies, by visits to the community, through movies and special exhibits; in short by bringing the community, or parts of it, to the campus.

> But not only do we want to bring the community to the campus; we also want to urge some or even many of our students to acquire part of their education off campus. This has been done by work-study programs, junior years abroad, community action programs, and many variants of these.

Merrill College has a similar social mission; all of its students are expected to spend anywhere from a few months to a year in full-time fieldwork, possibly abroad. A student may gain academic credit for this work if he prepares an intellectually acceptable report on his experience. Old Westbury has gone even further. The Urban Studies College requires students to have fieldwork experience, perhaps as early as the second term of the first year; offers seminars or independent study programs which both prepare students for and are a supplement to their off-campus work; and encourages faculty to conduct seminars or workshops off campus and thereby to become involved themselves in the life of the local community.

While these schools permit their students to go abroad as

part of their off-campus experience, some cluster colleges have a special commitment to international study. Two colleges at the University of the Pacific have developed the most radical programs of international study. Elbert Covell attempts to create greater appreciation for Latin American cultures by conducting all of its activities, including classes, in Spanish. About one-third of the student body comes from the United States, and about two-thirds are recruited from Latin American countries. This program serves students from developing countries in their native language, returns a sizable proportion of graduates to their countries to occupy middle-level jobs and bolster the middle classes of countries which typically know only the extremes of great wealth and great poverty, and prepares the Latin American specialists who can help the United States develop more ties with several countries in that part of the world. Callison also has an international mission, but with a somewhat different purpose and in a different part of the world. Callison sees the study of non-Western cultures as an integral part of a liberal education; in addition it attempts to create a group of specialists on Asia, a part of the world Americans have long ignored but which is of increasing importance to them. In order to implement these purposes several courses are offered on various aspects of Asian cultures, including basic languages, and each student spends a year abroad. During the sophomore year the entire class travels to the overseas campus at Bangalore, India, where they study Asian history, religion, literature, and society from Indian instructors.

Thus, some cluster colleges have rejected the idea of the campus as a place removed from the world in favor of a concept of a campus as an integral part of the world. They are attempting to tear down the artificial barrier that has separated the campus from the community and are attempting to gain for their students the enrichment and understanding that results when intellect is faced with real and practical puzzles.

The traditional procedures for governing institutions of higher learning have been attacked on all fronts. Their hierarchical structure, bureaucratic procedures, and centralized decision-making have been especially criticized. Although cluster colleges are located within the familiar bureaucratic university structure, many have attempted to devise a very different governing system within their own colleges. Generally, they attempt to substitute equality for hierarchy, participant democracy for bureaucracy, and reasoned authority for vested authority.

Again the context of these schools greatly affects the kind of governance arrangements they adopt. The small size, large amount of informal interaction, and the close community all imply that hierarchy and bureaucracy are both unnecessary and inappropriate. This context and the purposes running through the cluster colleges have led them to adopt governing procedures that rest upon the concept of shared authority and necessitate the active involvement of many members of the community. There are three main reasons given for adopting this approach. First, when the interests of all segments of the group are represented, the school can make better policy. Second, when persons participate in making policy decisions, they are more willing to accept and live with those policies. And third, deliberation among various segments of the campus is educational; it is an especially valuable pedagogical aid in teaching students about the practical art of governing an institution.

If this is the ideal of many cluster colleges, how do they seek to implement that ideal? One of the earliest and most fundamental ways is to involve a number of persons in the process of planning the new school. In the planning for Fairhaven, for example, a committee of faculty and administrators at Western Washington hammered out a general design. Then during the first year of operation a small pilot class of students was admitted and a few faculty were hired; together they designed the program. A similar approach was followed at Old Westbury, but it was hoped that it could be carried a bit further. Since there were to be several subcolleges at that campus a special class on college planning was to be offered so that students could be helping formulate plans for future colleges.

Once a college is planned, personnel must be recruited. Here again is a matter of general interest to the college, and often many persons are involved. Rather than relying primarily on their departmental colleagues (who are likely to be few in number even when the school reaches maximum size) to search out and interview candidates, most cluster colleges involve faculty colleagues in other fields as well as several interested students. In like manner, students and faculty may aid in student admissions; prospective students who visit the campus often have an opportunity to talk with faculty members, to sit in on seminars, or to stay in student dormitories. Similarly, students and faculty often help to select administrative replacements.

The ongoing affairs of the college are typically conducted in ways designed to assure that all voices are heard. For example, at the Residential College a central governing committee has been formed; it is composed of representatives of students, instructional faculty, and administrative faculty. This committee has established subcommittees on which each constituency is represented; the membership of each constituency is weighted in accordance with the area of concern. Thus, the committee with primary concern for the curriculum contains proportionately more instructional faculty and the committee concerned largely with student affairs has a larger percentage of students. Some schools, such as Paracollege, hold occasional "town meetings" of the entire college community; these meetings may either make policy or simply provide an opportunity for an exchange of information and viewpoints. In either event they provide an opportunity for anyone to voice his concerns and to present his ideas before the entire group.

The departmental administrative structure that carries much of the day-to-day administration of most colleges has given way to more encompassing structures. The faculty at many of the smaller colleges sit as a committee of the whole to make academic policy; in other schools divisions have become the effective administrative unit. And frequently faculty meetings are open to students who can bring their concerns into such sessions.

In summary, the traditional values inherent in the concept of a liberal education have been accepted by cluster colleges, but as a group they are critical of the traditional concepts and procedures by which most schools try to achieve those values. They have instituted a number of innovations designed to effect basic changes in the nature and organization of the learning experiences offered to undergraduates.

The dominant negative aspect of these changes is that they

remove the arbitrary barriers that have been erected between disciplines and departments, between students, faculty and administrators, between the academic and social segments of students' lives
and between the campus and the community. In a more positive
vein the changes are designed to foster an intellectual community
that will help students to develop an integrated world view from
the totality of their whole college experience.

Part Two

CONSEQUENCES

There has been agreement, both within and without the ranks of educators, that systematic investigation has much to offer. Indeed, there is agreement that massive, lasting changes in education cannot safely be made except on the basis of deep objective inquiry.

Lee J. Cronbach and Patrick Suppes
Disciplined Inquiry for Education

Chapter 3

Promises and Products

Jerry G. Gaff

Cluster colleges are typically new institutions that presume to offer new ways to educate college students. Their promises are often couched in persuasive philosophical and pedagogical analyses, are based upon cogent criticisms of the educational establishment, and are given substance in new academic structures.

But promises are one thing, and products are quite another. Sumner (1934, p. 106) long ago declared "it is the greatest folly of which a man is capable to sit down with a slate and pencil to plan out a new social world." One need not be as pessimistic as Sumner to recognize the difficulty of bringing about planned change in such historically conservative institutions as colleges and universities. But one must recognize that colleges must be judged primarily on the basis of their results rather than on the basis of their intentions. Certainly it does not follow that merely because a college is preceded by the new word *cluster* it is necessarily any better—or any worse—than other kinds of schools. Just because a college claims to be innovative is no indication that it offers significantly different experiences to its students (Martin, 1969a). And if it does manage to implement substantive innovations, that is no evidence that the new ways are more effective than those of traditional schools in achieving educational objectives. It is appropriate that now, after the decade of innovation, cluster colleges be put to rigorous empirical test in order to assess their actual effects.

Despite the persuasive innovative rhetoric it is at least possible that the new programs have not been enacted in the desired way. For example, a core curriculum may be as fragmented as traditional disciplinary courses; seminars may be merely another setting for faculty to lecture, albeit to a smaller group of listeners, or they may degenerate into rambling "bull sessions" devoid of intellectual content; expected close student-faculty relationships may not develop, either because faculty may still respond to the lure of research or because students fear close personal contact; and the delicate living-and-learning balance may be tipped either way resulting in living without learning or learning without living. In short, these several innovations may actually operate in a way quite different from what was envisioned.

Even if they have been enacted to create the kind of college environment desired, these innovations still may not have the expected kind of educational impact upon students. For example, close student-faculty contact may actually undermine student respect for the knowledge and experience of professors; students who have been raised on conventional courses for twelve years may lack the proper motivation to pursue disciplined independent study. Knowledge about the effects of their innovations may serve as a basis for improving the organization for learning in cluster colleges as well as in other colleges and universities.

Fortunately, several clusters of colleges offer ready-made settings for natural experiments which can provide some information about these issues. That is, when two or more undergraduate colleges on the same campus operate different programs, a comparative study of the colleges can provide valuable insights into the advantages and disadvantages of each kind of program. Studies of this sort may add to the fund of knowledge about the educational values of alternative educational structures.

If a systematic study of cluster colleges is both desirable and practicable, one must decide upon the nature of that study. Three main assumptions underlie the collection of empirical reports in Part Two. First, an assessment of cluster colleges is meaningful only in relation to a clearly formulated set of values or objectives. Perhaps the most reasonable set of objectives against which to evaluate a program are those it has taken as its own rather than those imposed upon it by outsiders, including researchers. To this end, the research reported herein attempts to determine how well the structures adopted by the colleges realize their own stated educational purposes, purposes which have been discussed in Chapters One and Two. More specifically, it is to the following questions the research reported in Part Two is addressed: Have cluster colleges created a greater sense of community and managed to provide a more personal approach to the education of undergraduates than more monolithically structured schools? Do the colleges on the same campus have different educational climates so as to provide in fact the structured diversity they sought? Have the internal innovations produced vital intellectual communities? Has the experimentation extended into other portions of the university? At what personal and economic price have the advantages been purchased? How much do students and faculty utilize the services and facilities of the other schools in the union?

Second, a thorough assessment should be based upon hard data. Dressel (1961, p. 6) has declared:

> There is no issue concerning the presence or absence of evaluation. When one is faced with choice, evaluation, whether conscious or not, is present. Failure to engage systematically in evaluation in reaching the many decisions necessary in education means that decision by prejudice, by tradition, or by rationalization is paramount.

The main concern is the quality of evidence with which to assess the consequences of a program. It goes almost without saying that such judgments should be based upon the most reliable evidence available; this means that the most sophisticated methods, measures, and standards of precision developed in the behavioral sciences should be used to gather information about the effects of cluster colleges. While several well-known criticisms have been leveled at these procedures, they do yield reliable evidence.

Finally, this assessment is focused upon a holistic rather than an elemental level. While every cluster college program is distinct from every other one either in its elements or their combinations, these variations of necessity will not constitute the core of this study. The focus rather will be on whole cluster college programs, their students, and their faculty in contrast to the more traditionally structured parts of the same school. The limitation of a holistic approach, of course, is that one never knows which elements or which combinations of elements are responsible for the observed results. Such limitations may be overcome in subsequent research; they become important only if there are differences between cluster and other colleges. It is to this prior and more holistic question that the present work is addressed.

Since the cluster college movement is so young, little systematic study of these schools has been completed. In a fundamental sense the movement probably is too young for a full assessment. But given the problems facing higher education and the cluster solution attempted by a number of schools, even a tentative early assessment might be valuable. In order to provide a research base for the holistic assessment of the extent to which cluster colleges realize their self-proclaimed purposes, five of the six chapters in Part Two contain reports of empirical studies. All chapters are previously unpublished reports of the most valuable research and the most valuable insights into cluster colleges. Collectively these reports provide at least a first approximation to a systematic study of cluster colleges, and they may serve as take-off points for future studies, which may provide more definite knowledge about these new forms of organization. A Harvard president is reputed to have said of his school, "This is not a good school; it's simply the best there is." Something of the same can be said of the research presented here. It inevitably fails to answer all the relevant questions about cluster colleges, but it is about as good as the art permits, and it does give a revealing look at the actual workings of cluster colleges.

The several contributing authors were invited by the primary author to write their chapters for a variety of reasons.

Paul Heist and John Bilorusky have studied the kinds of students who enter cluster colleges. In comparing the values, attitudes, and educational philosophies of students who enrolled in four subcolleges with their counterparts who entered more traditional portions of the same universities, they discovered many consistent differences. Mindful that the quality of a college is determined in large part by the kinds of students it attracts, they have considered some implications of this differential recruitment for cluster college educational programs.

Raymond College is one of the "first generation" cluster colleges, and I present a case study in which an innovative program is described, and which suggests that the innovations have been generally successful in achieving the kind of environment desired, one radically different from that found in the rest of the university. However, a number of unanticipated consequences occurred, and the report details the difficulties that resulted from a number of the innovations.

The chapter by Newcomb and his associates examines students in a subcollege of one of the nation's most prestigious universities. Using carefully selected matched groups of students at the University of Michigan, they found that the Residential College does make a difference in the education of undergraduates. Although they were able to report only on the freshmen, they found that the subcollege provides a learning environment significantly different from the rest of the university and that its students showed more personal growth after one year than did students in the other samples. They account for these different amounts of growth in terms of a theory of accentuation, a theory with considerable relevance to understanding student change both in cluster colleges and elsewhere.

Warren Martin, long a proponent of cluster colleges, has conducted a survey of faculty. Here he and Judith Wilkinson have compared faculty members in cluster colleges with their colleagues in other portions of three universities and found that faculty members with distinctive values choose to work in subcolleges. Their work suggests that cluster colleges may be a valuable way to group both faculty and students who share a common set of educational values. Their chapter raises the question whether clustering like-minded faculty members together may not be as educationally valuable as grouping similar students. Is it not as important to staff an innovative program with faculty whose values support it as it is to attract students whose values are consonant with it?

Harris Wofford, a former Peace Corps leader, was charged with the task of establishing a new campus of the State University of New York. The school was to be self-consciously innovative and was to make constructive responses to the current criticism of established ways. Wofford proceeded in an eminently rational way to plan the school. He consulted a number of nationally respected experts, elicited suggestions from persons representing all parts of the educational spectrum, set up a small planning group of faculty and students, established a posture of openness to all ideas, and started a pilot program featuring the best ideas. However, the forces unleashed by his policy of "organic planning" were greater than he—or any rational man—could have foreseen. In a moving existential statement he records some of the advice he received, tells which he took and which he spurned, and assesses some consequences—both good and bad—of his decisions. While some may want to do some "Monday morning quarterbacking" with Wofford's decisions, his message that giving birth to an innovative college is an extraordinarily complex task cannot be taken lightly.

Clifford Stewart and Herbert Kells have inquired into the practical matters of clustering independent colleges. Concentrating on the Claremont Colleges, they report the results of two studies. First, they examine the extent to which a particular kind of academic cooperation, cross-registration, occurs. Second, they attempt to determine the cost advantages of cooperating to support a number of central services and facilities. Their test of the hypotheses which are central to the federation of colleges confirms that cross-registration does occur and does extend the range of academic resources available to any one of the colleges, and that the sharing of central services generally produces lower costs and improved quality of service.

Chapter 4

A Special Breed
of Student

Paul Heist

John Bilorusky

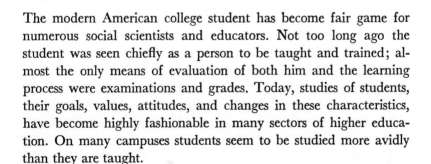

The modern American college student has become fair game for
numerous social scientists and educators. Not too long ago the
student was seen chiefly as a person to be taught and trained; almost the only means of evaluation of both him and the learning
process were examinations and grades. Today, studies of students,
their goals, values, attitudes, and changes in these characteristics,
have become highly fashionable in many sectors of higher education. On many campuses students seem to be studied more avidly
than they are taught.

71

Among the most challenging findings of the last fifteen years is the discovery of tremendous diversity in the student population, both among institutions and within institutions. Colleges and teachers are literally overwhelmed with an awesome multiplicity of mankind, in ability, motivation, attitudes, and interests (Heist, 1960; Darley, 1961). Student diversity seems to be so extensive that most educators beg their way out of the situation and the implications by negating or ignoring the established fact. Not being prepared to consider or accommodate the significant and meaningful differentiations among the increasing influx of students, educators commit a sin of omission in that they treat and teach the students as if they were all of one general mold.

Since the mid-fifties some educational leaders and administrators, as well as some faculty members, seemingly have begun to respond to the great diversity that exists among students. For almost a decade the idea of honors courses and programs was introduced in numerous institutions, although this idea had been given birth at least twenty years earlier. More recently, using the cluster concept, administrators have instituted two or more separate educational programs on the same campus. By adopting a pluralistic approach to the education of undergraduates, they have attempted to meet the needs of a wide variety of students.

Several fairly recent institutional innovations, all of which may claim to be some type of cluster college, provide the basis for the research reported in this chapter. The students entering four new cluster colleges, as well as those first-year students in the four associated institutions, are the major topic of consideration here. All four pairs of institutions have been involved in two different investigations conducted under the auspices of the Center for Research and Development in Higher Education at Berkeley. The major objective of this chapter, drawn from the Center studies, is to present a descriptive analysis of a variety of noncognitive characteristics that differentiate the enrollees in an innovative cluster college from those entering the parent or fostering institution. From these results, inferences are made about the processes that seem to underlie the selection of these institutions by the particular youth. A final objective is to explore some of the implications for programs which may or may not be successful in enrolling a special clientele.

Most of the eight institutions under consideration in this study have been mentioned in earlier chapters. However, to provide the necessary background for this chapter, the schools will be described in more detail. Two extreme regions of the country are represented—by Nasson College and Hofstra University in the northeast and by other schools in California. The vast majority of students in all cases come from homes in areas near the respective schools. The chief exception is found in the two University of the Pacific colleges, each of which enrolls a small minority of out-of-state candidates, whose homes are over 500 miles from the San Francisco Bay Area.

Starting with the eastern schools, Hofstra University, located on Long Island, is a comparatively young institution; it started in the mid-thirties as a branch of New York University. Although the enrollment has increased as rapidly as in many other schools since 1950, and even though a complex program accommodating a diversity of students' needs has developed, this university has managed to maintain itself on a relatively small, compact campus.

In the mid-sixties a special freshman program, titled New College, was initiated at Hofstra, with the major goal of offering and emphasizing intellectual challenges for capable commuting students who ordinarily receive few of the benefits and advantages of residential colleges. From its inception, New College was designed as a self-contained academic community, facilitating close student-faculty relations and stressing a climate and experiences conducive to learning, critical thinking, and personal growth.

In 1965, shortly before Hofstra was invited to participate in this study, the program of New College was converted to a three-year curriculum, culminating in a Bachelor of Arts degree. As in the one-year program, admission was open to interested students of above average to exceptional ability. These simple criteria, plus propaganda about the program emphasis, probably were seen as sufficient to attract an atypical clientele from the university's incoming student body.

The second college, Nasson, is located near the southern tip of Maine in the small semirural community of Springvale. It is nonsectarian and became a four-year institution in 1935 and coeducational after the Second World War. Like Hofstra, it is one of the member schools of the Union for Research and Experimentation in Higher Education. The justification for Nasson's membership was twofold: a long commitment to a strong, interdisciplinary, liberal arts curriculum, with a major concern given to developing "a certain cast of mind, a way of looking at things, which might be summarized as the responsible use of information in the light of experience . . ."; and the pending initiation of a second, separate but adjoining program, called New Division. This cluster institution began in 1965, the year preceding the start of this study.

New Division was presumably the first of an intended series of semiautonomous units of limited size which typified a form of planned expansion adopted by the board of trustees. The curriculum was to be "dedicated to experimentation and to the development of an increasing commitment on the part of its students to areas of universal social concern." Flexibility, individualization, independent inquiry, breadth of curricular experiences, and elimination of conventional grading were among the program innovations or emphases communicated to potential candidates in the New England area. In the earliest solicitation of students application was encouraged from any desiring a novel approach to liberal education.[1]

The College of the Pacific and Raymond College are two institutions in the growing assemblage of schools in Stockton, California, which association assumed the title of the University of the Pacific in 1961. The larger, parent institution, COP, is one of the well-known Methodist colleges in the nation, having achieved a national image largely as the result of its success in intercollegiate athletics in an earlier period. By the end of the sixties three cluster colleges as well as a number of other associated or semi-independent schools were included in a growing organization encompassed by the University.

College of the Pacific (COP), if it may be seen separate from the adjoining, associated schools, might be described as a fairly typical, modern, semi-sectarian college, with a number of

---

[1] After several years of "experimentation," the Nasson Board recently decided to unify the Nasson institutions and to assimilate the special program of New Division to the parent school.

common course requirements for all students in spite of a diversity of programs. More attention and emphasis seems to be given to the preparation for vocational and professional futures than to strong interdisciplinary liberal arts majors. The former emphasis is highlighted in the several on-campus professional schools, such as education, engineering, music, and pharmacy. A recent campaign by a campus committee to revise the COP curriculum has resulted in a plan to break with traditionalism and uniformity of programs and procedures, and to improve teaching-learning approaches with renewed emphasis in the liberal arts.

From its inception, Raymond College, the first of several cluster colleges to be adjoined to the university, represented a break with traditionalism, and, because of a fast and successful start early in the sixties, various aspects of its program have served as the models for more recent efforts at innovation. The philosophy of Raymond (1963), quite similar to the one expressed by the Nasson leaders, is exhibited in an emphasis on "a curriculum and methodology that aims to confront the student with ways of thinking; the meaning of personal identity, involvement, and social responsibility; and the necessity of hard thinking and good judgments."

Some of the features of the Raymond program are a special emphasis on the liberal arts, three courses per term, independent study, a de-emphasis of majors and concentration of work in one department, an integration of work across several disciplines, two comprehensive examinations, and an absence of any conventional grading system. Admission is determined by a flexible set of criteria, including grades and aptitude scores, but with greater attention given to motivation, personality traits, and background experiences.

The three innovative colleges described above can all be categorized as cluster colleges in the most commonly used sense of the term. Each was set up as an immediately adjoining unit to an established institution. Actually, although each had some form of separate housing, all were located on the campus proper of the parent institution. From this standpoint, the fourth pair of schools, both University of California campuses, represents a different form of association.

Santa Cruz is one of the most recent campuses to be constructed in a scattered university network, encompassing its own cluster of small institutions and exhibiting a host of innovations and experimentation. This complex of developing colleges, located on the outskirts of Santa Cruz, is beyond the proximity of the Bay Area and some seventy miles from Berkeley. In reality, the entering students at Santa Cruz could be compared to those at other university campuses, which could provide a reference base for the students on any new campus. The fact that Berkeley and one of the Santa Cruz schools were both in the Center's Student Development Study was an automatic determinant of their inclusion in these analyses, along with the fact that the Santa Cruz colleges in general have introduced numerous innovations in the overall context of an established university organization and program.

The students in this study were all of the entrants at Stevenson College, the second institution to be built at Santa Cruz. This campus opened in 1966. The major theme of the Stevenson program was directed to the social sciences: "their intellectual orientations, their interconnections with the other divisions of disciplined learning, and their role in the study and life of man." Like the other colleges in the Santa Cruz complex, Stevenson is an undergraduate, coeducational program, largely residential in its early years. Close communication between students and faculty, facilitation of student community, small classes and seminars, a liberal arts emphasis, independent study, numerous library facilities, access to courses and specialties on adjoining campuses, the use of comprehensive exams, and pass-fail evaluation—such are some of the characteristics of the academic program that the Stevenson men and women encounter. Such is not the general regimen for students on the Berkeley campus, where the curricula are fairly traditional and large classes are the rule, to the detriment of intimacy and community.

The university at Berkeley is a rather compact campus with an enrollment of over 27,000 students. The entering students on this and all University of California campuses are selected from the top 12 per cent of the high school graduates in the state. Thus, by aptitude and achievement they cannot be described as typical college freshmen. Since the same criteria apply to all campuses, differentiating characteristics among entering students, if they appear, would demand other means of explanation, such as population differences contingent with regional origins, or program differences that attract a different clientele.

The studies at the Berkeley Center from which these data are drawn were initiated as five-year studies in the fall of 1966.[2] Both investigations represent special projects concerned with student development, and the analyses in this chapter are incidental to the major objectives of the basic investigations.

The staff of both investigations used the same means of data collection. Two of the assessment instruments are the sources of information employed here. The first is the Omnibus Personality Inventory (OPI) (Heist and Yonge, 1968), which consists of fourteen psychological scales or dimensions that assess students' attitudes, opinions, and interests basic to measuring degrees of normal ego functioning, nonauthoritarian thinking, and interest in academic and intellectual pursuits. The second instrument is an extensive questionnaire through which a gamut of information is obtained regarding such matters as students' aspirations, socioeconomic and family backgrounds, religious and political preferences, previous and anticipated activities, perceptions of the institution, ideas about ideal institutions, academic and vocational goals, and reasons related to the selection of a college.

The assessments of students in the respective institutions included in the two studies were conducted on entering, first-year classes, on "samples" that represent 90 per cent or more of the entrants. The chief exception to this is the University at Berkeley where the number tested constituted two-thirds of the total freshman class.[3]

---

[2] The two studies are directed by Mildred Henry and Paul Heist. The authors extend their appreciation to Miss Henry for releasing data from the study conducted in institutions in the Union for Research and Experimentation in Higher Education.

[3] The actual sample sizes of those who responded to or completed the two instruments vary minimally from the following figures: Hofstra University, 308 males, 238 females; New College (Hofstra), 43 males, 37 females; Nasson College, 144 males, 88 females; New Division (Nasson), 45 males, 15 females; College of Pacific, 176 males, 241 females; Raymond,

The composite of diverse scales in the Omnibus Personality Inventory can be instrumental in differentiating between students in an established or parent institution and a new cluster college. The particular descriptions of students, as groups of males and females, will be taken chiefly from the obtained differences on individual scales and clusters of scales between the two types of institutions. Only the differences significant at the .05 level of probability or greater, using the t-test statistic, are the basis for the following descriptions.

At the risk of confounding the results of the comparisons for the reader, we present some of the general "story" of major differences first for all institutional pairs, to be followed by the more specific findings for each of the four pairs. The sequence of presenting the results is determined by a presumed logic of learning, which was basic to the development of the OPI. In the following order, this sequence includes a freedom or openness to learn and change, an orientation to or interest in learning, not unrelated to the first concept, and the perception and acceptance of self and others. Three or more related scales in the OPI assess each of these three conceptual areas. Where the obtained differences are minimal or are limited to one institution or to one sex group in a single institution, any interpretations will be slighted due to the fact that the results demand greater replication.

The first category of differences, a freedom or an openness to change, sometimes referred to as a derivative of the nonauthoritarian syndrome, is one major concept measured by the OPI. This openness is basic to a greater readiness to pursue and examine new ideas, as well as to learn them. Relevant to the objectives frequently underlying the creation of smaller, cluster colleges in recent years, it was of direct interest to see whether the students recruited, selected, or admitted could be differentiated accordingly from those in the larger and established counterpart institutions. In the latter, with their complexity of programs, we may find a lesser concern for the liberal arts and intellectual pursuits per se. The OPI includes two basic means of assessing this concept of freedom or openness in the Autonomy (Au) and Religious Orientation (RO)

---

37 males, 51 females; California (Berkeley), 1042 males, 1034 females; California (Santa Cruz), 105 males, 108 females.

scales and two correlated characteristics, according to a number of factor analyses, in the Practical Outlook (PO) and Complexity (Co) scales.[4]

The analysis of differences between the students in the two different types of institutions, the parent schools versus the cluster colleges, on this measure of openness led to consistent results across all four pairs. Specifically, differences were obtained in a direction that indicated that the cluster college youth were more open to change. These results were obtained for both male and female students on all four scales, with one exception—the differences between males in two pairs of schools (Hofstra and the University of California) on the RO scale were in the same direction but not significant (see Figures 1 through 8).

For the Hofstra samples, the differences on Au, RO, Co, and PO between the New College students and those on the university campus are all significant, with the above exception already noted. Judging by the mean scores for the two groups (see Figures 1 and 2), especially on Co, Au, and RO, the women who selected or were admitted to New College are more dissimilar from Hofstra female entrants in general than are the men. The New College women definitely exhibit a profile of characteristics, as a group, that would make many of them candidates for some of the prestigious or innovative colleges on the East Coast, if only considering their scores on this "openness for change" dimension.

Similar results were obtained for the women in the other eastern cluster college, New Division at Nasson. This small sample (N = 11) accentuates the points just made in that they are very much unlike the considerably larger group on their main campus, and again much more dissimilar than the males (see Figures 3 and 4). In general, comparing the differences among the institutional pairs on these four OPI anti-authoritarianism scales, Nasson appears to have been as successful as any of the four schools, if not more so, in admitting or assigning students to the special program who were ready for or open to new experiences. It remains to be seen whether this so-called openness is matched by a natural involvement in challenging academic and intellectual experiences.

[4] See the OPI manual for the rationale, defense, and statistics underlying this composite assessment via the particular four scales.

The results on these scales for the men and women on the University of the Pacific campuses fall approximately between Nasson and Hofstra, as far as the extent of the differences between the students in the two settings is concerned (Figures 5 and 6). At Raymond, in contrast to the first two colleges, the differences for the two sexes average out to be about the same across the four openness-to-change scales: that is, the women on this cluster campus do not show up to be somewhat more different from the College of the Pacific students than the men. Many of these students in the first three cluster colleges, with the possible exception of the Nasson women, could quite likely have enrolled in any of the three schools described without feeling that they had made a drastic change in the kinds of peers they would encounter.

The data on the rather special pair among the four, that is, the non-adjoining campuses of the University of California at Berkeley and Santa Cruz (Figures 7 and 8), indicate that both of these campuses recruit a little different clientele than the smaller institutions. These two groups of students are less dissimilar on the variety of characteristics measured by the OPI scales than those in the other paired colleges, presumably a result of common admissions criteria. Consequently, the fact of any differences in scores most likely could be attributed to some differences in the perceptions or images of these campuses and the self-selection process by students in the available pool of candidates.

The actual statistical results on the four characteristics do show that the students in Stevenson College (Santa Cruz) are sufficiently unlike the much larger sample at Berkeley; significant differences are obtained on all comparisons with exception of the males on the Religious Orientation scale. As before, judging by the amount of the differences, there is somewhat greater dissimilarity between the women on the two campuses as compared to the men.

The major interpretation to be drawn from the particular data reviewed, recalling the underlying concept theoretically assessed by these four scales, is that the entering students in the four new, innovative settings are significantly more open to new experiences and to the possibility of change, while being essentially nonauthoritarian in their thinking. More specifically, the major differences, in amount, on the Au and Co scales imply greater inde-

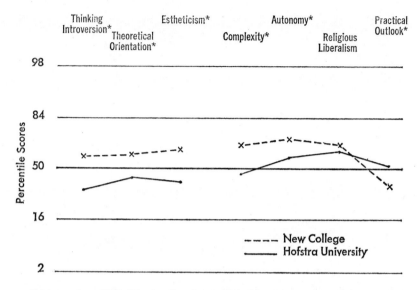

FIGURE 1. OPI Percentile Score Profiles for male students at Hofstra University. Significant differences: * = .01 level; ** = .05 level.

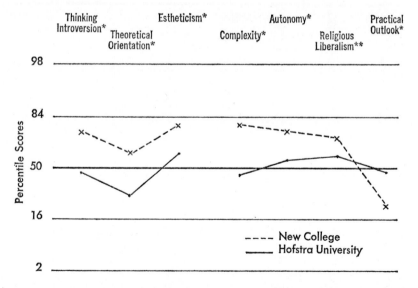

FIGURE 2. OPI Percentile Score Profiles for female students at Hofstra University. Significant differences: * = .01 level; ** = .05 level.

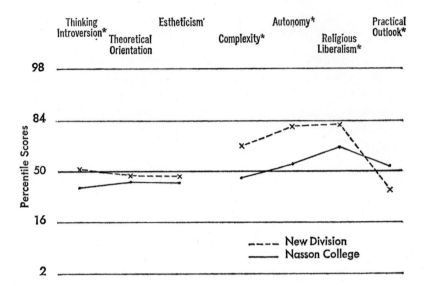

FIGURE 3. OPI Percentile Score Profiles for male students at Nasson College. Significant differences: * = .01 level; ** = .05 level.

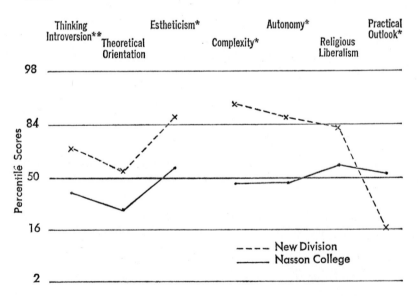

FIGURE 4. OPI Percentile Score Profiles for female students at Nasson College. Significant differences: * = .01 level; ** = .05 level.

pendence of judgment, freedom to consider social issues, tolerance of ambiguous and frustrating situations, and a lesser anchorage in their subcultural pasts, for example, family and church. The latter is substantiated in the RO scores, with the students in the cluster colleges tending toward liberalized religious beliefs and concerns, if not self-confessed agnosticism. However, the reference groups for comparison here, those in the parent institutions, also are not dogmatic fundamentalists. On a Hebraic-Christian basis, the great majority of freshmen in all eight situations are more liberal than conservative; but for those enrolling in the newer institutions, religious commitments have become a much lesser determinant of their thinking and decisions.

The consistent differences on the PO scale supplement and complement the distinctions based on the other three scales, largely highlighting the variation in authoritarianism. In essence, these results indicate also that the cluster college youth are less goal-oriented, less concerned about the immediate or future utility of their studies, and freer from concerns regarding the applied and practical.

The second question under consideration is whether the cluster college students exhibit interests in intellectual pursuits which complement their above average openness to new experiences and learning readiness. The analyses of the pertinent data have been made on the basis already introduced, that is, a comparison of the mean scores on a set of individual scales which together constitute an index of intellectual orientation.

The specific scales used for this index are Thinking Introversion, Theoretical Orientation, and Estheticism. Patterns on these three scales represent varied styles of thinking or orientations to the quest for knowledge. These variations range from a strong, intrinsic disposition (pattern of high scores) toward intellectual activity, including literary and esthetic overtones, to an anti-intellectual way of thinking, typifying those who view learning chiefly in terms of its application or utility. The Complexity scale, included in the openness-to-change concept discussed above, contributes to this intellectual index also.

In the fashion pursued in the previous section, the results on this concept are also reviewed, one by one, for the institutional

pairs, but without an initial, generalized appraisal of the findings
for all four. The reason for omitting the latter is that the common
findings are not as clear as they were for the openness concept.
Starting again with the Hofstra duo, New College had significantly
higher scores on the three primary intellectual scales, as well as on
Co (Figures 1 and 2). The amount of the differences is approximately the same between the men and women groups, but both
groups of women score higher on two of the three scales, implying
that both represent a somewhat more selective sample than the men.
The major point to be noted here briefly is that the cluster college
has enrolled a majority of students who have a stronger orientation
to intellectual involvement than those on the university campus,
with many of the women representing a rather atypical sampling
of the female gender.

The findings for the Nasson groups represent a very different story for the two sexes. The differences for the women (Figure
3) represent a pattern of results very similar to those observed for
Hofstra women, although the difference is not significant on the
TO scale. However, when combining the results on TI and Es for
this small sample with the large differences they showed on the
openness syndrome, these female entrants present themselves as
the most unusual subgroup in the four institutions.

The findings for the Nasson men are in considerable contrast
to the women, with the small differences on TO and Es not being
significant (Figure 4). These results are a good example where a
measured readiness for new experiences on the part of the New
Nasson males is not complemented by a comparable interest in
learning. However, the sufficiently high mean scores on Co, Au,
and RO would imply the *possibility* of developing a stronger intellectual orientation, given appropriate, conducive circumstances,
perhaps of the sort envisioned for New Division. But according to
the evidence from other studies, the odds are against such changes
in most colleges and universities. Also in interpretation, the majority
of these males will not pose the characteristics of a very challenging
social or academic environment for each other, and the women in
this class, obviously more highly motivated and committed, are too
few in number to vitalize the general situation.

The differences on the TI, TO, and Es scales between the

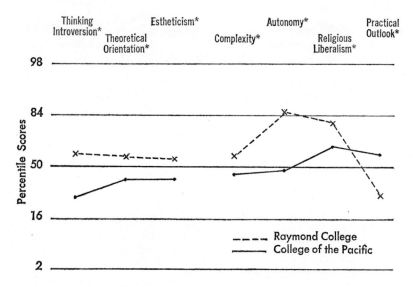

FIGURE 5. OPI Percentile Score Profiles for male students at University of the Pacific. Significant differences: * = .01 level; ** = .05 level.

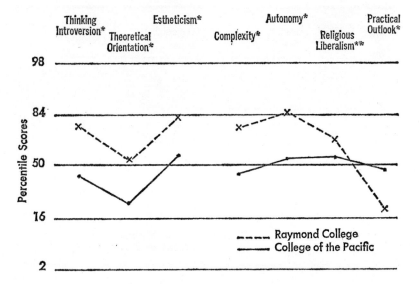

FIGURE 6. OPI Percentile Score Profiles for female students at University of the Pacific. Significant differences: * = .01 level; ** = .05 level.

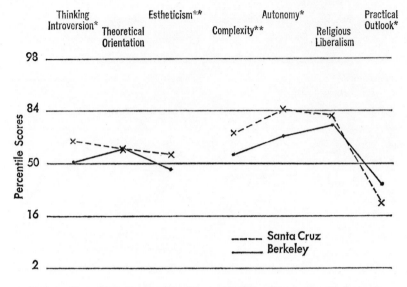

FIGURE 7. OPI Percentile Score Profiles for male students at University of California. Significant differences: * = .01 level; ** = .05 level.

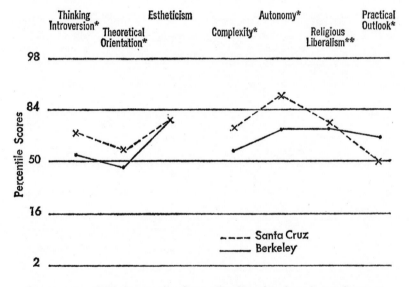

FIGURE 8. OPI Percentile Score Profiles for female students at University of California. Significant differences: * = .01 level; ** = .05 level.

students at the College of the Pacific and at Raymond result in much the same story as presented for the Hofstra institutions. Both the women and the men have mean score profile patterns very similar to the separate sexes at Hofstra, with significant differences on all three scales (Figures 5 and 6). Again the women at Raymond, especially when considering the Co scales also, have a stronger intellectual orientation than the men in this college. But the majority of both sexes are sufficiently different from the Pacific students, particularly with the supplementation of the male differences on the Au, RO, and PO scales, to provide a psychological foundation for a greater receptivity to challenging learning experiences and to create a quite different campus climate.

The men and women at Santa Cruz each show mean scores which are higher on two of the three scales, when compared to the Berkeley entrants, but the differences are not of such an extent that they would create a distinctive academic climate. In other words, what is different about life and learning on these two campuses would be much less determined by the intellectual orientation of students, if the Stevenson College sample may be taken as representative of Santa Cruz, than is the case in the other three paired colleges. But as indicated previously, the total combination of differences, when considering all OPI scales, cannot be overlooked; the clientele at Santa Cruz might be described as a more selective subsample of the type of students that matriculate in the undergraduate program at Berkeley.

For our third category, the OPI includes five scales which, when viewed or analyzed as a pattern of scores, permit interpretations about individuals' social adjustment, affiliative tendencies, concern for others, self-acceptance, and general psychological well-being. The five scales are Social Extroversion, Impulse Expression, Personal Integration, Anxiety Level, and Altruism. The general story on this complex is that the students in all eight institutions tend to be similar, with most groups showing patterns approximating the normative mean on most scales. One exception is found on the Altruism scale. The cluster college men and women at Raymond and Santa Cruz fall above the normative mean and are significantly higher than those enrolled in the comparative campuses.

Another exception is found on the IE scale. Both sexes at

New College present mean scores that are significantly higher than those on the main campus at Hofstra University. Differences on the IE scales between the two Nasson groups were more accentuated, especially for the small proportion of women in the sample. This sample of the New Division women at Nasson is the only one of the eight groups that has a profile of scores on the social-emotional *complex* of scales which deviates considerably from the normative mean. Along with their autonomy, readiness for new experiences, and above average intellectual concerns, a proportion of these women are more impulsive and less happy with or accepting of themselves.

What is the sum and substance of the differences in personality characteristics, as measured by the OPI, between the entering students in several cluster colleges and their counterparts on the campuses with which they are associated? First, the results demonstrate that these cluster colleges have enrolled a special breed of students, students who differ in their orientation to learning and styles of thinking from their peers enrolled in the associated parent schools. Significant differences for the comparisons between students in the paired institutions were obtained on nine out of the twelve characteristics under consideration.

Second, if one focuses on the size of all measured differences between the two student groups in all paired sets of institutions, the variations in openness to change and readiness for learning appear to be the most consistent and important finding. More specifically, the majority of the youth in the cluster colleges were less authoritarian, less applied and practical, less religious (in subscription to dogma and Hebraic-Christian practices), more independent in judgment, more tolerant of ambiguities, and more interested in the complexities of their environment. As a complement to this potential for change, with only two exceptions, those in the innovative schools also had a decidedly stronger disposition toward intellectual involvement. In a sense, significantly larger proportions had "learned to learn," or at least were ready to learn, and at age seventeen they had a real potential for intrinsic involvement in the process of inquiry.

Third, there was no consistent finding, for more than two

pairs of institutions, on a set of five scales assessing social relations and emotional well-being.

When one considers the fairly similar results across the four pairs of institutions, the obvious conclusion is that these particular innovative or experimental educational programs, for the most part, were recruiting or admitting atypical high school graduates. These young people brought advantageous orientations and greater motivation to the academic challenges and assignments posed for them.

If cluster colleges do indeed differ from most colleges in their educational missions, and if such differences are made known, then it might be expected that these colleges will be selected by freshmen for whom these special goals have a particular appeal. The educational attitudes and objectives of the freshmen in the four varied cluster colleges in this study suggest that such a relationship exists. Although these data also indicate a number of differences between the freshmen in the parent institutions and those in the cluster colleges, usually consistent with OPI measurements, most of these differences may be subsumed under two major differentiations. The students in the cluster colleges are less vocationally oriented, particularly with respect to their education, and more predisposed to taking an active role in their education.

In answer to the question, "Which of the following objectives do you hope to gain in college?" the cluster college students were much less likely than those in the parent school to state that vocational preparation was their primary objective. Instead, they were more likely to emphasize the development of either critical thinking or of a "broad general outlook," in line with the differences in intellectual orientation presented in the previous section. Consistent with the vocational orientation of the non-cluster college students was the emphasis they placed on the certification process, as was manifested in their concern with grades. For example, the non-cluster college students acknowledged that good high school grades in certain courses played an important role in their selection of a major. More than the students who selected cluster colleges, these students also indicated that they liked to compete for grades and that making superior grades was more important than other activities. The cluster college students, on the other hand, rather than being concerned about good grades, showed a highly consistent tendency to endorse the following type of participation: "Expressing my true feeling, ideas or knowledge even when they contradict the instructor's." This preference appears to be related to the other major tendency for cluster college students to desire to take an active role in their education.

The freshmen in the cluster colleges stated that they like to write papers and indicated that they preferred that the topics and approach of their classroom assignments be left up to them, rather than being fixed and definite. For example, 73 per cent of the students at New Division, as compared to 50 per cent at Nasson, wanted to take the initiative in doing their assignments; the results for the other pairs of institutions were similar. Furthermore, the students at New Division and Santa Cruz (more than the students at Nasson and Berkeley) believed that students should be given very great freedom in the selection of their studies and that they should "participate significantly in the content and organization of courses, academic policy decisions, and matters of this sort."

Cluster college students also reported a greater tendency to lend support to or become active in protest movements on their campuses—particularly those in "support of civil rights" or in "opposition to the war in Vietnam." Interestingly enough, Santa Cruz freshmen are much more "protest-prone" than Berkeley freshmen. Finally, and also in line with OPI results, it should be noted that cluster college students seemed to have a more "open" and exploratory attitude toward their future educational experiences. They were more likely to be undecided about their majors, and the Santa Cruz and Raymond freshmen were more likely than their peers at Berkeley and COP to plan to transfer to another college before graduation.

The above results indicate that large proportions of freshmen at cluster colleges tended to have somewhat distinctive educational attitudes and goals, with many seeking active involvement in the educational process, while de-emphasizing the vocational and certification aspects of the college experience. These concerns are consistent with the relatively high autonomy, readiness for new experiences, and intellectual orientation of these students. Thus far, it would appear that these cluster college students are in search of and ready for certain kinds of relationships with their educational environment, as manifested in the personality and attitudinal characteristics described above, and that these desired relationships are highly consistent with some of the stated objectives of these institutions.

The kinds of relationships cluster college freshmen desire to have with the social aspects of the total institutional environment are revealed in their descriptions of "an ideal college." The students in the four cluster colleges (as again compared with the students in the other colleges) wanted their ideal college to be experimental in most respects, as would be expected. Also, they tended to prefer an institution stressing discussion classes over lecture classes and encouraging independent study. And perhaps less expected, they opted for the stepped-up quarter system rather than the semester system, a pass-or-fail system of grading, and a de-emphasis of competitiveness for grades (see Table 3).

Regarding the admission of students, they preferred a policy of selection on the basis of personal qualities rather than grades and test scores, while still desiring to be in an institution where most students would be highly intelligent. Their ideal college would be small and academically oriented with the emphasis on general education (rather than specialization), while intercollegiate athletics and fraternities would be de-emphasized. They also preferred a place encouraging involvement in off-campus politics to campus activities.

In summary, the cluster college freshmen, when compared with their peers in the parent institutions, can be described as more academically than vocationally oriented. They are more eager to participate actively in the educational process, and this includes interest in experimental programs and approaches. With reference to their extracurricular interest, these students are more likely to actively demonstrate their concerns about contemporary social and political issues, while rejecting the more "traditional" campus activities.

These data on educational attitudes indicate that the kinds of relationships cluster college students desire to have with their environment appear to form a consistent and coherent pattern.

Table 3

Descriptions of "Ideal College" Selected by Freshmen

Ideal College Characteristic	Institutions[a]			
	Nasson	California	Pacific	Hofstra
Lectures vs. discussions	ON > NN	B > SC	COP > R	NH > OH
Residential		SC > B		NH > OH
Small		SC > B		NH > OH
City (location)		B > SC		OH > NH
Fraternities		B > SC	COP > R	OH > NH
Intercollegiate athletics	ON > NN	B > SC	COP > R	
Admission by grades	ON > NN	B > SC	COP > R	
Pass vs. no-pass evaluation	NN > ON	SC > B	R > COP	NH > OH
Off-campus politics	NN > ON		R > COP	NH > OH
Independent study	NN > ON		R > COP	
Church affiliation			COP > R	
Quarter system		SC > B	R > COP	NH > OH
Traditional (not experimental)	ON > NN	B > SC	COP > R	OH > NH
Competition	ON > NN	B > SC	COP > R	
Live at home		B > SC		OH > NH
Community		SC > B		
General education		SC > B	R > COP	NH > OH
High intelligence		SC > B	R > COP	

[a] The differences between the pairs of institutions at the .05 level of probability (or greater) and the direction ($>$) of the differences are noted, where significant, in each case. The letters O and N in the school symbols represent the old and new campuses respectively; B stands for Berkeley and SC for Santa Cruz.

Moreover, these preferred relationships seem to be similar to the dominant orientations and objectives of the cluster colleges, and it is important to know whether cluster college freshmen see their institutions as emphasizing these desired relationships. Consequently, the images of these institutions, as perceived by these entering freshmen, become an added area of interest.

The students in each of the cluster colleges were more likely than those in each of the related institutions to say that their institution has "some special quality that distinguishes it from other colleges and universities." One hundred per cent of the Raymond students, but only 72 per cent of the College of Pacific students, saw their institution as being distinctive. Similarly, 83 per cent of the New College and 40 per cent of the Hofstra students viewed their institutions in this way. Not surprisingly, most of these freshmen said that an experimental feature of the institution was responsible for this special quality. Moreover, there were additional differences between the parent institution–cluster college pairs, with respect to perceived distinguishing features. For example, the freshmen at New Division and Raymond (more than those at Nasson and COP) identified a permissive climate and concern for individual development and growth as distinctive aspects. However, the students at Nasson, Berkeley, and Raymond (more than their peers at the three comparable institutions) saw the academic-intellectual aspects and the social character (for example, sense of community) to be the distinctive qualities of their colleges. Since Raymond is a cluster college and Nasson and Berkeley are not, this is a good example of the fact that a uniform role is not played by each factor involved in the image and selection of cluster colleges. Therefore, later in this chapter, consideration will be given to those factors which seem to be particularly important in the selection processes in each of the four pairs of colleges.

Consistent with the distinctive images of these cluster colleges is the finding that the entering freshmen in these institutions indicated that they knew more than the freshmen in the other institutions about most aspects of their colleges, with the exception of their academic reputation. This exception is not surprising, however, since the parent institutions are older and have had the opportunity to develop an academic reputation. Specifically, more than the non-

cluster college students, the cluster college students said they knew
about the innovative features of their college's curricula and the
institutional objectives. They were more aware of the ratio of required work to free electives, the availability of independent study,
the amount of individual help, and the amount of informal contact
with the faculty. Moreover, they were more likely to know a lot
about the general philosophy of their institution and the college's
academic expectations of students.

Thus, the images students have of different cluster colleges
are similar in several respects, despite variations in the areas of
special emphasis which make each institution unique. Experimental
curricula, particularly as manifested in the concern for individualization of education, give cluster colleges distinctive images, even
though their academic reputations are not yet as clear and established as those of the older, comparable institutions. These data
again illustrate a great parallelism between the acquired images of
cluster colleges and the orientations of the entering freshmen, which
emphasize the desire to be active agents in the educational process,
along with a rejection of some of the vocational and collegiate
aspects of a college education. In line with this similarity, an examination was made of the congruence between student orientation
and institutional image to see whether it was made more explicit in
the reasons given for the selection of a college.

Before the reasons the students in the four pairs of colleges
gave for selecting their college are examined, it is of interest to
determine what persons or events influenced the students in their
decisions. The cluster college freshmen were more likely than the
other students to say that the most important influence was "reading about the college in its catalogue" and that the second most
important influence was a "staff member from the college." This
would seem to indicate that cluster college freshmen were more
influenced from "within" the college in their selection of their
college, with the students enrolling in both cluster and parent colleges being influenced about equally by their parents, high school
teachers and counselors, and friends. We would expect, then, to
find a high degree of similarity in the images held among cluster
college freshmen, as well as among their orientations and the
reasons given for selecting a college.

The students in cluster colleges were more likely to say, as already mentioned, that an important reason for the selection of their college was the opportunity to participate in an experimental and individualized program. They were also more likely to say that career reasons or a particular department were *not* important, and the general extracurricular activities and location of the campus were also less likely to be given as important reasons (Table 3).

An additional clue to the students' reasons for selecting their colleges is the description of anticipated sources of personal satisfaction. The students in cluster colleges were more likely to mention "individual study or research," "getting acquainted with faculty members," "development of self-insight," "individual artistic or literary work," and "off-campus politics" as anticipated sources of satisfaction. On the other hand, the non-cluster college freshmen were more likely to say that student government, athletics, and "other student activties" would be important sources of satisfaction.

It becomes quite apparent that the reasons given by cluster college students for selecting these special institutions seem to be related to several basic orientations or themes. To iterate, cluster college students are seeking neither a vocational nor a specialized education (in the usual sense of *specialized*), but rather an experimental and *individualized* education. They are not interested in participating in the more traditional or collegiate types of activities; however, they do expect their institutions to be concerned with their individual growth and development, permitting them to have the freedom to play an active role in their own development and in off-campus politics.

These findings demonstrate that the entering freshmen in four cluster colleges are differentiated from their peers in four comparable institutions with respect to orientations and attitudes, perceptions of their college's image, and reasons given for the selection of a college. Some very similar and recurrent themes can be found among these differences. Furthermore, these differentiating themes are related to the stated objectives and characteristics of these four cluster colleges and, in fact, are representative of some of the more prominent and common features of cluster colleges in general. Before suggesting some of the implications of these com-

Table 4

FRESHMEN'S REASONS FOR SELECTING COLLEGE
(Percentages)

Institutions

Reasons	New Division	Nasson	UC, Santa Cruz	UC, Berkeley	Raymond	College of Pacific	New College	Hofstra University
Career reasons	16	47°	15	41°	29	47ᵇ	43	46
Closely-knit college community	67	76	88	12°	82	72	67	40°
Extra-curricular activities	7	23	12	21ᵇ	1	18°	5	24°
Financial reasons	5	14	7	21°	26	20	26	31
Friends attending	2	6	2	10ª	0	6	1	7
General academic reputation	20	36°	74	87°	74	47°	39	53
Geographic location, climate, etc.	18	42°	52	62	16	33ᵇ	47	56
Influence or wishes of parents	7	17ª	17	21	10	20	17	22

Opportunity for great deal of freedom in personal life	44	25[a]	44	45	38	20[b]	29	20
Opportunity to live away from home	25	33	42	39	37	37	18	10[a]
Opportunity to participate in experimental programs	77	10[c]	71	11[c]	38	3[c]	66	3[c]
Opportunity to pursue individualized academic program	81	26[c]	60	35[c]	59	26[c]	65	24[c]
Parents attended the college	3	2	0	5	1	1	0	1
Variety of elective courses	32	22	7	47[c]	0	12[c]	25	24
A particular department	7	22[a]	7	24[c]	1	5	12	30[b]

[a] .05 level of significance
[b] .01 level of significance
[c] .001 level of significance

monalities and relationships, the four colleges should be examined separately. Indeed it has been hypothesized that the selection of each of these institutions is related to some particularly dominant themes which are particularly characteristic of that institution.

Which characteristics are most "distinctive" in the selection of each of the four cluster colleges under study? Several criteria are used to determine these most distinctive factors. First of all, those particular responses to a given question (for example, "How important was each of the following considerations to you *in selecting* the college you are now attending?") which yield the greatest statistically significant differences between the cluster college and the comparable institutions are identified. Second, the items most frequently responded to in a positive way by the cluster college students are examined. And finally, some consideration is given to those items which reveal a uniform pattern of responses for three pairs of colleges but not the fourth.

The students at New Division seemed to place the greatest emphasis on individual development and individualized education. They differed considerably from the students on the main campus, usually beyond the .01 level of significance, in the following ways. Eighty-nine per cent of the freshmen at New Division said that their ideal college would have a pass-or-fail system of grading and that independent study would be emphasized. Eighty-one per cent said that an important reason for their selection of New Division was the "opportunity to pursue an individualized academic program." The development of self-insight was listed an important source of anticipated personal satisfaction by 80 per cent of the New Division freshmen. Moreover, 81 per cent said they knew a lot about "the extent of informal student-faculty contact," and 68 per cent knew a lot about the availability of independent study. Finally, it should be noted that 33 per cent of the New Division freshmen listed factors related to the encouragement of individual development as distinctive qualities of the institution.

While many University of California students selected Berkeley because of its well-established academic reputation, the entering freshmen at Santa Cruz seemed to be seeking the opportunity to have their educational experiences in an intimate atmosphere. Interestingly enough, the mass media was the factor

which most influenced the Santa Cruz students to enroll; so that
even though the Berkeley freshmen were more likely to say that
they knew a lot about their institution's academic reputation, the
Santa Cruz freshmen were more likely to say that they knew a lot
about the general philosophy of their institution.

A number of other highly significant differences were found
between the two groups of freshmen. For example, 97 per cent of
the Santa Cruz students said that their ideal college would be
residential in nature, and 83 per cent said that they selected Santa
Cruz because of the desire to be in a "closely-knit college community, [with the] chance to know students and professors." On
the other hand, 85 per cent of the Berkeley freshmen said they
selected Berkeley because of its academic reputation. They also
said that career reasons, a variety of electives, and a particular department were important for them. *138730*

However, 87 per cent of the freshmen at Santa Cruz said
that an important anticipated source of satisfaction was the development of self-insight. Off-campus politics, bull sessions, and
the opportunity to get acquainted with the faculty were also given
as particularly important anticipated sources of satisfaction. Berkeley students were much more likely than the Santa Cruz students
to list academic or intellectual characteristics as the distinctive
quality of their institution, while Santa Cruz students showed a
greater tendency than the Berkeley students to mention the distinctiveness of the physical characteristics of their college.

More than the freshmen of any other cluster college, the
Raymond freshmen emphasized the academic reputation and
quality of their college. This fact may be a result of the college's
history, short as that may be. Two other distinctive characteristics
also appear: individualized education and an emphasis on general
education. This is shown by a number of significant differences between the students at Raymond and the College of Pacific.

All of the Raymond freshmen said that their ideal college
would have mostly discussion rather than lecture classes. Ninety-
eight per cent said that independent study, general education, and
academic reputation would be emphasized at their college. The
Raymond students were more likely to say that they selected their
college because of the individualized nature of the education and

its academic reputation. They were also more likely to mention "individual study or research" and "getting acquainted with faculty members" as important sources of satisfaction.

Ninety-two per cent of the COP students anticipated that their major courses would be an important source of satisfaction, but 86 per cent of the Raymond students said that "course work in general" would be important. In addition, 23 per cent of the latter listed characteristics related to individual development as being distinctive of Raymond, and 34 per cent listed academic and intellectual characteristics.

In examining the more prominent differences between New College and Hofstra University, it is more difficult (than in the above three cases) to find one distinctive pattern. However, it would appear that students select the New College program with the expectation that the educational curriculum encourages a greater concern for the individual student. Sixty-seven per cent of the freshmen at New College said they selected the college for the opportunity to be in a "closely-knit college community, [with the] chance to know students and professors." Sixty-five per cent gave "opportunity to pursue an individualized academic program" as an important reason. Moreover, the opportunity to become acquainted with faculty was an important anticipated source of satisfaction, and these cluster college freshmen said they knew a lot about the amount of individualized help at their college. They also said that the curriculum was distinctive of the college, and 87 per cent said that their ideal college would be on the quarter system.

The contents of this chapter have been devoted chiefly to the presentation of a variety of comparisons, fairly consistent for the most part across four paired settings, between entering students in established institutions and those in associated cluster colleges.[5] Some diversity in the type of academic settings under considerations permitted an exploration for common findings, that is, a search for generalizations regarding possible distinguishing characteristics of those young men or women who desire more experimental, flexible,

[5] Studies of the students at three cluster colleges at Michigan State University (Olson, 1968, 1969) and at Callison College at the University of the Pacific (Mason) have obtained results which are consistent with those reported here.

and challenging learning experiences, presumably more frequently found in cluster colleges.

The major result of this study is the factual delineation of numerous differences, in selected personality characteristics, goals, attitudes, institutional preferences, and reasons for selection of a college. The student who chooses and accepts admission in an innovative cluster college, as represented in the above four somewhat varied examples, tends to exhibit a gamut of differences from his counterpart in the more conventional educational institution. However, these results are based on computed differences in average scores or in frequencies of responses. Such data permit conclusions only on the basis of the average student, a possible statistical artifact, or what a proportion or majority of a sample indicate about themselves. In other words, in line with human variation, not all students are different or as different from the reference groups as these types of analyses might lead one to believe. However, the proportions of differentiated "types" in the two compared groups are such as to permit us to venture several conclusions and implications.

The fact of the numerous differences, between students in the associated colleges, leads to a guarded conclusion about behavioral correlates of certain basic orientations or perceptual sets, but not so much about specific characteristics as about the *fact* of a number of related characteristics. For example, given a youth at age seventeen who has an intrinsic interest in intellectual pursuits and who is very much a non-authoritarian, a host of other things about him tend to fall into a pattern, as to what he will say or do at the moment, and as regards previous experiences and those he is likely to seek out in the future. The students who declare themselves candidates for an innovative college also declare numerous other things about their behavior on campus, their aspirations, their associations, and what they will frequently communicate to their associates. Thus, a special college environment and climate becomes in large part the characteristics of those who compose it. The entering students will tend to reinforce in each other that which a sufficient proportion already are or seek to become; this tendency also implies a likelihood of further development in a direction already established. For others, different in orientation, the predominant type of student will often pose a challenge, perhaps as a model to emulate or reject.

It may be that the greater autonomy and openness reported about cluster college students is a primary factor in the selection of these institutions, since the main perceived reputation of most of these innovative settings promises new and different experiences for students. This is less likely to be the image of the parent institution, even when it is a respected, renowned institution of reputed high academic quality. Since the cluster colleges have yet to establish and confirm an academic reputation, these students are taking a "risk" in selecting these experimental institutions; yet, as their personality characteristics indicate, they are capable of doing just that. Moreover, they seem to be prepared to de-emphasize vocational education and traditional academic and collegiate activities for the chance to have new and different experiences, as well as the opportunity to play an active role in the development and creation of these experiences.

Taking another approach and recalling the variety of data reviewed in this chapter, there is some available information about the "objective" environment such as is found in the stated goals of the institutions; there is information about the way students view the environment; there are indications about the kinds of relationships students desire to have with educational environments (for example, as shown by their ideas of an ideal college and educational attitudes); and there are the findings about the personality orientations of the students. From these different sources of information and data a principle of congruency may be introduced, in that the goals of the cluster colleges seem to imply an emphasis on certain kinds of relationships between students and their educational environments (for example, autonomous behavior, intellectual involvement, active roles in the educational process, new experiences and experimentation, and individualized treatment). Certain students seem to perceive these emphases, which correspond to the kinds of relationships they desire to have with their educational environments in particular and environments in general, as witnessed in their views of an ideal college, their educational attitudes, and their personality. Moreover, the importance of these emphases, as seen in the above congruencies, is made explicit at least in part in the reasons the students give for having selected their particular college.

A principle of congruency may be needed then to consider both the matter of choice of a college and its ongoing function. Accepting the premise that individual student decision was highly involved in either choosing a college or accepting the "invitation" to enroll, the student's goals and conception of learning were apparently congruent with what he perceived in the description of the place and program. This seemed to have been the case in a couple of the cluster schools even when the college bulletins provided only an intimation, rather than an explicit description, of what could be expected. Enough was conveyed to a sample of high school seniors about an anticipated situation, sufficiently in keeping with their ideas and desires, to lead to a positive decision. A conveyed image was adequate to drawing students congruent with at least some of the ideas and goals of the college.

The congruency basic to admission becomes a determinant of the congruency of associations and communication. Presumably a social and, in part, an academic climate have been imported with the entrants, at least by the proportion who came in direct response to the described program. The success of the four innovative cluster colleges in this study in admitting a majority of freshmen unlike those on the parent campuses should give some cause for exploration and examination. Not only should the power and function of a propagated image be examined, especially of new institutions with a special mission, but also the role of admissions staff in fully comprehending the characteristics of whom they recruit, attract, accept, and reject.

The image of many a college might well be more important than the criterion of ability in that the former may attract a special type of student desired, who in being congruent with the campus goals will contribute more to a conducive learning environment than a high ability "nonintellectual" or a well-practiced achiever. More significant to the objectives of a college, by recruiting a sufficient proportion of students sympathetic to the objectives, the whole process of learning and academic attainment is facilitated. It may be inferred that cluster colleges are meeting the challenge posed by the great diversity of students entering institutions of higher education, with the resulting need for individualized education, in the following manner. The educational program of a cluster college represents a special kind of program, designed for a relatively homogeneous and special group of students. Moreover, many of the students who select cluster colleges exhibit personality characteristics which are seemingly consistent with the objectives of the programs of these colleges. Future studies might be aimed at ascertaining the effect of "isolating" the less intellectual and less autonomous students in the parent institutions. Does this decrease the likelihood of their changing in the direction of greater intellectuality and autonomy? Or does it provide the faculty of the parent institutions with the opportunity to develop programs especially suited to stimulating certain kinds of development in those students who may be initially less open to change?

Among remaining questions, the faculty of the cluster colleges should at least be introduced as a relevant and important concern. Obviously they too must be congruent in attitude and concern with the objectives of a college, particularly one focused on a special program, and the organization and styles of instruction. And indeed, there is some evidence that the faculty may be so inclined (see Chapter Seven). Probably of equal, if not greater, importance, however, is their comprehension of the perceptions, aspirations, and motivation of the students. Should they fail to recognize the special qualities of the student body, much of the potentiality of utilizing the advantages created by the establishment of an innovative program may well be lost. The importance of the cluster college student and his unusual orientation and characteristics has been more than implied in the comparative analyses reviewed. The learning is done by the individual student, and it is his advanced openness to change and intellectual interests that should be understood and accommodated; it is also the campus culture and climate that he lives in that cannot be ignored by all who serve in the teaching capacity.

Chapter 5

Making an
Intellectual
Community

Jerry G. Gaff

The year 1960 was a pivotal one for the school then known as the College of the Pacific. A small, private college affiliated with the Methodist Church, College of the Pacific had been historically committed to the teaching of undergraduates. It had long operated a liberal arts program and maintained schools of music and education, but it recently had expanded the scope of its undergraduate offerings by adding schools of pharmacy in 1955 and engineering in 1957. A modest graduate program was operated, mainly in the field of education. COP (as it was usually referred to) was perhaps best known for its football exploits; Amos Alonzo Stagg, Eddie LeBaron, and Dick Bass all left their marks on the school. Fraternities and sororities dominated the social life, and among many on the West Coast COP enjoyed a better reputation as a "party school" than as an intellectual center. This was the College of the Pacific at the turn of the decade.[1]

But changes were in the air. California was expanding its extensive public education institutions; the increased number of University of California campuses, the expansion of the state colleges, and the spreading junior college movement posed a challenge to all of the state's private colleges. The place of an institution like COP within the context of an expanding state system was anything but certain. In addition, the costs of providing a college education were spiraling. Like other private schools, COP was increasing tuition and conducting even more aggressive development efforts, but there was some question as to how long small colleges could continue to cope with the rising costs. With the increased availability of "free" public education, it was feared that COP might find itself operating at a greater competitive disadvantage.

Size posed another problem. Although the College of the Pacific enrolled only a total of 1,655 full-time undergraduates in the fall of 1959, this was 74 per cent more than in 1951; furthermore, all the statistics pointed toward a veritable student avalanche in the near future. While COP was a small college, it was suffering the same growing pains, in terms of both enrollment and number of programs, as many larger institutions. Perhaps these pains were felt more acutely because of the school's traditional commitment to a small, friendly, religious, and even familial campus catering primarily to undergraduates.

In reflecting upon the role of the small, private college in the context of the state's ventures in public higher education, President Robert E. Burns (1959) recognized that his school could not compete in the areas of university strength—research, graduate

[1] The research reported in this chapter was undertaken pursuant to a contract with the United States Office of Education. Some of the material contained herein is also available in my earlier work (Gaff, 1967, 1969).

training, and professional consulting. But perhaps, he thought, the small size and limited resources of Pacific could be used to advantage. It could specialize in undergraduate education by providing the sense of community, the close student-faculty relations, and the personal touch usually lacking in larger schools:

> Let us grow larger by growing smaller. Let us develop about the University a cluster of colleges which will retain the values we cherish so much, and yet will, at the same time, make it possible for us to accept some responsibility for educating the increasing numbers of young people seeking to enter institutions of higher learning in California. Let us follow the Oxford and Cambridge system and expand by establishing small, interrelated colleges clustered together to draw strength from each other and from the University.

One way the school might compete effectively with public institutions and still respond to its own past growth and expected future demand for its services would be to develop a cluster of colleges around the periphery of the existing campus; by adapting the Oxford-Cambridge model the institution could, in the words of the president, "grow larger by growing smaller." The board of regents approved his plan and at the same time changed the school's name to the University of the Pacific. At once California's oldest state chartered institution of higher learning became one of the most innovative.

The year 1960 was also an important one for the cluster college concept in the United States. Of course, the idea of a federation of colleges had been applied first in 1925 in the Claremont Colleges, but the subcollege form was just beginning to emerge. Wesleyan had established its specialization colleges, but they were not conceived of as complete and autonomous colleges. Efforts were under way at Monteith College at Wayne State University to experiment with a special college program for commuting students, but the university was to have only a single experimental college as an appendage. Hofstra University was planning a similar special program for commuters but at that time it was only an intensified freshman year; not until 1965 did it develop into a full college program. And there was talk within the University of California about creating a new campus composed entirely of semiautonomous colleges. The cluster college idea was definitely in the air, and Robert Burns acted quickly to apply the idea and to begin creating a cluster of semiautonomous undergraduate liberal arts subcolleges under the same central administration.

Once the general plan was formulated and adopted, the focus of attention on the now UOP campus shifted to the design of the first cluster college, Raymond College. President Burns and the then academic vice-president Samuel L. Meyer decided that the first school would be an innovative liberal arts college having about 250 students and twenty-five faculty members. After having worked out the basic outlines of the college, they selected Warren Bryan Martin, a thirty-six-year-old chaplain and chairman of the religion department at Cornell College, as the first provost of Raymond. This triumvirate planned the details of the program. The selection of Martin, a dynamic young educator with a bent toward educational philosophy, altered the original direction of the cluster college idea at the University of the Pacific. Although it was expected that the new schools would be innovative, Burns saw them primarily as a technique to provide a personalized education within the context of an expanding university; and while Martin recognized their value as close educational communities, he saw them primarily as devices to attempt substantive academic innovations. Thus, Martin picked up the theme of innovation and carried it further than had been originally expected; when Raymond opened its doors in the fall of 1962, it was a radically innovative cluster college.

The purposes of the new school were summed up in the phrase *liberal education*. They have been articulated in a college brochure (Raymond College, 1963, p. 1):

> To train the mind and discipline the emotions; to encourage curiosity and imagination, creativity and personal authenticity; to bring man into contact with the records of the past and the realities of the present; to help the young student recognize and carry through his obligation to his fellow men and to society; to help him make the most of all that is around him and all that is within him, so that he may be equal to the challenge of the future; to help produce, in a word, better men and better citizens—these have always been regarded as the prime functions of liberal education in America.

If these goals were traditional, the means by which Raymond sought to realize them were not. If the school has made any contribution to American higher education, it is because it devised alternative educational structures to achieve these goals.

The basic structure of the academic program was a 3-3-3 plan; students took three courses per term, for three terms per year, for three years. Colleges had come to recognize the educational liabilities of the semester calendar which had been in vogue for years. It contained two "lame duck" sessions in the first semester—between Thanksgiving and Christmas and between Christmas and the end of the term—and it caused economic waste when facilities were idled during the lengthy summer vacation. In the wake of such criticism the quarter system and the trimester calendars had been tried out, but each had its own attendant difficulties. The quarters were very short time periods, and the summer trimester proved to be rather unpopular. Raymond proposed yet another way to divide the school year. Operating within a thirty-nine-week academic year, the fall term began during the last week of August and ran without break until the Thanksgiving recess; the winter term started a week later and lasted until mid-March with only the Christmas interruption; after another ten-day vacation the spring term commenced and ran until mid-June. It was expected that this calendar would allow a concentration of instruction with only a single interruption by a major holiday; it would provide a short breathing spell between terms; and it would still ensure a longer nine-week summer vacation.

The three-year aspect was perhaps the boldest of all the innovations. It must be clear that although the school was prepared to offer a Bachelor of Arts degree after three years, its program was not an accelerated program; it did not attempt to cram into three years what other schools do in four. It was conceived of as a different program, one almost totally dedicated to general education. For example, while Raymond was able to offer some specialized work in the academic disciplines, it did not require an academic major; it was content to leave to the graduate schools and the professional schools the task of providing disciplinary specialization. If its students could acquire a broad general education, develop critical intellectual tools, and appreciate methods by which knowledge is produced; if they could become sensitive to themselves and to others; and if they could develop personally satisfying and socially useful identities, then Raymond would have achieved its purposes. It was felt that most students could make substantial progress toward these objectives in three years. Then, if they wanted more work in an academic discipline, students would be free to begin that specialized training in the fourth year.

Originally there was some apprehension about adopting a college program only three-fourths as long as the conventional one, and in order to justify this innovation in traditional "contact time" terms, some inventive figuring was done (Raymond College, p. 5).

> Each term is twelve to thirteen weeks in length, and each term provides 62 or 63 sixty-minute class meetings. With five meeting periods of sixty minutes each week the Raymond student has more "contact time" with the professor and the class than the student who follows the conventional semester schedule where there are 70–75 class days per semester (with examination days and other special events often included in this total) and only fifty minutes for each class meeting. Each term at Raymond, therefore, has the weight of a semester. The total program includes nine such terms rather than eight semesters.

Although the Raymond community never regarded contact time as a reliable index of a student's education, this arithmetic did serve to justify its departure from tradition in terms of the rationale underlying that very tradition.

Having rejected the idea that a student's educational growth can be reckoned by the amount of time he spends in contact with his professors, the unit system based upon that rationale was not defensible. A course system was adopted in its place; this arrangement had the advantage of allowing a student to concentrate his intellectual efforts in fewer courses at a given time than is generally possible under the unit system. The particular course plan adopted at Raymond allowed students to take only three courses per term; it was hoped that such concentration would make each course a deeper and more rewarding intellectual experience for the students.

The curriculum was unusual in a number of ways. First, it was very limited; there were just twenty-three standing courses, probably the smallest number of courses offered by any college in the country. Second, every one of these courses was required of all students. In addition, this core curriculum contained a balance among the traditional divisions with five courses in mathematics and natural science, nine in the social sciences, and nine in the humanities. Finally, each student was expected to take four courses in some intellectual specialization, not necessarily an academic discipline.

The heavy emphasis on the core curriculum did not rest upon the assumption that every educated man must have each course, nor was it an attempt to introduce students to a survey of the knowledge contained in all the useful disciplines. The knowledge expansion had reduced these arguments to mere cliches. The rationale was simply that the minds of students could be broadened by bringing them into contact with some—not all—of the major facts, theories, perspectives, methods, and values which have emerged within the context of several relevant disciplines. By requiring a balance of work in the major divisions of knowledge it was hoped that students would come to see intellectual relationships which more narrowly trained persons might miss, and they might come to develop an appreciation for different fields of knowledge which would prevent their encapsulation within any of the many useful but inevitably narrow specializations. The core curriculum consisted of the following courses:

Introduction to the Modern World (A unique offering, usually team-taught, interdisciplinary, and focused on some themes of the contemporary world, taken in the first term of the first year)

Written and Oral English (Primarily writing instruction, taken in the first term of the first year)

Language (French, German, or Spanish, three terms, taken in the first year)

Readings in World Civilization (A history of Western civilization, two terms, taken in the first or second year)

Readings in World Literature (Largely European and American literature, two terms, taken in the first or second year)

Mathematics (Through calculus, two terms, taken in the first year)

Physics	Chemistry
Biology	Philosophy

Readings in Non-Western Civilization	Religion
	Fine Arts
United States History	Economics
Political Science	Sociology
American Civilization	Psychology

Although most courses carried prosaic disciplinary titles, it should not be assumed that they were conventional offerings. Since Raymond required no major, each course was freed from its disciplinary straitjacket. There was no need for the introductory course to prepare students for advanced work in the field, and the entire effort of the teacher could be directed toward the "interested layman." And while the course titles were disciplinary, the Raymond ethos was interdisciplinary. The rhetoric emphasized that intellectual interests cannot be confined within disciplinary categories, that each course should focus upon only a selected portion of the field, and that students and faculty should attempt to relate ideas gained from one course to that of other courses; this rhetoric permeated the community and helped to produce courses which approximated this ideal.

Although many general education programs have been criticized because they were superficial, Raymond constructed some built-in safeguards against superficiality. First, the school adopted as a guideline the slogan, "Do only a few things but do them well." Applied to the courses this meant that most courses featured a block-and-gap approach; several valuable topics were skipped entirely so that certain other topics could be examined in sufficient detail as to yield truly useful knowledge. Also, the student's work was concentrated by virtue of his three-course load and uninterrupted term. The seminar classes and the living and learning environment were planned to enhance the impact of the curriculum and thereby to add intellectual depth to the student's classroom experience.

Finally, it should not be supposed that because most courses were prescribed students had no academic choice or that a core curriculum precluded intellectual diversity. In the Raymond plan courses were to be open-ended so that students might pursue their own special interests within each one, and they were to have porous boundaries so that information from other courses and from personal experience could be brought in. While the choice of courses was removed from students, they were to enjoy the freedom to explore the relevant issues, to develop and defend their own personal stances in seminars, and to follow their own intellectual leads within the context of the courses.

If the core was designed to develop a broadening of students' intellectual horizons, the specialization portion of the curriculum was designed to deepen their understanding of some delimited portion. Specialization did not mean developing a traditional major; cross-disciplinary and integrative study was encouraged. But if a student desired a conventional major, he could take all of his four specialization courses in the same discipline. Because each course was assigned an equivalent weight of five units for transfer or graduate school purposes (internal bookkeeping disregarded the unit idea), a student could earn twenty units in specialization; this, combined with his core course or courses, would give him a total of twenty-five to thirty units, enough for a major at most schools.

The most common form of specialization was through the mechanism of ad hoc courses; these were offered as independent study, tutorials, or irregular seminars. Some students chose to enroll in regular courses elsewhere in the university. In this way individualized instruction was made an integral part of the curriculum and not merely an appendage to the rest of the program; and it was made available to all students, not just the ones who had "proven themselves" in more traditional courses.

A word must be said about the instructional process at Raymond. The entire curriculum was oriented to seminars, tutorials, and independent study. All classes save one were small, generally ten to fifteen students. With lectures the exception rather that the rule and with the entire program oriented to discussion methods of teaching, it was expected that students would become actively involved in intellectual dialogue. It was thought that only with such student involvement would the ends of a liberal education be realized, and it was assumed that if students were invited to be active participants in their education, they would accept the invitation and the challenges it posed.

Raymond also abandoned the customary letter grading system; for each course a student received either a "Satisfactory" or

"Unsatisfactory" designation on his official records. In order to supplement these simple designations, the student also received a "term letter" from each of the professors. The letter, which ranged in length from a single sentence to several pages, was usually a paragraph in length and contained the professor's assessment of his performance. This letter, which also was part of a student's official records, was thought to provide more relevant feedback to the student than the usual letter grade and might help him learn how to improve his work in future courses.

Since the original plan called for little formal evaluation during the term, because the institutional rhetoric opposed common use of formal classroom evaluation procedures, and because the frequent personal contact between faculty and students made such conventional evaluation practices unnecessary, it was thought that one or two rigorous examinations might be useful. Accordingly, comprehensive examinations were required for students at the end of the freshman year and near the end of the senior year. After a short period of confusion about the senior examinations, it was decided that seniors would have to pass a test in their specialization, complete a special research project, or write a quality essay. One specialization course was to be used for these senior activities.

The concept of community was central to the entire Raymond program. The small size, the residential quality, and the concentration of all buildings within a compact corner of the university fostered a sense of community. There were no separate academic and residential buildings; faculty offices were in student dormitories, and the dormitory lounges served as seminar rooms. Student-faculty contact was further enhanced in a variety of ways. Teachers were provided with five free meals per week in the college dining hall; a group of students and faculty performed a play once or twice a year; there was a weekly dinner (which all were expected to attend) often followed by a program; periodic all-college town meetings were held to discuss matters of concern to the community; occasional off-campus retreats were held to delve into some problems more deeply; and there were a host of informal and spontaneous contacts between faculty and students.

Raymond attempted to secure the support of the faculty for this innovative program in a number of ways. First, it tried to recruit faculty whose educational philosophies were consonant with the program, and considerable discussion with prospective professors centered on their place within the total program, not merely on their "departmental" responsibilities.

Second, it provided the human satisfactions which can but often do not accompany undergraduate teaching. Unlike most professors who see students for one class during their college career, the Raymond faculty members could get to know the students well, they could see them grow and develop in and out of class over a period of time. Also the departmental structure was abandoned since there was usually only one teacher responsible for each course; each professor was given a wide latitude within which to operate. Further, each faculty member was encouraged to participate actively in the crucial policy decisions which determined the posture of the new college. Because the departmental structure was abandoned, the faculty conducted most of its business by meeting weekly as a committee of the whole. It was expected that their involvement might lead to their implementing the purposes of the school and pave the way for them to develop primary loyalty to teaching and the school rather than to research and their professional guilds. Further, the school adopted the practice of rewarding classroom professors with promotions and salary increases on the basis of their teaching effectiveness and their contributions to the college. Although this policy in no way solved the ever-present riddle of exactly how to evaluate good teaching, the compactness and intimacy of the environment made it possible to detect a professor's contribution and to reward him accordingly.

Some innovative schools have faltered because their weak financial base has required the faculty in effect to subsidize the college by accepting low salaries. Although the University of the Pacific had been moderately low on the American Association of University Professors pay scale, Raymond faculty were paid somewhat more than their colleagues in the older portion of the university because the three-term academic year required them to work at least five weeks longer. It was hoped that this moderate salary combined with the psychic rewards available from teaching in that novel college would be sufficient inducement to attract and to retain a competent faculty of teacher-scholars.

This radically innovative Raymond program stood in contrast to the more conventional practices of the more established divisions of the university. The units historically identified as the College of the Pacific used a semester calendar and utilized the unit system. While the schools of liberal arts, education, music, engineering, and pharmacy had some of their own degree requirements, all students receiving the baccalaureate degree had to complete a minimum of 124 units. Because COP utilized the familiar letter grading system, all graduates were required to compile a grade-point average of 2.00 (C).

The curriculum was organized according to academic disciplines, and there were a few curricular requirements for all students. Regardless of the school in which they were enrolled, all were required to complete six units of freshman composition, three units of speech, six units of Western civilization, four units of religion, and two units of physical education. In addition to these general requirements, the liberal arts college awarded Bachelor of Arts degrees to students who: (1) completed a six-unit mathematics sequence if a non-science major or a ten-unit sequence if a science major, or achieved a second-year level of competency in a foreign language; (2) obtained an academic major by taking twenty-four units in some department, or an interdepartmental major by compiling forty to sixty units in two or more departments; (3) took six units in the humanities in two of the following three areas: music or art, literature, or philosophy or religion; (4) finished six units in social science in two of these areas: economics or business administration, history or political science, psychology, sociology or home and family living or geography; and (5) took eight units in a natural science, including biological sciences, chemistry, physical geography, geology, and physics.

Predominantly a residential school, COP required all undergraduate women and freshman and sophomore men to live on campus unless they stayed at home or with close relatives. Approximately two-thirds of the students resided in dormitories, while most of the remainder were housed in five social fraternities and five sororities. Numerous extracurricular activities were available to the students, including a non-required weekly religious chapel, various religious organizations, a campus YMCA–YWCA, student government, several intercollegiate athletics, intramural sports for both men and women, dramatics, forensics, a campus radio station, musical groups including an orchestra, band, and choir, a campus newspaper, honor societies, student professional associations, and special interest clubs. Despite its rapid growth, the school was still sufficiently small that most students knew a substantial proportion of the student body and the faculty. The students and the faculty combined to create a friendly small college atmosphere.

Because COP was so much in step with most widespread practices in higher education and because Raymond was so much out of step with that beat, those two segments of the same university provided an excellent setting for a natural experiment. A scientific study of the consequences of those two alternate programs promised to add to the accumulating knowledge of the process by which young adults acquire a liberal education.

Man's best plans may not be implemented as conceived; well-implemented plans may not have the desired results; and programs which do realize the desired results may also produce unanticipated consequences. For all of these reasons it was decided to conduct an empirical study of some of the actual outcomes of the cluster college experiment. Such a project was begun in the spring of 1966 and completed in the summer of 1967; that research forms the basis of this portion of the case study.

The basic research design called for a comparison of students in the cluster college with a group of students in the older portion of the university and a comparison of Raymond students at various stages of their careers with a class of entering freshmen. A battery of four highly structured objective questionnaires was administered to the entire Raymond student body as the second class was about to graduate in the spring of 1966, to a sample of students from throughout the rest of the university at the same time, and to a sample of the freshman class as they entered Raymond in the following fall. Since the details of the method, instruments, and complete results of the study have been discussed elsewhere (Gaff, 1967, 1969), only a capsule summary of the results is presented here. The focus is upon the differences between the perceived environments of Raymond and of College of the Pacific.

Two major questions were asked about the environment of

the schools: How does the climate of the cluster college compare with the climate of the other portions of the university? And have the innovations of the new school fostered the kind of atmosphere for which they were designed?

The primary method was to administer two questionnaires which have been used extensively to study college environments, the College Characteristics Index (CCI) and the College and University Environment Scales (CUES). They were distributed to the entire population of 153 students at Raymond in May, 1966, and 139 or 91 per cent returned completed questionnaires. A non-random sample of ninety-seven students enrolled in the College of the Pacific completed questionnaires at the same time. Although non-random, the COP sample was drawn from all segments of the school. Earlier research (Pace and Stern, 1958; McFee, 1959, 1961; Pace, 1963) suggests that a random sample is not necessary to obtain a valid description of the college environment.

One of the first discoveries from the CCI was that there was a difference in the degree of consensus between the Raymond and COP samples. A total of ninety-three of the 300 items were answered in the same way by 90 per cent or more of the Raymond student body, and another seventy-two items elicited a consensus of 80–89 per cent of the students. By contrast, only seventeen items elicited agreement of 90 per cent or more of the COP sample, and thirty-one statements were answered in the same way by 80–89 per cent of the group.

A sampling of the items which resulted in this consensus showed that over 90 per cent of the cluster college students but less than half of the COP students said such statements as the following were true of their school:

> Students are encouraged to criticize administrative policies and teaching practices.
> Channels for expressing students' complaints are readily accessible.
> Students here are encouraged to be independent and individualistic.
> In talking with students faculty members often refer to their colleagues by their first name.

And likewise 90 per cent of the Raymond sample but less

than half of the COP sample said such statements as the following were *not* true of their college:

> There are lots of dances, parties, and social activities.
> A lecture by an outstanding literary critic would be poorly
> attended.
> Students are more interested in specialization than in a general
> liberal education.
> Most students are interested in careers in business, engineering,
> management, and other practical affairs.

The best way to summarize the results of the CCI is to
examine a school's score on several scales which have been derived
by a factor analysis. Two general dimensions, labeled Intellectual
Climate and Non-Intellectual Climate, have been identified, and
each of these are summaries of other subordinate scales. Scores
have been calculated on each of these measures for each school in
relation to a national normative distribution, and they are contained in Table 5.

CUES provides a measure of five environmental variables.
Scores of each school on these scales in comparison to a national
normative group of institutions. These results are shown in Table
6.

Both instruments demonstrated that Raymond College and
College of the Pacific maintained radically different learning environments. The fact that the two schools differed in a statistically
significant way on all thirteen of the CCI factors is impressive evidence of this divergence. Indeed, two more different segments of
the same university, both claiming support of the same goals,
probably can not be found anywhere in the United States. It is
immediately apparent that the cluster college organization led to the
structured diversity called for in the university plan.

In addition, the evidence indicates that the innovations
adopted by the cluster college have produced in general the kind
of atmosphere desired. First, Raymond did effect a homogeneous
community, as inferred from the high degree of consensus on the
CCI items. But the term *community* is ambiguous. If one implies
by that term an atmosphere characterized by warmth, friendliness,
politeness, and cooperation, then Raymond could *not* be characterized as a community. The low scores on Social Form and Group

Table 5

PERCENTILE RANK OF RAYMOND AND COP SAMPLES ON CCI[a]

SCALE NAME	Raymond	COP
Intellectual Climate	93	9[b]
Work-Play	67	13[b]
Non-Vocational Climate	98	36[b]
Aspiration Level	96	7[b]
Intellectual Climate	90	14[b]
Student Dignity	94	9[b]
Academic Climate	52	7[b]
Academic Achievement	89	5[b]
Self-Expression	96	4[b]
Non-Intellectual Climate	3	60[b]
Self-Expression	96	4[b]
Group Life	23	44[b]
Academic Organization	0	52[b]
Social Form	5	70[b]
Play-Work	33	87[b]
Vocational Climate	2	64[b]

[a] Based on normative data contained in Stern (1963).
[b] Statistically significant difference using t-test and .01 level of confidence.

Table 6

PERCENTILE RANK OF RAYMOND AND COP SAMPLES ON CUES[a]

SCALE NAME	Raymond	COP
Practicality	5	26[b]
Community	69	37[b]
Awareness	95	9[b]
Propriety	23	18
Scholarship	96	12[b]

[a] Based on normative data contained in Pace (1963).
[b] Statistically significant difference using chi-square test and .01 level of confidence.

Life all point to an extremely free, individualistic, and even ego-
centric ethos; they indicate that students failed to perceive pressures for them to exercise restraint, to attend to proper social form,
or to cultivate what to them may be regarded as a superficial social
impression. To the extent that this notion of a close community is
more than a romantic vision, to the extent that it is characteristic
of real colleges, previous research with the CCI indicates that it is
found in the less intellectually productive schools.

But if *community* is taken to mean a group of persons
bound together by a common set of values and regulating themselves by social structures for the purpose of achieving desirable
goals, then Raymond was not only a community but a distinctive
one. Both the CCI and CUES demonstrate that students perceived
the community to be based upon intellectual values. This intellectual community, like most of the other schools which score high
on the CCI Intellectual Climate factor or the CUES Scholarship
scale, was abrasive. The educational climate supporting intellectual
investigation was characterized by intellectual and personal freedom, tolerance for nonconformity, the encouragement of high aspirations, active student involvement in their education, and the
joining of intellectual activities of students with their personal and
social activities.

When these data are interpreted to mean that Raymond
students perceived their school to be based upon intellectual values,
one must be clear about what that phrase means. Intellectuals have
been thought by some to value discipline, order, and attention to
detail and to advocate the exhaustive, detached, value-free study
of abstract and personally irrelevant academic matters. This sense
of the term is more a caricature of a social type than an actual
description of living and working intellectuals; but if this definition is used, Raymond simply was not conducive to their development. The personal vivacity as shown by the high CCI score on
Self-Expression, the low score on Academic Organization, and the
high CUES Awareness score are dissonant with this image of the
orderly scholarly type. But if the phrase *intellectual values* implies
that a college encourages students to develop a curiosity about
ideas, to pursue ideas to the neglect of other responsibilities, to

critically analyze social conventions, to think about new ways of living and acting, and to act on the basis of their convictions (even when such actions may be frowned upon), then Raymond does appear to have created a community founded on intellectual values.

If one pole of the Raymond ethos was perceived by students to be pressures for them to develop and sharpen their intellect, a second pole was pressure for them to develop and enhance their existential selves. Students saw that the climate of the new school stimulated high aspirations of personal achievement, especially in a broad array of intellectual and esthetic activities, urged them to expend great effort to realize those ambitions, accorded them personal dignity, involved them in both the academic and social life of the college, encouraged self-examination, fostered the awareness of impulses, and tolerated the behavioral expression of many of those impulses. It appears that in the Raymond community the intellectual development of these young adults was part and parcel of their personal development; like Narcissus, students looked for their own reflection in the books they read, the papers they wrote, the teachers they knew, and the friends they made. They seemed to see that thinking, reading, and talking could not only sharpen their minds but help to develop their personalities as well.

These data indicate that at the same time Raymond intellectualized and personalized undergraduate education, it overcame the academic regimentation, the peer-group accent on fun and games, and the vocational orientation so predominant on most campuses. Such are the perceptions of the Raymond students when compared with their counterparts at other schools. It should be no surprise that the climate of the subcollege was perceived to be a community with pressures toward intellectual analysis and self-examination. The small size of the school, the primacy of dialogue, the opportunity for personal encounters, the absence of conventional academic trappings, and the living and learning arrangements are all innovations which attempted specifically to foster intellectual investigation and to expand the individual consciousness of each student. The innovations were especially designed to provide an intellectually sound and personally relevant education. These data indicate that they have done just that, and to a degree uncommon in American colleges.

What seems to be lacking in the Raymond environment are the values of discipline and order, respect for and commitment to institutions, patience and a future time orientation, sympathetic tolerance for the failings of others (especially those in positions of authority or contented with the status quo), humility about one's own ideas, social propriety, and a sense of practicality. In short, the self-restraining virtues seem to be weak or absent.

COP, like most denominational colleges, was perceived to be a kind of community too, but it was very different from the brand found at the cluster college. The scores on the CCI factors of Play and Social Form indicate the most typical quality of COP is its sociability. Campus life seemed largely oriented toward dating and partying, casual and formal social events, and friendly affiliation. The school was perceived to have a friendly atmosphere featuring the common forms of student extracurricular amusement.

A second student view was a weak press of intellectuality. Every one of the eight factors comprising the Intellectual Climate measure was negative; seven were more than a standard deviation below the mean. This is not to say there were no academic demands, nor does it mean there was an absence of learning; but these data do indicate that students perceived more pressures from the total institution to participate in social life than to engage in academic matters.

Associated with high social and low intellectual demands is a perceived lack of student freedom. The low factor scores of Student Dignity and Self-Expression indicate an abundance of academic and social rules and regulations which effectively controlled the activities of students. Students perceived authoritarianism and paternalism on the part of the campus authorities, however well-meaning they may be. But it was not only the authorities that were perceived as restricting the freedom of students; there is some indication that students themselves preferred this type of well-structured environment. They reported that their student colleagues paid considerable attention to social impressions, had little respect for nonconformity, emphasized order, restraint, and inhibition of impulses, and supported formal and organized group activities; these data suggest that COP students may have been well-fitted to their perceived college.

The presence of sociability and the absence of intellectuality and freedom are obviously interrelated. In a college tightly structured academically, where lectures and grades predominate, teachers are perceived to be authority figures and are separated from students by a variety of academic structures, students probably will feel that intellectual matters are to be endured rather than devoured. In a school where social rules are thought to be made by "the administration" students may perceive little opportunity to think and act on the basis of their own versions of right and wrong. One might hypothesize that when students perceive restraints from the formal structure of the institution, they will create an informal peer-group culture in which they can escape the watchful eye of the authorities, set their own standards, express their impulses, and enjoy the thrills of late adolescent life. If this peer-group culture has values antithetical to the values of the formal academic and social structures, it probably represents little loss to the students who could not find satisfactions there in the first place. These data suggest that something of this sort has probably happened at COP.

This tremendous difference between two colleges on the same campus is truly amazing. It is even more amazing that a school such as COP, never before known for its intellectual attainments, has spawned a college which in a very few years has, with its various innovations, created a climate which appears to be very similar to that found in some of the nation's leading liberal arts colleges. Obviously this development has had a significant effect upon the main campus, and these effects are explored later. For now it is sufficient to note that it is inconceivable that the addition of this handful of students and faculty could have had such a profound impact upon the University of the Pacific except through the device of the cluster college.

Indeed the difference between these two schools is so amazing that one must wonder whether something else is reflected in the data. Is it not curious that the two schools are perceived to have such diametrically opposite emphases? Raymond is highly intellectual and COP nonintellectual; Raymond provides much freedom for students and COP little; Raymond has little collegiate peer-group activity and COP much. The fact that these two pieces of data fit together like two halves of a puzzle suggests that students at each school may have highlighted and accentuated the special characteristics of their school in comparison with the other. Thus, in comparison with Raymond the COP students could describe their school as nonintellectual and Raymond students could say their school had little social life compared with COP. While the measured differences appear to be real, the cluster college setting probably encouraged each group to accentuate the "real" differences.

The findings derived from the other instruments may also be mentioned briefly. An objective personality inventory, the Activities Index, showed that Raymond students, compared with other college populations, appeared to be more emotionally alive, to have a more personalized and independent intellectual style, to hold higher aspirations in intellectual and cultural areas, and to possess a greater sense of self-consciousness. A questionnaire constructed by the author indicated that Raymond students held very liberal attitudes concerning a variety of social, political, economic, religious, and sexual matters, and had a low level of authoritarianism. Their subcultural identifications were almost exclusively with either the academic or nonconformist group while the vocational and collegiate orientations were virtually nonexistent.

In addition, the Graduate Record Examination Area Tests have been administered to all graduating seniors. The means on the social science and humanities tests were at the ninety-ninth percentile of the institutions which compose "use norms" (as opposed to representative national norms) for each of the first three graduating classes. The means on the natural science portion were at the ninety-seventh, ninety-eighth, and ninety-ninth percentiles during the three years.

The entirety of these data demonstrate that the innovations launched by Raymond College were remarkably successful in terms of both its own purposes and the classic ideals of a liberal education. The high scores on the Intellectual Climate factor of the College Characteristics Index; the high ranking on the Awareness and Scholarship scales of the College and University Environment Scales; the personalized and independent intellectual styles of students and their relatively advanced stage of emotional development as measured by the Activities Index; the liberal attitudes and the relatively low level of authoritarianism of the students; the exceptional performance of seniors on the Graduate Record Examination Area Tests—all of these empirical findings coalesce to validate the radically innovative philosophy and program adopted by Raymond.

In order to be perfectly clear about these results, they *do not* prove that any of the educational structures adopted at Raymond were necessarily better than those found in more conventional schools. This is so for several reasons. First, Raymond was not altogether successful nor equally successful with all students. Second, whatever success the school may have enjoyed may have resulted as much from its newness and from the enthusiasm generated over its innovations as from the innovations themselves. Third, since all of the program formed an integrated whole, it is impossible to know with exactitude which practices were most responsible for the results obtained. Fourth, since the survey employed a cross-sectional design, it cannot be known to what extent the school obtained the above results from educating its students or from merely attracting the kind of student which "fit" with the values of the program. Fifth, it is logically impossible to draw conclusions about the effectiveness of these institutional practices from a single instance. Any of these several practices which worked well at Raymond may, in a different context, prove to be ineffective; and if they had been infused with different values or manned by different people, they may not have been effective even at Raymond. Finally, it is quite possible that very different philosophies of education and the structures they dictate may reach similar ends, and they may conceivably reach those ends more effectively or efficiently.

What *can be* concluded is this: the combined innovations were generally effective in producing the kind of environmental conditions and the kinds of students desired. Also, the evidence demonstrates that the traditional goals of a liberal education can be realized with very different academic mechanisms than currently found in most colleges. And, despite the handicap of not knowing exactly how students changed during their college experience, they appeared in general to be more broadly educated and more emotionally mature than students in all but the choicest colleges in the United States. Finally, these favorable results were achieved in only five years on the campus of a school never previously noted for its academic achievements, one which functioned with traditional academic structures. This accomplishment has been possible only because of the cluster college structure.

In short, the main values of the cluster college form of organization were generally realized at the University of the Pacific. The subcollege provided an opportunity to innovate; the innovations collectively were effective in producing a close community founded upon intellectual values; and Raymond was the first step in providing a series of truly diverse liberal arts programs on the campus.

Merton (1957) has argued persuasively of the need to examine both the intended and unanticipated consequences of social systems. The empirical study has demonstrated that the innovations were relatively successful in achieving the avowed purposes of the school, but a full report of the results of the college's innovations must also contain a discussion of the unanticipated consequences. Unless these unexpected outcomes are examined, full knowledge of the effects of the structures will be lacking.

The three-term calendar adopted by Raymond College provided relatively long periods of uninterrupted study, and in that respect it was an improvement on both the semester and quarter system. The evidence has indicated that the students acquired a broader scope of knowledge than most college graduates and that they were more emotionally mature than most—evidence which tends to validate the three-year aspect. And the fact that more than 90 per cent of the students reported that they planned to work for advanced degrees would appear to reinforce the assumption that the college could serve to provide a broad general education as a base on which specialized training at other schools could be built, perhaps in the fourth year.

But there have been difficulties. The breaks between terms, lasting only seven to ten days, proved to be all too brief for students who had spent days and nights during the last weeks of the previous term writing long papers; often they were not prepared to start the first day of the new term with vigor. And there were some difficulties with the three-course arrangement. Faculty knew they were entitled to one-third of each student's academic commitment at any given time, and they demanded a large amount of work; students felt that none of their three courses could be slighted, and they had no opportunity to take easy courses that would balance the more difficult ones. While most students were stimulated to intellectual and personal growth in this setting, they found that the concentrated pressures which led to that growth—academic demands, intimate social interaction, and personal examination—difficult to endure for the long ten-month academic year and for three uninterrupted terms.

From the faculty viewpoint, the problems were similar. The break between terms was spent correcting papers, writing term letters, planning the next term's classes—all of which left little time for physical or mental recuperation. Although the summer vacation provided some respite for both students and faculty, it allowed teacher-scholars little time to do substantial research or writing. Each faculty member was required to teach only two courses per term and, consequently, was allowed adequate time for preparation, in the long run probably making classes more effective. The faculty favored the three-year program largely because they felt that any longer period would almost automatically require them to provide more specialized courses, to increase the diversity of faculty viewpoints represented in each discipline, and probably to become departmentally structured, all of which would undermine their ideal. In addition, the faculty felt a college with only 250 students could not begin to provide comprehensive specialized education economically and at that time they had little confidence that more than a few students could take a profitable specialization in the other portions of the university. Almost all elements of the school, accordingly, accepted the three-course, three-term, three-year structural foundation of the college despite the difficulties it produced.

The twenty-three-course required core curriculum helped students gain a broad intellectual education. Though the courses were mostly introductory, generally they were taught in sufficient depth to make each a significant introduction into the thought-ways of some people in each discipline, and students apparently took their lessons to heart and grew personally as a function of this cognitive experience. Apart from an occasional student's prior difficulty with a particular subject such as language, math, or science, and with the exception of an occasional "personality conflict," students did not object to the twenty-three-course requirement of the curriculum.

However, it is also true that just as the core liberated the minds of students from their earlier bias and ignorance, so did the broad curriculum make it difficult for them to focus their thoughts on a specific and limited concern. To be sure many did find a focus in a problem, theme, or even academic discipline, but many found themselves going in every direction and thus in no direction at all. For all its faults, the disciplinary major does provide an intellectual focus for the student.

A related matter is that since the college did not require students to complete an academic major and most students took only a single core course in most disciplines, no student had the advantage of having already taken upper division work in his major, and hereby competing on favorable terms with nonmajors in some of his classes. Without the focus, security, and self-confidence that a major provides, and with the expectation to engage in frequent dialogue about several new and unfamiliar areas, students have been placed in a precarious, even threatening, position which perhaps increased their anxiety and reduced the amount of learning.

It is curious that neither faculty nor students collectively talked much about the independent study aspect of the program. Perhaps this relative silence indicated that all were satisfied; perhaps it meant that independent study was not as valuable, or perhaps just not as visible, as the core.

Still some things are clear. It was discovered that few faculty and students were committed to "independent" study—most preferred "cooperative" study. The typical Raymond College student usually wanted or needed some guidance, and often he wanted to share his developing ideas with his teacher. The professors tended to feel, with some justification, that if the student was not supervised periodically throughout the term, he might waste time following unproductive paths of investigation or even neglect that work in favor of the more regular demands of the courses.

Also, students chose to study with a non-random group of teachers. For example, in one spring term eight faculty members supervised 112 student courses, nine supervised 25 courses, and four had no independent study load at all. In addition, independent study, because it was not originally thought to be "cooperative" study, was never made a part of the faculty's formal teaching load. No teacher received any compensation or "release time" because of his efforts in independent study. For all of these reasons this innovation proved to be more burdensome to some faculty than originally anticipated.

The seminar teaching method widely used throughout the curriculum succeeded in getting nearly all students to participate actively in their education; it probably motivated them to study more than they might otherwise; and it helped them to personalize the knowledge gained.

But here, too, the results were ambiguous. It must be stated in all candor that while practically every course save one was organized around the seminar, the most influential course probably was that single lecture course. It was called Introduction to the Modern World, an interdisciplinary, team-taught course given in the first term to all new freshmen; it was structured around three or four lectures plus a discussion section weekly. The most striking features of the course were its immediate and concerted intellectual attack on conventional social, political, and religious beliefs, and its outlining of the basic ground rules of intellectual investigation in general and of Raymond College in particular. Incidentally, it was discovered that team-teaching, another minor innovation, occasionally impeded this impact; it was found that some students "tuned in" when the teacher with their own biases appeared and "dropped out" when one with opposing ideas spoke.

In several ways the seminar proved not to be a panacea. In the first place few teachers have been trained to conduct a group discussion, and the seminar is a very difficult device to manage. Indeed, the seminar teaching method probably can be ruined in more ways than nearly any other technique. When the discussion is unfocused, it may give no one an integrated sense of what has been discussed; when it is too tightly focused, the students may feel like they are simply giving the answers desired by the instructor. When the leader is open to student reflection, it may easily degenerate into a bull session; when he is closed, it may become simply another setting for a lecture. Raymond College undoubtedly had its share of poor seminars.

Student reaction to the seminar was mixed. Some withdrew from discussions because they feared exposure, because they were unprepared, because of personality conflicts, and for numerous idiosyncratic reasons. Other students came to think that merely because they were encouraged to share their ideas, they should say something about everything and that everything they said was important. Although the model of the teacher at one end of the log and the student at the other may be appropriate for some kinds of teaching by some teachers for some students at some times, Raymond learned that it is not necessarily the best for all at all times.

The elimination of letter grades led to intrinsic study motivation; it did not destroy the initiative of students so long reared on grades; it eliminated cheating; and students had little difficulty being accepted into the best graduate and professional schools without a grade-point average.

But educational problems did not disappear; they simply changed their forms. A term letter proved to be much more personal and relevant to the student than a letter grade as he tried to assess his performance in a course, but it was also vague. He may have learned that he showed superb understanding of a particular book, ought to be less critical of certain authors and more appreciative of their strengths, should take some position more seriously, and so on, but he may have been unable to grasp either his achievements or his evaluation with definiteness. Letter grades, for all their faults, are naively definite. A Raymond student could not have the security of knowing exactly where he stood in a class, the confidence of being better than his classmates in some of his courses as verified by an objective grade, or a precise sense of overall evaluation by teachers who may have come to be of great personal importance to him.

More interesting, however, is that the elimination of grades did not eliminate competition, as many expected. Students still competed for the respect of their colleagues and for the favorable reaction of teachers, respect which came from making insightful and relevant contributions to the class; students competed not for an extrinsic grade, but for the very real intrinsic reward of being judged more intelligent by knowledgeable authorities, by their peers, and by themselves. Sigmund Freud long ago observed that the demands made by one's own conscience are much more severe than those imposed by others. Thus, as the Raymond students became intrinsically motivated, they set their own personal standards at a high level and ruthlessly drove themselves to attain them. The competition was removed from a superficial level of a social game, but it was transformed into a potentially more vicious intrapsychic struggle. When this occurred, there was no way for students to rationalize failure by saying academic grading was only a game; in the psychic realm evaluation of oneself is not a game but the essence of life.

The faculty, too, had their problems with the new evaluation scheme. The term letters, because they were so individualized, made it virtually impossible to obtain an objective comparison between students. When they selected honors candidates or members for all-university honorary societies, or when they considered students in academic difficulty, the faculty found itself embroiled in lengthy discussions about the relative merits and demerits of students. Letter grades with all their defects are at least one objective measure of some kind of achievement, and as such, they permit the bureaucratic handling of students so that faculty can be freed to do more teaching or research. In addition, the term letters required a considerable investment of time to compose, even for groups as small as, say, thirty students; inevitably faculty had to do this work during the short and treasured "vacation" periods.

The residential college and all the devices to bring the faculty and students together produced close faculty-student relations, personalization of academic life, intellectualization of student social life, and a strong sense of community—all desired results.

Yet surprisingly these very consequences have produced some of Raymond College's most pressing problems. The school was structured to maximize social interaction, but it almost totally failed to provide for privacy. This omission was probably the single most important problem at the student level. Because they had so little opportunity to closet themselves from the omnipresent other, to reflect upon and recoup from one encounter and to prepare for the next, some of these young adults acquired social masks and played stereotyped roles to protect themselves from each other. Facing enforced public exposure, some students turned inward in search not only of self but also of an inner freedom unspoiled by others; some became introspective, sometimes morbidly so, and spurned social activities. In these ways the attempts to create a close community passed the point of diminishing returns and actually worked against the very community they were designed to foster.

In addition, students quickly spotted the marked contrast between substantial academic freedom and the restrictions on their nonacademic life. The requirements that all had to live in dormitories during all three years, that they could not have alcohol in their rooms, that they could not entertain members of the opposite sex in their rooms (except at a few specified times and under special conditions), and that girls' dormitories were to be locked at a designated hour were perceived by students to be inconsistent with the freer academic practices. These strongly independent students chafed under the school's more conventional social restrictions. In this situation, the social rules, unlike the academic rules, came to be accepted only by a minority, and there were few student norms supporting them. The fact that Raymond students had more social freedom than their colleagues at College of the Pacific —that is, minimal regulations on dress, later women's hours, and a limited inter-dormitory visitation plan—mattered little to them. The existence of these regulations was perceived to be entirely inconsistent with the freedom found throughout the rest of the school, a confession of a basic mistrust of them, a restriction on their treasured freedom of movement, and a further blockade of their attempts to gain privacy.

Most faculty found the constant contact with students fulfilling but often draining. When faculty were on campus, it was difficult for them to turn away students in favor of their own personal work; their professional advancement was made difficult. Being so accessible, teachers frequently found themselves discussing with a student his deepest problems in a quasi-psychiatric fashion; this is a role for which none were trained and in which some were not interested, however effectively they may have performed that function. It was learned that familiarity may at times breed contempt, and overexposure may actually limit the impact a teacher may have on a student. And of course, this personal involvement produced additional psychic and physical fatigue which seemed to culminate near the end of each term and especially near the end of the long academic year.

The entire story of the cluster college development at this institution cannot be written yet as Elbert Covell College was established in 1963 and Callison College opened its doors as recently as 1967. Both of these innovative colleges at the University of the Pacific, as well as Raymond, are still in their infancies. But a few results are clear. True to the hopes for a cluster college, Raymond did provide the community missing in most schools; it experimented with new ways in higher education; and it has had a significant effect upon the established school. Further, by most educational criteria the collective innovations of Raymond College must be judged to have been generally successful. Indeed, the University of the Pacific. which has never enjoyed a high academic reputation, found it had spawned a college which from all available evidence was a newcomer to the ranks of highest quality liberal arts colleges in the United States. It is inconceivable that some twenty-two faculty and 200 students could have had such a profound impact on the campus in any way other than the cluster college arrangement.

And yet here too have been a number of unanticipated consequences. First, the diversity inherent in the cluster college plan soon became polarized into "good" and "bad." One half of this story is that Raymond's pioneers were captives of their innovative spirit. This phenomenon can be understood in terms of Erik Erikson's conceptual framework; his discussion of an identity crisis, although meant to refer to individuals, has utility in describing this group reaction. As a fledgling school, Raymond College attempted to create an institutional identity. One of the ways a positive identity can be created, according to Erikson (1962, p. 102), is first to form a negative identity, that is, an image of what one would not like to be under any circumstance. As Raymond established its own identity as an innovative college, members conjured up an image of traditional educational practices, and assumed their own new ways to be better than the old ones. This symbolic image of inadequate traditional undergraduate liberal education was concretized, for the innovators, in College of the Pacific, the more conventional portions of the university. After the cluster college made College of the Pacific into a specific negative identity, whenever it advanced its own ideals, it implicitly criticized its neighbor.

The other half of the story is a parallel phenomenon within the College of the Pacific. This development may be briefly chronicled. When the cluster college plan was announced and while the Raymond program was being planned, many in College of the Pacific were curious, sympathetic, and even overtly proud of the venture. Undoubtedly this curiosity, pride, and good wishes covered an apprehension about their status in the context of an expansion plan which devoted so many of the limited resources of the university to other parts of the institution. Soon the curiosity and pride turned to less constructive emotions as several of the faculty in the established sector came to fear that their own programs would lack support in favor of the cluster college. Envy was aroused; some faculty attempted unsuccessfully to join the staff of Raymond, and many longed for the smaller classes, newer facilities, brighter students, special program, and greater attention from both local and national educators which Raymond College received and which they might well have used. Finally, fear and envy found a common denominator in hostility. The new school threatened to stagnate or destroy the existing school; it drained the institution of limited resources; and it relegated them, the faithful of the past, to the position of second-class citizens on the campus. In this way the cluster college produced an unexpected intergroup conflict situation; the emotion-laden psycho-logic dictated that one school was "good" and the other was "bad."

Second, Raymond College has produced an institutional identity crisis. When the cluster college plan was formulated, the College of the Pacific changed its name to the University of the Pacific. The old images of a religious school and a football power were strained even to Pacific, although they tended to linger as the church ties were weakening and football was de-emphasized. College of the Pacific had been known as a "playboy school" by students on the West Coast, a reputation foreign to life in Raymond. Perhaps the most popular internal image within Pacific was the "family," a small, close, friendly, protective, homogeneous school; but Raymond was too free, abrasive, and independent for this image to be accurate. In point of fact, the cluster college program made the resulting institution too heterogeneous to be saddled by any of these old images. It had become a pluralistic *University* of the Pacific complete with a differentiation of structure and a specialization of function. The full implications of this change in institutional identity were just beginning to emerge, and some confusion resulted from this identity crisis.

A third curious consequence is that through the academic year of 1966–67 there had been little change in the education offered in College of the Pacific since the establishment of Raymond. Contrary to the original thoughts, the cluster college did not produce any significant reform in the existing school. Perhaps the major reason for this resistance to innovation was that the psychology of those in the older school was defensive; they understandably preferred to protect and rationalize their own institutional arrangements rather than to revise or modify them. The original vision of the cluster college as a technique of reforming the existing school assumed a higher degree of rationality than the intergroup conflict situation thus far permitted. It was expected that as more time passed and as Callison and additional colleges developed, passions would cool and substantial innovations might occur in College of the Pacific. And there is some evidence that such innovations may now be in the offing, as COP has instituted an entirely new freshman year program.

The Raymond College faculty and administration and the administrators of the University of the Pacific preferred to work with these problems which their own educational order has created rather than with conventional ones. But they learned the crucial lesson that innovation is a matter of dealing with one set of problems instead of another set, that it is more than a matter of solving educational problems once and for all, as they had earlier naively assumed.

Chapter 6

Self-Selection
and Change

Theodore M. Newcomb, Donald R. Brown,
James A. Kulik, David J. Reimer,
William R. Revelle

In 1967, five universities (The University of California at San Diego and at Santa Cruz, the University of Kansas, the State University of Florida, and the University of Michigan), each with newly instituted "living-learning complexes," formed a research consortium for the study of residential-academic units. The purpose of this consortium is to gather data over a five-year period on the programs, institutional environment, characteristics of entering students, and students' experiences during college, among other factors. This chapter reports findings from the initial year of data collection. Since the University of Michigan obtained data from a wider range of control populations than did the other four cooperating universities, the present report deals only with research results from that institution.[1]

In 1967, following several years of planning, a semiautonomous undergraduate unit of the College of Literature, Science and the Arts (LSA), officially known as the Residential College (RC), received its first freshman class. The original designers—a faculty-student committee—planned the new college to house 1,200 students who would live and dine together, and especially during the first two undergraduate years, would follow a separate curriculum. Although RC and LSA curricula had similar objectives, the RC course of studies was to emphasize the humanities and social sciences. Most of the classes would be held near residential quarters. Students, far from forming an elite population, would represent a random, stratified population corresponding to the freshman population of the parent college. Only students who asked to enter the Residential College were considered. Faculty members were recruited from the parent college on a voluntary basis, a few devoting their full time to RC.

The new college would be governed by the RC community, although the original plan did not stipulate in advance the procedures for governance. These decisions were made by the first entering class, which voted to establish a Representative Assembly to be elected by constituencies and consisting of eight students, four faculty members, two administrators (including the dean, who, as chairman, has the power to veto), and two resident fellows. Its purview would include all matters of policy, including curriculum.

The findings reported below are based upon responses to

[1] The research described in this chapter represents an interim report of only one portion of a more inclusive enterprise. A more detailed version entitled "A Small Residential College Compared with Three Control Populations" provides the statistical information from which this condensed version is drawn. The longer report is available on request from CRLT, 1315 Hill Street, Ann Arbor, Michigan, 48104. The authors express their thanks to Elinor Foulke and Barbara Bluestone for their assistance in preparing these materials.

standard scales and inventories, to questionnaires of our own devising, and to interviews, and for the most part are limited to
freshmen entering the university in 1967, the first year of the
Residential College. The four populations from which responses
were obtained on entrance in the fall of 1967 were: the "experimental" group, or all 217 Residential College entrants, of whom
91 per cent responded; Control A, a random sample of 200 Residential College applicants (from LSA) rejected only for reasons of
space (excluding Honors students), of whom 87 per cent responded; Control B, a random sample of 200 students who, although eligible for the Residential College, enrolled instead in the
College of Literature, Science, and the Arts, of whom 82 per
cent responded; and the Honors group, a random sample of 100
freshmen enrolled in the parent college's Honors Program, of whom
72 per cent responded. The LSA students differ from the experimental RC group in two ways: they have not sought admission to
RC and none are enrolled there. The RC reject group differs from
RC students only in the latter respect. Honor students differ from all
other populations because they are drawn from approximately the
top 10 per cent of freshmen entering the parent college using a
combined criterion of SAT scores and high school grades. (Approximately 10 per cent of RC students were invited into the
Honors Program, but declined.)

Initial responses were obtained generally by mail not long
before entering freshmen arrived on the campus. Proportions of
respondents at later times declined somewhat, especially in the three
control populations; hence effects of "volunteerism" in these populations cannot be excluded. The freshmen responded to four instruments: the Omnibus Personality Inventory (OPI); the College
and University Environment Scale (CUES); the College Student
Questionnaire (CSQ-1), which is issued by Educational Testing
Service especially for entering freshmen and includes a wide range
of questions dealing with high school experiences, family backgrounds, plans and hopes in college, and interests, attitudes, and
values; and an inventory developed at the University of Michigan
labeled Inter-University Survey (IUS).

In the spring of their freshman year, samples of all four
populations completed four additional instruments: "A Student's

Time," a short questionnaire which asks the student to respond to items based on the general question, "With whom did you spend how much time doing what, and where?"; CSQ-2, designed for second-semester freshmen or more advanced students. Certain items in this form are identical with those in CSQ-1, so that changes over a seven-month period could be observed; CUES, administered again, but this time with standard instructions to respond in terms of one's own experience, rather than in terms of expectations, as before; and IS, the Interview Schedule, administered in the spring of 1969 to a sample of thirty sophomores from the Residential College and thirty students rejected by the RC. IS deals with academic matters, relations with faculty and with peers, and satisfactions with various aspects of university experience, and was conducted in seven sessions each separated by two to four days. The intervals were described by a time budget kept by the student and brought to each interview.

Our general strategy was first to obtain reasonably full information about input characteristics before the freshman's arrival at the university. Seven months later we obtained information from which individual change could be inferred, and information based upon freshman experience during the interim. Twenty months after entrance, intensive reports were obtained from small, representative samples of all groups. At every step, comparisons were possible between the experimental and one or more of the three control populations.

Each of the 8,895 applicants seeking admission to the University of Michigan's College of Literature, Science and the Arts (LSA) for the fall of 1967 received by mail a two-page description of the new "college within the college," its facilities, educational atmosphere, climate for living, and academic programs. The brochure explained that the Residential College was to "combine the environment of a small college with the resources of a large, cosmopolitan university." The students of the college were to live in quarters designed as centers of an academic-residential community where they would study, play, dine, and pursue mutual interests. Their course of study would include a core curriculum designed to provide a common intellectual experience for all students. The applicant was then asked to indicate whether he was interested in applying to the Residential College.

Almost 20 per cent of the applicants to LSA indicated that they wished to be considered for admission to the Residential College. Fewer than one-quarter (217) of the qualified applicants, a representative sample of the LSA student body in terms of sex, geographical area, and scholastic aptitude, were accepted. Not all students invited to the Residential College accepted the offer: some changed their minds and entered LSA; others accepted invitations to the university's Honors Program; others turned down the University of Michigan entirely for different colleges. Such defections, and similar ones from the conventional LSA program, distorted the match between students in RC and in LSA.

Although no particular type of student was encouraged to apply to the Residential College, there is evidence that the RC entering class differed from the rest of the LSA freshmen in subtle ways—in goals, personal dispositions, and attitudes. These differences and their ramifications are important. College administrators and researchers in higher education are aware that the quality of an institution is determined in large part by the quality of its applicants. Information concerning what kinds of students choose a particular kind of college, what the needs of those students are, and how their needs differ from those of students applying to other programs is important to their decision-making. We therefore identify some of the personal qualities of students attracted to a residential setting for their higher education.

Incoming students in our LSA and RC samples, as well as in a representative nationwide sample of students (using data from the CSQ manual), were asked directly about their "personal philosophies" of higher education. They were asked to rank-order four philosophies, each described in a paragraph, according to the accuracy with which the philosophies portrayed their own point of view. The philosophies embodied the norms of four college subcultures described by Clark and Trow (1966), and can be labeled Vocational, Academic, Collegiate, and Nonconformist. Two of these educational types, the Academic and the Nonconformist, are concerned with ideas; the other two, Vocational and Collegiate, seem less intellectually oriented. The choices of our three major samples on this criterion are summarized in Table 7.

Table 7

EDUCATIONAL ORIENTATIONS OF INCOMING FRESHMEN
(Percentages)

	Nationwide Sample	*Residential College*	*College of Literature, Science, Arts*
Vocational	28	18.1	22.0
Academic	20	37.7	26.2
Collegiate	42	31.2	45.7
Nonconformist	4	13.1	6.1

More than one-half of the RC males and females choose the Academic or Nonconformist philosophies to best describe their personal philosophies of higher education; fewer than one-third of the LSA control group make this choice—a statistically significant difference. RC students most often use the Academic philosophy to describe their educational orientation. They also identify the Collegiate philosophy as matching their idea of a college education much less often than either of the two control groups, and they choose the Nonconformist philosophy at least twice as often.

Both LSA students and the nationwide student sample select the Collegiate philosophy more often than the other three as best defining their own. However, the nationwide sample tends to choose the Vocational philosophy more often than the LSA group and on the whole is less often academic in orientation. Using the criterion of educational philosophy, RC students are clearly more intellectually oriented than students preferring a more conventional program throughout the nation in general and at the University of Michigan in particular.

When the educational orientation of students entering the RC is compared with freshmen entering the Honors Program at the University of Michigan, we find that Honors students are definite in their preference for educational philosophies that emphasize concern for ideas. Nearly 62 per cent of the Honors group choose Academic and Nonconformist philosophies while 51 per cent of the RC students and only 32 per cent of the LSA students prefer them. The Honors Program, however, accepts only the top 10–12 per cent of the student body (using SAT scores and high school percentile rank), most of whom enter the program, live in separate units and attend special classes. RC students, then, although unlike Honors freshmen in scholastic aptitude, approach them in their concern for ideas.

Another interesting pattern emerges when the three groups above are compared to a fourth sample—students who initially indicate an interest in the Residential College but are not admitted because of space limitations and who enter the LSA program instead. The choices of this group most nearly coincide with those of the LSA sample rather than the RC students. This finding can be partially explained by noting that students in LSA are more likely to join the Honors Program when invited than are RC students. About twenty freshmen who were invited into the Honors Program chose RC instead, whereas the LSA groups included almost no Honors caliber students. This in itself supports the hypothesis that residential education captures the imagination of many of the more intellectually oriented of the University of Michigan's students.

Further distortions occur because some of the qualified but rejected applicants to RC decide to pursue their education at other colleges and universities. Many choose small liberal arts colleges, similar in some respects to the Residential College. Such defections probably eliminate from the pool of qualified, rejected applicants those with the strongest commitment to residential education.

To determine the personal dispositions of these students, a total of forty-one standard psychometric scales were used as the basis for comparing the RC group and the LSA students samples. These were developed in a variety of ways—empirically, rationally, and factorially—and were grouped into clusters using a hierarchical technique devised by Kulik and Revelle (1969). Each of these clusters describes a series of personal characteristics. The four major clusters that emerged from this analysis were labeled and can be described as follows:

Conventional Adjustment: High scores on scales in this cluster are characterized by a lack of tension, worries, and anxiety, and show a conventional "good" adjustment.

Intellectual Openness: Scales in this cluster indicate intellectual and esthetic interests, flexibility and complexity in thinking, and anti-authoritarian attitudes.

Sociability: Scales in this cluster indicate extroverted social attitudes and sensitivity to the welfare of others.

Interpersonal Independence: High scores on these scales show a generalized autonomy in relation to family, peers, and religious orthodoxy.

In terms of educational philosophy, we have already indicated that RC students are more intellectually oriented than students choosing a conventional large university environment. An analysis of the personal characteristics measured and categorized into clusters corroborates this finding. The characteristics that most decisively separate RC and LSA students are those that indicate an interest in ideas, in the flexible use of intelligence, and in esthetic interests, the cluster we have labeled Intellectual Openness.

It should be noted that RC students are significantly higher than LSA students on SAT Verbal scores, probably as a result of the "defections" noted. This variation, however, does not explain the difference in Intellectual Openness between the two groups. Even when verbal ability is statistically controlled, RC students score significantly higher than LSA students on measures of Intellectual Openness.

Comparisons of RC students with qualified but rejected RC applicants reveal differences that are consistent with our findings regarding educational orientation. RC students rate higher than RC rejects on most of the scales measuring Intellectual Openness. Since this variation cannot be attributed to admissions procedures, it is apparently the result of student self-selection following notification about admission to RC. These self-selection factors do not explain the difference between unsuccessful applicants to RC and the sample: the former, although lower on Intellectual Openness than RC students, are still significantly higher ($p < .05$) on this factor than LSA students. The Honors group, as we expected, was the highest of all groups in Intellectual Openness.

Why do students wish to enter a residential college? What

factors lead some of the most intellectually oriented students among University of Michigan applicants to enter the RC, despite attractive alternatives? We have no foolproof answers to these questions, although we have some challenging and paradoxical results. The findings reported below are more tentative than those preceding, but they are nevertheless suggestive.

Students in our samples provided us with their stereotypes of the UM and the RC before matriculation by responding negatively or positively to statements about the college environment they were about to enter (CUES). Since both the LSA sample and the group that qualified for, but was rejected by, the RC were entering LSA, their responses are pooled in the description below.

Before comparing the expectations and actual experiences of the several UM student groups, it is important to note that UM students as a whole hold expectations for their university that are substantially above the national norms reported by Pace (1969) in the areas of Awareness, Scholarship, Campus Morale, and Quality of Teaching and Faculty-Student Relationships (see Figure 9). Future RC students showed strikingly high expectations on the latter scale. In the areas of Practicality, Propriety, and Community, their expectations are similar to those of the nationwide sample. After two semesters of college, scores of the Michigan groups on all scales but Awareness drop somewhat (Figure 10). Awareness and Scholarship remain substantially above the national average. RC students maintain their expectations of Community and Quality of Teaching and Faculty-Student Relationships and show the greatest drop on the Practicality scale.

Feldman and Newcomb (1969) have isolated three sets of determinants that influence student responses to the CUES: the larger university environment; the specific unit of the university to which students are attached (department, residence, and so on); and personality disposition. Since both RC and LSA students are entering the same university, the larger university environment presumably does not contribute to differences in responses. The effects of the other two factors were separated statistically using the analysis of variance technique.[2] The differences in students' re-

[2] See the fuller report for details.

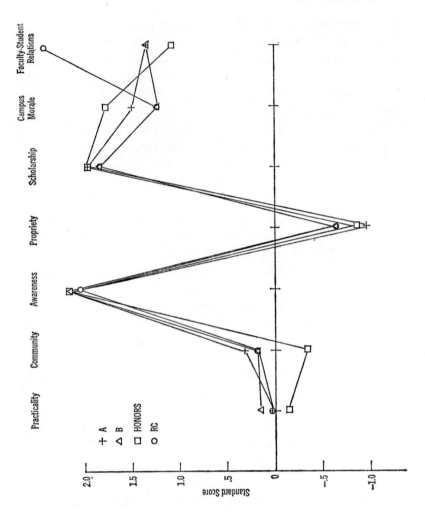

FIGURE 9. Standardized fall testing CUES scale scores for all groups plotted against the national norms with the 66+ 33— scoring method.

sponses that could be attributed to differences between the image of a residential and a conventional college are statistically significant ($p < .05$) and are reported below.

RC students indicated higher expectations of the environment they were about to enter than LSA students on three of the seven CUES scales: Practically, Community, and Propriety. Ac-

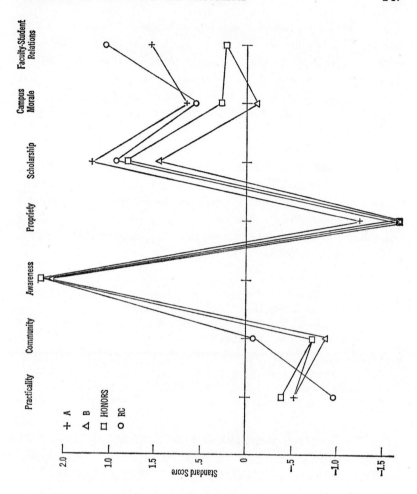

FIGURE 10. Standardized spring testing CUES scale scores for all groups plotted against the national norms with the 66+ 33— scoring method.

cording to Pace (1969), the Practicality scale describes "an environment characterized by enterprise, organization, material benefits, and social activities." The items on the Community scale "describe a friendly, cohesive, group-oriented campus," while the items in the Propriety scale "describe an environment that is polite and considerate." These scales emphasize congeniality and fairness in social and academic relations.

The four remaining scales—Scholarship, Awareness, Campus Morale, Quality of Teaching and Faculty-Student Relationships—in one way or another characterize environments with a high degree of intellectual commitment and academic emphasis. On these four scales, however, no differences emerge between students entering the residential and conventionl units of the University of Michigan.

The specific expectations of students entering RC are further revealed by the individual items they endorsed. On sixteen of the 150 items of the CUES, statistically significant ($p < .05$) differences occur which cannot be attributed to personality factors, and therefore presumably reveal discrepancies in students' images of the two educational units. RC students are more likely to describe their professors in the following terms:

> Standards set by the professor are not hard to achieve.
> The professors go out of their way to help you.
> The professors regularly check up on students to see that assignments are being carried out properly and on time.
> Professors usually take attendance in class.

LSA students more often subscribed to such statements as these:

> Faculty members rarely call students by their first names.
> Most of the faculty are not interested in students' personal problems.

In summary, then, although RC students are more intellectually oriented than those in LSA, they do not expect intellectuality to be more heavily stressed in RC than in the larger university setting. The bright, intellectually oriented student appears to be more distressed by the loss of human scale in our large universities. He expects to find congeniality, clarity of expectation, and fairness at a residential college and appears to see residential education as an alternative to the relatively impersonal, competitive, and confusing educational experience at a large university.

Institutional environments such as the Residential College can be and sometimes are planned to take into account theoretical and pragmatic assumptions about the relationships between student behavior and environmental press. In contrast, the ambience of the larger university generally develops gradually over many decades in response to a wide range of events and influences. Since students tend to be as selective in their perceptions of environmental press as most other people, we asked our groups to fill in the CUES a second time, in terms not of their expectations but of their actual experience after one year on campus. The results give a picture of life at the university as informal, intellectual, esthetic, and unconventional.

We have seen that, when the personality dimension of Intellectual Openness is controlled for, entering RC students expect the RC to be more congenial and fair in social and academic relations than entering LSA groups expect LSA to be. After spending one year at RC, students describe the environment they actually discover as warm and intellectually and academically oriented. They are significantly ($p < .001$) higher than LSA students on the Community, Campus Morale, and Quality of Teaching and Faculty-Student Relationships scales of the CUES. Again, the Community scale measures "a friendly, cohesive, group-oriented campus." However, the Campus Morale scale, while also describing group cohesiveness, "at the same time [describes] a commitment to intellectual pursuits and freedom of expression." The Quality of Teaching and Faculty-Student Relationships scale describes "teaching infused with warmth, interest, and helpfulness towards students."

When we look at the difference between student expectations and actual experience on campus in the college environment, with controls for Intellectual Openness, the only consistent difference between RC, LSA, and Honors groups is that the Honors students fall below their Michigan peers on all scales. However, the differential effects of the year in the RC itself result in large variations on Practicality, Community, Campus Morale, and, most of all, Quality of Teaching and Faculty-Student Relationships scales.

In the spring of their freshman year, RC students were much *more* likely to endorse the following items than were the LSA groups:

$p < .001$
The professors go out of their way to help you.
$p < .01$
Most of the professors are very thorough teachers and really probe into the fundamentals of their subjects.

Most people here seem to be especially considerate of others.

This school has a reputation for being very friendly.

It's easy to get a group together for card games, singing, going to the movies, and so on.

Channels for expressing students' complaints are readily accessible.

Course offerings and faculty in the social sciences are outstanding.

$p < .02$

Many courses stress the speculative or abstract rather than the concrete or tangible.

The big college events draw a lot of student enthusiasm and support.

Everyone has a lot of fun at this school.

$p < .05$

Most students show a good deal of caution and self-control in their behavior.

Students are sometimes noisy and inattentive at concerts or lectures.

The school offers many opportunities for students to understand and criticize important works in art, music, and drama.

Second semester RC students were much *less* likely to endorse the following items than were LSA students:

$p < .001$

Faculty members rarely or never call students by their first names.

Proper social forms and manners are important here.

$p < .01$

There is a lot of apple-polishing around here.

Student rooms are more likely to be decorated with pennants and pin-ups than with paintings, carvings, mobiles, fabrics, and so on.

Everyone knows the "snap" courses to take and the tough ones to avoid.

The history and traditions of the college are strongly emphasized.

Most of the faculty are not interested in students' personal problems.

Many of the natural science professors are actively engaged in research.

Dormitory raids, water fights, and other student pranks would be unthinkable here.

$p < .02$

> There are lots of dances, parties, and social activities.
>
> Students have many opportunities to develop skill in organizing and directing the work of others.
>
> Frequent tests are given in most courses.
>
> In many classes students have an assigned seat.
>
> Students' mid-term and final grades are reported to parents.
>
> $p < .05$
>
> People around here seem to thrive on difficulty—the tougher things get, the harder they work.
>
> The school is outstanding for the emphasis and support it gives to pure scholarship and basic research.

Again, the picture is clearly one of faculty-student involvement in a supportive intellectual community.

In order to determine what, in fact, students do in their environments, we asked them to keep track over a five-day period of the amount of time they spent in various activities, including study, discussion, grooming, eating, sleeping, and so on. We discovered that for all four groups approximately one-third of the time is spent sleeping, one-third in studying and attending class, and the remaining one-third in eating, grooming, and maintenance activities.

Looking now at statistically significant differences between Residential College and both LSA and Honors, we find that the RC students report less time attending classes and less time going to and from classes (because their residence halls house their own classrooms). However, the Residential College students report more hours in study outside of class and less time in recreational activities.

In addition to the areas referred to above, the time budget provided information on thirteen subareas of the academic week's activities, directed at where, how, with whom, and about what activity time was spent, and what types of topics were talked about with whom and where.

These data confirm the picture painted by the CUES. When Intellectual Openness is controlled for, RC students are significantly higher than LSA groups in the amount of time they report spending in bull sessions, interacting with the faculty, and remaining in their residence halls. They report spending significantly less time by themselves, or in discussing personal problems. Therefore, although they entered RC expecting a more social atmosphere, after one year RC students describe their college as more academically oriented than LSA students; they spend more time in contact with their faculty and in discussion groups with their classmates, while still maintaining a high degree of community.

As we have already seen, college environment contributes substantially to student development. But the personality of the student and the interaction between student and residential environment are also integral factors in any study of college environment. We next deal with the correlation between measures of student satisfaction and change and various types of college residence arrangements, and with the relationship between personality at entrance to college and subsequent satisfaction, personality change, and several types of behaviors.

We began our study with the expectation that the environment of the Residential College would be more conducive to student growth and development than that of the larger university. RC students therefore would probably show more evidence of change than our LSA samples on such attitudes as maturity that discriminate between upperclassmen and lowerclassmen. We also predicted that, because of the more informal living and studying arrangements at their college, RC students would be more satisfied than LSA students with their faculty, administrators, and fellow students.

Finally, we felt that students with certain personality traits would be more receptive to change than others. Newcomb's theory of accentuation (Feldman and Newcomb, 1969) in particular predicts that, in appropriate environments, students with high initial ratings on a trait will show greater increases on those ratings than students with low initial ratings. Specifically, then, students initially high on our dimension of Intellectual Openness should show greater change than students with low scores on the attitudinal scales of the CSQ. The following results involve only the RC and the combined LSA sample (rejected RC students and LSA students); the Honors group was excluded for this purpose because of the unique basis on which its members are selected.

The satisfaction of a college's students is one component of a school's success. Our data clearly show that seven months after the beginning of the academic year RC students are more satisfied than the LSA population with faculty, students, and administration, as measured by CSQ scales. They also show higher scores on twenty-nine of the thirty items making up these scales (significant at .01 for more than half of the items). RC students are more likely than LSA students to say that their faculty is composed of superior teachers, who are genuinely interested in their students' personal and academic progress. RC students think that their administration fairly enforces the campus regulations, which are logical and necessary. Finally, RC students feel that their fellow students are honest and not overly involved in extremist or nonconformist activities.

If the RC experiment is to be considered successful, however, it must not only satisfy the student body; it must also aid the maturational process of its students. One of the consistent developmental trends during college that Feldman and Newcomb (1969) report in undergraduates is toward greater independence. In all of our groups, scores on measures of Family Independence (FI), Liberalism (L), Social Conscience (SC), and Cultural Sophistication (CS) increase during the first year and they increase more substantially for RC students than for the LSA samples.[3] Changes on Liberalism and Family Independence are significant beyond the .05 level. On measures of change in Peer Independence (PI), however, there is hardly any difference between the schools, although RC students score slightly lower than those in LSA. Raw scores on this scale decrease for all groups.

The personality cluster that most discriminates between RC and LSA samples, as we reported earlier, is that of Intellectual Openness. This cluster relates negatively to Satisfaction with Administration and positively to Satisfaction with Students: on the one hand, the more intellectually open students are more critical of rules and regulations than are less intellectually inclined students; on the other, they do not feel that the student body is too nonconformist, extreme in political beliefs, or extreme in behavior— they feel that the student body is concerned politically, academically honest, and neither over- nor under-competitive.

RC students initially high on the intellectual cluster show

[3] For more detail on how measures of attitudinal change were developed, see the fuller report.

greater change on the Family Independence, Liberalism, and Social Conscience scales of the CSQ than do RC students with low initial scores on this cluster. They also tend to show greater change on the Cultural Sophistication scale. This result supports our initial hypothesis of accentuation: students with high scores on a dimension relevant to their subsequent experiences will increase their scores on those dimensions still further as they progress. The patterns of change, however, are not identical for the RC and LSA groups. At RC, initial intellectualism is most often related to changes on the Liberalism and Social Conscience scales, while LSA students initially high on the intellectual cluster change most on Peer and Family Independence scales; that is, they become more self-reliant. (RC students high on intellectualism tend to become more Family Independent, but there appears to be no relationship with Peer Independence.)

Because RC and LSA groups differ significantly upon entrance on the personality cluster we have labeled Intellectual Openness, and because this cluster relates to some of the dependent variables of satisfaction and change, we used statistical controls for this cluster when considering any differences in impact between the two groups.[4] Under these conditions, RC students change more than the control groups on the Liberalism scale alone. Their scores also tend to rise (at the .1 level of significance) on Family Independence. Intellectually open students become more peer independent and more socially conscious.

Although neither the Conventional Adjustment nor the Independence clusters relate to satisfaction or change measures, the personal characteristics in the Sociability cluster proved to be among the more important variables. For the RC sample, it enabled us to relate personality, behavior, satisfaction, and change. At present, however, we will restrict ourselves to its correlations with change.

RC students who are more socially oriented showed greater

---

[4] A two-way unweighted means analysis of variance allows us to examine simultaneously the variations in the dependent variables attributable to differences in personality and college. See the fuller report for details and supporting data.

change on the Liberalism, Social Conscience, and Cultural Sophistication scales of the CSQ. This finding does not hold for LSA students. The explanation for this difference may lie in the fact that students who enter RC are more intellectual, more liberal, and more sophisticated than the LSA students we sampled; the more socially oriented RC students are probably more involved with the RC and interact more with their fellow students and are, therefore, more affected by the liberal RC environment. (Indeed, corroboration for this explanation appears later in this paper.)

Although sociability is significantly related to change, the pattern of relationships between the cluster of characteristics that defines sociability and the CSQ satisfaction scales is not clear. For the RC sample, however, sociability does relate to Satisfaction with Faculty: those students who are more socially oriented view the faculty as comprising academically superior, tolerant teachers who come to know the students personally. RC students lower on the sociability dimension do not share this view of the faculty as strongly. There is a tendency, not a particularly strong one, for students who rate high on sociability to show somewhat higher satisfaction with their fellow students.

While it is relatively clear that students at the Residential College change more on our variables than students at the LSA, the question of causation is somewhat more difficult to resolve. Is it, as our two-way analysis of variance suggests, merely because RC students initially are predisposed to change, or is some other factor at the RC aiding the change? From the preceding discussion on environmental differences, we know that there is more faculty-student interaction at the RC than at the LSA. And from our data on RC students, the degree of faculty-student contact shows an impressive, positive relationship to change and impact. At the RC, those students who have more faculty contact become more liberal, more socially concerned, and more culturally sophisticated. Because this finding does not hold for the LSA groups[5] the discussion below will be limited to sources of change at RC only.

[5] That faculty contact relates more to change at the RC than at LSA is probably due to the greater range of scores found at the RC. While the RC means are higher on most of the behavioral measures, there are still

Change in Liberalism, Cultural Sophistication, and Social Conscience relates positively both to amount of faculty contact and to time spent in residence halls. This fact, and the finding that RC students are initially higher on the intellectual openness cluster, together imply that students who spend most of their time at the RC associating with students who are initially higher than average on the intellectualism factor become even more intellectually open than those students who spend less time at the RC. On the other hand, students who spend more time in their residence halls become more dependent upon their peers.

A third major group of behaviors that relates to change is general talkativeness and outgoingness—students who talk more at the RC become more liberal, more socially concerned, and more culturally sophisticated. This finding simply indicates that students who interact with their environment, and particularly with people in that environment, are more affected by those people. And these data in turn suggest that students who participate more in the college experience gain more from it. Again, as we noted earlier, students who talk more and are more outgoing become more dependent upon their peers.

For LSA students, however, the most striking correlates of behavior and change are those along our independence dimension. That is, specifically, LSA students who talk about literary and artistic activities become much more independent of their families, and students who spend a good deal of their time in their residence halls become more dependent upon their peers. Conversely, LSA students who report more home visits become even more dependent on their families. While no strong relation exists between talkativeness and our various change measures at LSA, a strong correlation shows up between talking about social issues and change in Liberalism, Social Conscience, and Cultural Sophistication. Thus it seems that, in LSA, students who are talking about socially relevant issues are the only ones who are experiencing change, whereas at the RC

---

students who do not report taking advantage of the possible faculty-student interaction and other students who do report taking full advantage of this possibility. The greater variability at the RC thus increases the chance of finding interpretable correlates of behavior.

the prerequisite for change is simply talking and interacting with other students.

Those students at the RC who interact most with the faculty like them the most. Oddly enough, this same relationship does not exist at the LSA, possibly because so few LSA students report much contact with faculty. Satisfaction with Faculty at RC also relates to the amount of time spent in the residence halls, although this relationship does not hold for LSA.

Is there a relationship between satisfaction and change? Are students who are satisfied more likely to show change? Are they more likely to be affected by their environment than less satisfied students? Looking at the scales measuring satisfaction with faculty and administration, the answer is strongly negative. The lack of correlation between Satisfaction with Faculty and our change measures is surprising in view of the fact that Satisfaction with Faculty is the variable that most strongly separates RC and LSA groups. For both LSA and RC students, satisfaction with fellow students relates strongly to change in Liberalism, and, at the RC, to change in Cultural Sophistication.

We have already indicated that Residential College students who are more outgoing, have more faculty contact, or spend more time in their residence halls become more liberal, more socially concerned, and more culturally sophisticated. Furthermore, students who are upon entrance more intellectually open or more people-oriented become more sophisticated in their attitudes than those students initially low on these two dimensions. Can we now relate initial personality to such behavioral variables as faculty contact, outgoingness, and residence orientation?

For the RC students, the answer is clearly yes. On the intellectual dimension, high scorers date more, interact more with the faculty, and talk to a much greater extent about social issues, about such topics as sex, drugs, or alcohol, and about literary and artistic subjects, than do low scorers. (These are the activities that relate to development as measured by the CSQ.)

On the sociability dimension, RC students who score high on social orientation date more, go out more, interact more with the faculty and resident fellows, spend more time participating in activities in their residence halls, and talk about everything more than do low scorers. Socially oriented RC students do spend more time at the RC, whereas no such relationship holds for the intellectually-oriented LSA group.

From the above discussion it is possible to develop a rather simple model of the dynamics of change. Students who are initially more socially or intellectually oriented interact more with the faculty and student body and spend more time in the Residential College than students not so predisposed. Those students who do spend time at the RC, who interact more with each other and with the faculty, experience more change in their attitudes and beliefs than do those students who interact less with their environment.[6]

While this model is overly simplified, it summarizes the relationships between initial student characteristics, self-reported student behavior, and observed final differences in attitudes. Although the correlations with change upon which this model has been constructed are statistically significant, they are all quite small. This is presumably due to the very low reliability associated with the measure of change. Current work is being undertaken to improve the change scales by analyzing the nature of change at the individual item level. Clusters of change scores should be found with higher reliabilities and should allow us to discover more conclusive correlates of the process of student development.

Our initial prediction—that RC students initially high on the intellectual dimension would change more on the attitudinal scales of the CSQ than would students initially lower on this dimension—has been substantiated; and another interesting finding resulted that may be considered an addition to accentuation theory: students who are more socially oriented interact more with their environment, and when fellow students in this environment are initially higher on a dimension, those socially oriented students will change more on attitudes relevant to that dimension.

In summary, let us recall that the program and setting of the Residential College appealed particularly to entering students high in academic and nonconformist interests; in these respects they resembled Honors students more closely than rank-and-file students

---

[6] These conclusions are further supported by analysis of patterns of factor loadings; see fuller report.

in the parent college. (These differences cannot be accounted for by the fact that the RC population included about 10 per cent of Honors-caliber students, while the LSA groups included few or none.) Further, the thirteen (among fourteen) scales that differentiated between RC and LSA groups at high levels of significance were precisely those that had high loadings on a general characteristic labeled Intellectual Openness, as identified by cluster analysis.

There were few differences in anticipatory images of RC and LSA freshmen with regard to intellectual and academic aspects of their respective college environments. But RC freshmen, whose anticipations were in many respects not very accurate, did view their future "college home" as an alternative to a relatively impersonal, competitive, and possibly confusing experience of a large university. Their general intellectual openness was associated with expectations not of a particularly intellectual environment, but rather of one characterized by friendliness and fairness, with promise of responding to their own needs for personal development.

Toward the end of their first year in college, RC students consistently reported more satisfaction with faculty, with administration, and with fellow students than did their contemporaries in LSA. These diverse evaluations of demonstrably different college environments represent one kind of impact; however, a more educationally relevant dimension has to do with changes in Family Independence, Social Conscience, Cultural Sophistication, and Liberalism. In spite of the fact that RC freshmen initially scored significantly higher than either LSA control group on each of these four scales, the increases by RC students were greater than those of the controls (at significance levels ranging from .1 to .001). Such accentuation of characteristics on which RC freshmen were initially high appears to be a joint outcome of the fit between their intellectual dispositions and the college environment and their relatively great sociability, which facilitated their exploration of that environment.

Furthermore, the individuals in the Residential College who changed most in these ways were those who were initially most open, intellectually and socially, and who later most fully exploited the resources of an environment congenial to those dispositions—

an environment which, in fact, they helped create. Others in that college, being less open, did not use its resources in the same ways, thus resembling students in the conventional control populations who were typically less open, initially, and whose environment did not offer similarly congenial impetus to change.

Chapter 7

Making a Difference

Warren Bryan Martin
Judith K. Wilkinson

There is nothing singular about cluster colleges. Although we speak of the "cluster college concept," there is no specific concept—no stated philosophy of education, no collection of goals or objectives, no set of attitudes or values operates as an accepted, essential rationale for these colleges. Although we speak of the "cluster college movement," there is no specific movement—no purpose or cause, no single direction, no step or style, characterizes the march of these colleges. Not all of them even bother to cluster.

We can say that these schools are, generally speaking, liberal arts colleges, committed to vitalizing and personalizing both teaching and learning. However, the same can be said for more than a thousand colleges in this country. Surely the cluster concept, if it is to earn special attention, must offer something better than a reiteration of the academic's traditional equivalent to the politician's commitment to god, mother, and country.

Is it the ability of the cluster colleges to give new or contemporary expression to classical themes, or to give specific application to historical generalizations, that sets off the concept and unifies these schools into a movement? Perhaps the essential distinction is that these colleges are centers of innovation and experimentation. They challenge departmental compartmentalization of faculty and students, the rigidities of conventional admissions criteria, course requirements, and evaluative mechanisms. They feature improved methods of instruction in appropriate facilities, as well as encourage personal identity and social community through involvement and sharing. Cluster colleges swing.

Do they? Do they swing in ways different from other colleges and universities? Every innovation or form of experimentation employed today in cluster colleges was created elsewhere and is today duplicated nearly everywhere. The departmental organization of knowledge has long been under attack, as have fixed admissions standards, course sequences, testing and grading procedures. To name Antioch, Bennington, Reed, Sarah Lawrence,[1] is to begin to list precursors of innovations whose epigones are now legion. Revised methods of instruction, better facilities, and improved governance arrangements designed to create learning environments in which self-realization is matched by group commitments and social responsibility are not new phenomena. We have only to reflect on Oxford, Cambridge, the colonial colleges, and the nineteenth-century denominational colleges to know how old and persistent is this concept of collegiality. And the College de France, the Uni-

---

[1] In the introduction to his book *Students Without Teachers*, Taylor (1969) recalled that in the thirties Sarah Lawrence had "an open curriculum, with no system of required courses, lectures, examinations, grades, credits, formal departments, faculty hierarchy, or other educational impediments, and a student body whose members were thoroughly involved in making college policy and running their own lives."

versity of Berlin, the University of London, and the American land grant colleges testify to the enduring concern to keep institutions of higher education identified with, and responsive to, societal and technological needs.

The sixties have been called the decade of innovation. That phrase is serviceable yet needs qualifications, as was shown by the research of Brick and McGrath (1969). They sent a questionnaire to 1,209 liberal arts colleges asking for information on institutional experience with specific forms of innovation, within four broad categories of concern: curriculum, instruction, organization and student services. From 882 usable responses, these researchers reported that curricular innovations such as interdisciplinary studies, independent study, non-Western studies, community service, work-study, off-campus and overseas study programs—all of which are innovations presently featured in cluster colleges—were in effect before 1961 at 90 to 250 institutions, depending on the particular curriculum scheme. After 1961, these innovations were accepted by even more schools, and by 1968 various innovations were in use at over 80 per cent of the liberal arts colleges reported in the Brick-McGrath study.

Instructional innovations, as tabulated by the Brick-McGrath research, were also widespread. Comprehensive examinations, team teaching, and interinstitutional cooperative programs were used as early as, and in number equal to, the already mentioned curricular innovations. Fewer schools made attempts before 1961 to introduce variations in grading practices, or used new instructional media, or extended the academic program to dormitories, but even in such areas scores of colleges were trying one or more of these innovations before the last decade. And the totals had greatly increased in all categories by 1964 when the cluster college movement began to get widespread attention. The story is different in degree only in the Brick-McGrath categories of organization and student services. Variations in academic calendars, experimentation with facilities, student participation on committees, special admissions arrangements, and other innovations were used rather widely before 1961 and were obligatory at most colleges by 1968.

The cluster colleges hardly have a corner on the innovation market. It is true that we have just completed a decade of innova-

tion and, for good or ill, nearly every institution of higher education has been affected.

Could it be that the point about the cluster college concept,
the thing that shows unique potential for good, is its emphasis on
small colleges: the idea of institutions growing smaller while getting
bigger? After all, the huge, monolithic university exacerbates the
modern student's tendencies to alienation and hostility. The problem of size can be solved by the small college, where individuality,
personal involvement, and a sense of community may replace
anomie.

This justification for cluster colleges is hardly better than the
other attempts to define the cluster concept or delineate the movement, and there are three reasons for this. First, the colleges in operation or proposed under one or another of the cluster plans vary in
size from less than 200 students to more than 3,000. There is no
agreement on what constitutes a small college. Second, if colleges with
less than 2,500 students are the hope of American higher education, it is hard to understand why our rapture has been so long
deferred. Of the 2,483 institutions of higher education operating
in this country in 1968–69, 1,827 of them had enrollments of under
2,500 students. And 1,200 of them enrolled less than 1,000 students
each. Though in the fall of 1968 there were twenty-five universities
with an enrollment exceeding 30,000, ten years earlier there were
only four such institutions (Grant, 1969, p. 33). This nation has
had ample experience with small colleges. That fact is, no doubt,
one reason for the popularity of large ones. The small college,
viewed historically, has often provided an opportunity for faculty
and students to practice mediocrity in an intimate setting.[2]

The third reason why the comparatively small size of cluster
colleges will not serve as the key component in a theoretical justification of this movement is the fact that exponents of the cluster
concept always balance their emphasis on the small college with an
equal emphasis on the virtues of the bigness provided by the clustering arrangement. Advocates are usually as much concerned to have
the subunits, or federated colleges, cooperate together as they are

[2] For more extensive coverage of the problems of small colleges,
particularly cluster colleges, see Martin, 1967.

to have them retain their separate identities. But to take up the federal model is to take on its problems: for example, balancing the rights and interests of the individual units off against those of the collective good. In academe today, as in the general socio-political realm, it is hard to resist tendencies to centralism. The cluster college notion may provide a corrective, but it threatens its own solution by also advocating cooperation in the achievement of services that only large size can give.

If cluster colleges are not unique in their commitment to the indefinable liberal arts, or in their concern for the improvement of teaching and learning through innovations, or in the individual or collective size of their institutions, are we to conclude that cluster colleges make no difference? Or, could it be that while they are no different in the sense of having unique features, they can make a difference for other reasons, particularly for their own faculty and students, and are at least different in the context of the sponsoring university of which they are a part?

This was, in fact, the conclusion of the Institutional Character study.[3] Certain attitudes, values, interests, and endeavors of faculty and students associated with the cluster colleges in this research project were sufficiently different from those of faculty and students in other colleges to make inescapable the conclusion that the clustering arrangement either effected changes in individuals or provided a setting where those with a particular value orientation could come together. Colleges that were not different from other colleges, in various details of their programs, turned out to be different in their effect on some people and to be different because of the presence of other people.

Differences were mainly in two areas. First, the cluster college faculty and students were more concerned about the institution's educational philosophy and were more knowledgeable about it than were their counterparts elsewhere. Second, the faculty and

[3] The Institutional Character study was sponsored by the University of California, Berkeley, Warren Bryan Martin, project director. The research report submitted to the U.S. Office of Education was entitled *Institutional Character in Colleges and Universities: The Interaction of Ideology, Organization, and Innovation.* A revised and condensed version of this report appeared under the title, *Conformity: Standards and Change in Higher Education,* San Francisco: Jossey-Bass, 1969.

students at cluster colleges were more open to the idea of challenging conventional approaches to liberal education. Innovation and experimentation were discernible characteristics of life in the cluster colleges.

The Institutional Character study questionnaires were distributed in the fall of 1966 and the spring of 1967. Of 2,669 faculty members in the eight participating institutions, 1,098 received the faculty questionnaire. A total of 577 questionnaires was returned, giving a representation from 53 per cent of those polled. Some variation of the cluster college idea had become operational in three of the eight institutions studied—the University of California, the University of the Pacific, and Hofstra University. These are the institutions evaluated here. Questionnaires were received from a total of sixty-seven faculty members in the five cluster colleges and from 325 faculty members in the four traditionally organized colleges of the same university systems.

For the purposes of this analysis, faculty from cluster colleges as a group were compared to their traditional counterparts as a group, then individual pairs of colleges within the same institutional system were examined to see if the general conclusion was supported in the specific example. Institutional comparisons were as follows: At the University of the Pacific, all but one of the Raymond faculty ($N = 18$) was matched with 44 per cent of the College of the Pacific faculty ($N = 38$), 78 per cent of those faculty to whom the questionnaire was mailed. In the University of California system, Stevenson College faculty ($N = 16$) from the Santa Cruz campus were compared with 22 per cent of the Davis faculty ($N = 151$) and then with the Santa Barbara faculty ($N = 94$). Return rates for these three campuses were 53 per cent, 65 per cent and 56 per cent respectively. The Davis and Santa Barbara samples were then compared to 47 per cent of the sampled faculty at Cowell College ($N = 14$), also on the Santa Cruz campus. Faculty respondents from the third University of California cluster college, Revelle College at San Diego ($N = 14$) were also compared with the Davis and Santa Barbara faculty samples, though the response rate from Revelle was only 22 per cent. Finally, at Hofstra University, five of the six faculty members then at New College were compared with faculty from the College of Arts and

Sciences (N = 42, a 58 per cent return). Since an N as small as 5 makes statistical significance especially difficult to achieve with a chi square test, New College and the College of Arts and Sciences are not included in the accounts of individual college comparisons. The general conclusion of every item reported here, however, was supported in the percentages of the Hofstra comparison.

Student questionnaries were received from more than 90 per cent of the entering freshman students at the following institutions: Davis (1523) and Santa Barbara (2676), College of the Pacific (416) and Raymond (88), New College (80) and the College of Arts and Sciences (546). Cowell College students were not studied, but questionnaires were received from 213 freshmen at Stevenson and 480 at Revelle. (Much of the data collected from the student questionnaires is reported at length in Chapter Four.)

One assumption of the study was that institutional character would be defined by respondents, whether administrators, faculty, or students, in terms of the stated goals and purposes of their colleges or universities. We expected that in a vital institution there would be good congruence between professed and perceived objectives as well as between individual and institutional goals. It was our concern, therefore, to ascertain how much project participants knew about the philosophy and objectives of their schools and what they thought to be the importance of these matters for their colleagues.

One item in the faculty questionnaire invited respondents to indicate the extent to which their institution's educational philosophy and general objectives were emphasized during the negotiations that went on before they were employed. Sixty-nine per cent of the faculty at the cluster ("experimental") colleges reported that "institutional objectives were treated at length" while only 5 per cent of the faculty at the non-cluster ("control") colleges answered this way. Fifty-two per cent of the faculty from the control colleges said that, on the contrary, when they were being considered for employment "the emphasis was clearly on the work of the department." A comparison of individual colleges, pairing experimental with control units, showed that the result just mentioned was the case on each campus (Table 8).

Another item asked faculty to estimate the proportion of

their colleagues who were seriously interested in the educational objectives that were supposed to give direction and character to the institutions with which they were associated. Cluster college respondents said that "almost all" of their faculty members were seriously concerned with institutional purposes. Meanwhile, faculty in the control colleges were split between answering that "well over half" or "about half" of their colleagues were concerned, while 18 per cent said that this was the case with only "one-fourth or so."

And, as before, the greater emphasis placed on institutional objectives by faculty in cluster colleges was maintained at the level of specific institutional comparisons ($p < .01$). Revelle was the only exception to this; it differed from Davis ($p < .05$) but was not different from Santa Barbara.

When students entering the colleges under consideration were asked, "How much do you know about the general philosophy of the college you are attending?" the same pattern of differentiation that has been seen in the faculty samples was repeated (Table 9). Forty-seven per cent of the freshmen at the experimental colleges professed to know "a lot" about their school's educational philosophy, while the youth at the control schools varied from claims of "a little" knowledge (70 per cent) to claims of no knowledge at all (12 per cent). The same result came from a questionnaire item in which students were asked whether they thought their college had a distinctive quality. Eighty-eight per cent of the cluster college respondents thought this to be the case, compared to only 57 per cent of the others ($p < .01$).

Whether consideration is given to students or faculty, then, persons in cluster colleges were more likely to be knowledgeable about institutional objectives and educational philosophy, and to show interest in their institution's distinctive features, than were students or faculty in the non-cluster settings.

In considering the broad aims of the undergraduate experience, about 60 per cent of the faculty in both of the samples agreed that the most important aim was to develop in the student an ability to think and to understand the consequences of his actions. A second, similar goal favored by faculty was to develop in the student a capacity for good judgment. Vocational or professional training for both types of schools ranked low, with only 10 per cent

Table 8

EMPHASIS ON INSTITUTIONAL
OBJECTIVES VS. DEPARTMENTAL DUTIES OF FACULTY

	Emphasis on Institutional Objectives	Emphasis on Work of Department
	Percent	Percent
University of the Pacific		
Raymond[a]	78	0
COP	13	26
Hofstra University		
Hof New[a]	100	0
Hof A&S	5	48
University of California		
Cowell[a]	79	0
Stevenson[a]	69	6
Revelle[a]	36	7
Davis	4	60
Santa Barbara	4	51

$p < .01$

Raymond > COP
Cowell > Davis, Santa Barbara
Stevenson > Davis, Santa Barbara

$p < .05$

Revelle > Davis, Santa Barbara

[a] Cluster college.

of the control faculty and 1 per cent of the experimental faculty choosing this option.

Entering students as groups in both the cluster and the non-cluster colleges, on the other hand, accepted vocationalism as the first goal of their educational experience. Forty-four per cent of the non-cluster college students and 38 per cent of the students from cluster colleges chose this option. Thus, a definite tension existed between the goal favored by faculty and the one most important to students. It is instructive to notice, however, that this difference was reduced in the cluster colleges. There, more than on the non-cluster campuses, freshmen showed a stronger intellectual orientation, 33 per cent of them compared to 24 per cent of the

Table 9

STUDENTS' KNOWLEDGE AT ENTRANCE OF INSTITUTIONAL PHILOSOPHY

	Know a Lot Percent	Know a Little Percent	Don't Know Anything Percent
University of the Pacific			
Raymond[a]	61	35	1
COP	17	72	9
Hofstra University			
Hof New[a]	36	55	9
Hof A&S	19	69	10
University of California[b]			
Stevenson[a]	61	36	1
Revelle[a]	40	52	4
Davis	20	69	10
Santa Barbara	12	70	15

[a] Cluster college
[b] No student data for Cowell

non-cluster students answering that their objective was "to acquire and use the skills and habits involved in critical and constructive thinking." An examination of the individual cluster college samples shows that students at Raymond and Stevenson definitely chose the intellectual over the vocational objective while students at New College, Hofstra, were split 30 to 31 per cent between these two goals. Revelle students were the only cluster college student sample to show a preference for vocational goals. An imperfect but better congruence thus existed between faculty and students in the cluster colleges regarding the aims of the educational program than was the case in the more conventional institutions.

Faculty in the cluster colleges seemed aware of this value congruence, just as their counterparts in the non-cluster colleges were aware of the disparity. In one part of the questionnaire, four types of students were described: professionalists, collegiates, intellectuals, and disaffiliates. Both faculty groups agreed that collegiates were the least rewarding group to teach and that they would like to see the intellectuals increase in number on their campus. But when asked to describe the student group dominant in influence on their campus, the control group most often named collegiates while the experimental group chose intellectuals. The cluster college faculty apparently see their students as approximating their ideal, but the non-cluster college faculty are mainly involved with the students they find least rewarding to teach.

At a time of societal change, it was expected that all respondents in the Institutional Character study would equate institutional vitality and distinctiveness with the capacity of their colleges or universities to identify with the current mood of change and to show interest in specific forms of change. But, in fact, the attitude of the cluster college faculty toward innovation was markedly different from that of the faculty of non-cluster colleges.

When respondents were asked to indicate whether their colleagues would be "willing to participate personally in experimental educational ventures," 63 per cent of the faculty sample in the cluster colleges said that "most" of their associates were so inclined. Faculty at the more established campuses, meanwhile, were much more likely to say that "some" (50 per cent) or perhaps "about half" (22 per cent) of their peers would participate personally in experimental educational ventures. This conclusion was sustained in a comparison of individual colleges (Figure 11).

Respondents at cluster colleges thought the description "not hostile to innovation but unwilling to get involved personally," was true for only "some" to "very few" of their colleagues, while at the control institutions the weight of the response pattern went to the side of "about half" to "most" ($p < .01$). When specific institutional comparisons were made on this item, the outcomes varied only slightly. Stevenson (Santa Cruz) differed from both Davis and Santa Barbara, and Cowell (Santa Cruz) differed from Santa Barbara ($p < .01$). Differences at the .05 level were found between Raymond and College of the Pacific, and between Revelle (San Diego) and Santa Barbara. In the comparisons of Cowell and Revelle with Davis, the requirements for statistical significance were not satisfied but the general thrust of the other comparisons was retained.

Support for innovation and experimentation was found among the students of cluster colleges as well as the faculty. Student respondents were asked whether "an opportunity to participate in experimental educational programs" was an important consideration in the selection of the college they were then entering. Such an opportunity was a much more important criterion in the selection of colleges for the cluster college group than for the non-cluster students. Thirty-three per cent of the cluster college students compared to only 4 per cent of the control group said this was "important." Individual college comparisons are shown in Figure 12.

When freshmen were asked to describe their "ideal college," and were queried on whether it would be "traditional" or "experimental," students in the non-cluster colleges described their ideal college as one that would be traditional while students in the cluster colleges chose to describe their ideal college as experimental.

From one perspective these findings from student data appear obvious. Of course students at innovative colleges will describe their ideal college as experimental and declare that an opportunity to participate in experimental programs is important to them. To say otherwise would be to refute their choices and confound their situation. But the point not so obvious, yet very important, is that structural provisions for change, innovation, and experimentation, as concentrated in the cluster college, are shown to be effective in drawing together like-minded people or in producing an anticipatory identification with the ideal of the college by the students who come there. And in so doing the opportunities for institutional change should be improved.

While interdisciplinary contacts at the faculty level, or cross-disciplinary teaching arrangements are hardly new ideas, the departmental and disciplinary mentality has become so deeply entrenched in the preferences and habits of American professors that a show of willingness by faculty to encourage such contacts or teach under such arrangements must be taken as evidence of an openness toward change. Therefore, we report here on two items in the faculty questionnaire dealing with these themes.

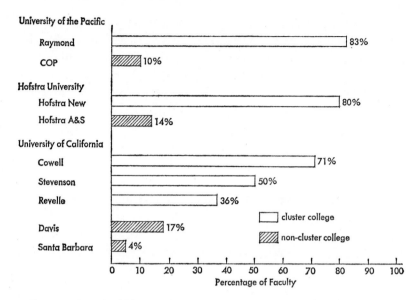

FIGURE 11. Faculty judging that "most" colleagues would be "willing to participate personally in experimental educational ventures."

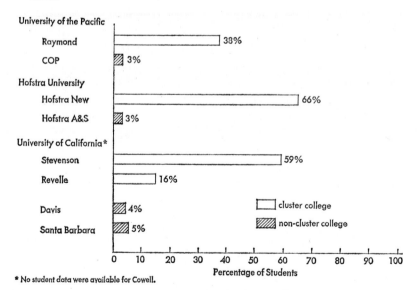

* No student data were available for Cowell.

FIGURE 12. Students saying that opportunity to participate in experimental educational programs was important in their selection of college.

When faculty respondents were asked to indicate the importance for themselves of "interdisciplinary faculty contacts and teaching opportunities," those persons at the cluster colleges expressed a greater interest in such interdisciplinary arrangements than did faculty in non-cluster college settings ($p < .01$). Seventy-three per cent of the experimental group, compared to only 30 per cent of the non-cluster faculty, said this was "very important." And, once again, the general picture remained clear when attention was focused on its several parts. Comparisons of Stevenson versus Davis or Stevenson versus Santa Barbara, Raymond versus College of the Pacific, and Cowell versus Santa Barbara, all showed the cluster college sample more interested in interdisciplinary contacts and teaching opportunities ($p < .01$). The .05 level characterized the difference between Cowell (Santa Cruz) and the Davis campus. The trend of findings at these colleges and at those previously reported was retained, but without statistical significance, in the Revelle comparisons.

Support for relational learning was also found in the questionnaire item in which faculty were asked how important cross-disciplinary teaching was for them on a theoretical level (that is, without regard to their actual professional obligations). Respondents at cluster colleges were more interested in this form of innovation, 49 per cent of them saying it was "very important," compared to 21 per cent of the controls. In both of these related items, respondents were also asked to judge how important these arrangements were for their colleagues. The cluster college faculty responded that these arrangements were just "somewhat important" to their colleagues. But in the perceptions of colleagues, as in the self-ratings, cluster college faculty were seen as more favorable to these innovations than were non-cluster college faculty.

Cluster college faculty were also more likely to favor changes in the degree of control over students' personal lives that colleges have traditionally shown. On the item, "The concept of *in loco parentis* is unnecessary and undesirable because students should have the freedoms and responsibilities of adults," a majority of faculty in all schools represented in the project tended to support the idea, but the degree of support was stronger in the cluster colleges (64 per cent) than in the non-cluster college group (50 per cent). In the institutional comparisons, Raymond differed from College of the Pacific and Stevenson (Santa Cruz) differed from the Davis faculty ($p < .05$). In two other comparisons—Stevenson versus Santa Barbara and Cowell (Santa Cruz) versus Davis, the general conclusion was supported but not at the level of statistical significance. Cowell versus Santa Barbara showed a tie, as did the Revelle (San Diego) versus Davis match. The only comparison producing a reverse trend was the result from Revelle versus Santa Barbara.

"Should students at your college participate more than they do at present in the formulation and implementation of academic policies?" This question brought the same response from the cluster colleges as from the non-cluster colleges: "No." But the results must be interpreted in the light of the actual practices of the colleges involved. The degree of student participation that cluster colleges encourage is considerably greater than is the case at the non-cluster colleges. So for the cluster colleges, "No" may have meant "No more of a good thing," while the negative response from the non-cluster colleges indicates that they did not favor more than token student participation.

Several other items on the faculty questionnaire had some measure of importance for the question of climate and related attitudinal considerations, but they were also difficult to evaluate due to the influence of local conditions. College of the Pacific faculty, for example, were more favorably disposed than Raymond respondents to the item calling for a reduction in the academic emphasis given to grades, units of credit, and rigid course requirements. But the situation in the College of the Pacific regarding these constraints of order was much more conventional than the situation prevailing at Raymond. So, College of the Pacific faculty may have been reflecting an interest in the liberalization of conservative policies for these areas while Raymond faculty were indicating hesitation at the point of having radical innovations carried any further.

Another questionnaire item which was difficult to interpret read: "More effort should be made to bring students and faculty together in unstructured, personal encounters." Control faculty were more likely than experimental faculty to "agree" or "strongly agree" with this statement. But at the cluster colleges considerable effort had already been made to encourage informal contact between faculty and students. The added support from the non-cluster colleges for this question, therefore, was probably not a matter of their greater enthusiasm for personal encounters so much as an indication of their dissatisfaction with established procedures.

It may be noted that in each of these three items the cluster colleges have indicated that their conditions are about as unstructured as they would have them be—the innovations have been carried far enough. The non-cluster colleges, on the other hand, seem to be aware of the need for certain changes that would modify existing structures. There is a limit to the changes that they would see take place, however, as was clear when they were questioned about student involvement in the formulation of academic policies.

It may be that the limits that cluster colleges set on the changes they are willing to make are formed because of their ignorance of change options. This ignorance was revealed by an item in the faculty questionnaire of the Institutional Character study which asked respondents to list colleges and universities at which, in their minds, the most promising innovations in undergraduate education were taking place. They were not given multiple choice response options but were instead presented with two blank columns, one for the listing of institutions and the other for the innovations themselves. When the responses which showed some knowledge, however vague, of innovations taking place outside of the respondent's own school were compared with those responses which showed no knowledge of such innovations, the cluster college faculty showed more familiarity with educational innovations than did the non-cluster college faculty ($p < .05$). There remains a gap, however, between the sparse knowledge that even the cluster college group had and the amount of knowledge of change options needed to encourage confidence and flexibility. Less than half of either group (40 per cent of the controls and 47 per cent of the experimentals) were able to name both an innovation and the school in which it was taking place.

In both their awareness of educational philosophy and their openness to change, innovation, and experimentation, faculty in the cluster college samples were noticeably different from their counterparts in the more established institutions of the same educational systems. And they were different, we think, in ways likely to be relevant to the reforms, changes, and improvements that are more and more regarded as mandatory to the success of American higher education in the future.

There were, to be sure, many areas in which cluster college faculties showed values similar to faculties elsewhere. Their attitudes toward research and publications, for example, were slightly different yet surprisingly conventional. Faculties everywhere, including those working in cluster colleges, are in the grip of professionalism and are judged, therefore, by the conventional criteria of excellence (Martin 1969a).

Furthermore, as was emphasized in the early section of this essay, it is hard to find structures and functions in cluster colleges that are unique or even especially characteristic of them. Everything they plan or do has its antecedent and equivalent elsewhere.

Nevertheless, as the data show, non-differences somehow make a difference. Why?

The commitments of the cluster college need not be new in an absolute sense. The creation of an organizational unit, with its own program and facilities, makes it possible for conservative or even reactionary ideas to hit persons who have been charged with the responsibility of being different with the weight of newness. Old ideas seen from a different perspective seem new. Innovations that are elsewhere being tried separately, partially, or in a less holistic fashion may be regrouped or revised in such a way as to produce a vital hybrid.

Substantive change requires a social matrix that is, on the one hand, sufficiently favorable to the proposed change to give it impetus and some protection but is also sufficiently critical of the proposed change to keep it under constant review. Because the cluster college is sponsored by an existing university or college, it is likely to have a social matrix capable of providing both challenge and response.

Another prerequisite to change at the institutional level is a motivating ideology. The cluster college usually has a sense of mission and is quite self-conscious about it. In a day when most institutions of higher education have had no time or stomach for the articulation and implementation of institutional purposes (being too busy with quantitative criteria and too skeptical of ideologies to be philosophically oriented), the new and avowedly innovative college such as the cluster college is compelled by the necessity for action in the context of rapid sociopolitical change to decide at least provisionally what it is for, as well as what it is against. Such a college is driven back to the eternal questions. In the competition for funding and status it dare not be content to sing a me-too tune. The college has been commissioned to be different in order to be relevant and this means trying to shape some timely answers to those eternal questions.

While that which students and faculty bring to a college is important to the character of the institution, that which the college brings to the person is important to the character of the individual and, as an ancillary benefit, to the character of the college. In the cluster college, students and faculty bring with them a high degree of courage and commitment—they are, after all, taking risks—and in turn, the college that has been forced by its circumstances to be self-conscious, critical, and definitive has something special to give these students and faculty.

It is in the interaction of individuals and institutions that the old becomes new and that which in itself is a difference that makes no difference becomes a non-difference that makes a difference.

Chapter 8

New College
at Old Westbury

Harris Wofford, Jr.

If confession is good for the soul, then a candid account of an experiment should be good for anyone seeking to learn from it. At Old Westbury our academic vice-president and first professor of physics keeps forcing us up against the wall—of honesty—by reminding us that in an experiment you must be ready to acknowledge failure, and then to assess what went wrong. That is painful to do when people are involved, when a living organism is at stake such as the life of a college. But an organism may contain a cancer cell that is out of control and require drastic surgery; and there are fates worse than death. So let me try to give a critical case study of the experiment in college-making and liberal education called Old Westbury.

Not long ago a father wrote to his young son that he was going to visit Old Westbury. The son wrote back: *Who* is Old Westbury? This account may give some clues.

A new college at Old Westbury sounds like the title of a Western movie, and already there has been some melodrama, especially during a six-day sit-in at the end of our first school year in May, 1969. An SDS leader has called me "The Green Slime" and a less political student has called me a tragic hero (no compliment intended, she insists, because she means I have a fatal flaw: I am blind and do not understand her or her generation and the depth of their alienation). Even with bad vision I can see and concede some major mistakes and some things I do not understand, but despite the funny and sad things that have happened to us on the way to our full opening for 1,000 students in 1971, we have probably not yet produced the comedy or tragedy of good drama. We may have learned enough, however, about the problem of liberal education for this late twentieth-century American college generation to make a public accounting worthwhile.

In the summer of 1966, Chancellor Sam Gould of the State University of New York asked me if I would take on the assignment of planning and creating the university's newest college, ultimately to be for 5,000 undergraduates and an undetermined number of master's degree graduate students. On the beautiful 600-acre wooded and rolling estate of Columbia dropout F. Ambrose Clark on the North Shore of Long Island, an hour from New York City, we were to build one of the most up-to-date campuses in the country, costing about $100 million; and to match it we were to design a new curriculum and academic organization that would "pay heed to the individual student and his concern with the modern world." The university's 1966 Master Plan further stated that, "Since the campus is to be built literally from the ground up, the President, and the faculty members the President recruits, will have an almost unrestricted opportunity for innovation and creativity." Specifically, Chancellor Gould, in the announcement of my appointment in November, 1966, added that he expected us "to review all the conventional ingredients such as admissions policies, grades, course systems and academic divisions, and break whatever barriers may stand in the way."

"Stand in the way" of what? That was not defined, except that we were to be a college of liberal arts and science. So the mandate was to search for the right ingredients for good liberal education. As one who sees universal liberal education as the central revolution of our time, and as one who saw the Peace Corps as a University in Dispersion and had been trying to make it a more effective form of higher education, I found that invitation irresistible. Looking across the steeplechase field around which the clusters of the new college would be built, my first colleagues and I said to ourselves: "There is no one to blow this but us."

Let me amend that. For a brief moment, before I asked anyone else to join me, I looked over those fields and said: "There is no one to blow this but me." So I should begin by conceding that I made some Himalayan miscalculations (as they put such confessions in India). Knowing how little I knew, I went far and wide for advice, and then proceeded to disregard or discount critical parts of it.

From Chancellor Gould or his key staff in Albany came the following counsel: Take your time—you are not supposed to open until 1970. Begin by finding the best possible men to head your main academic departments, then let them later locate the junior faculty. Make your first programs so academically convincing, even conventional, that you will be accepted by academia before you experiment with novel programs. Do not arouse undue expectations of student power—and never let students call you by your first name.

From Stringfellow Barr, Scott Buchanan, and Robert Hutchins at Santa Barbara came a different warning: Beware of the winds of conventional academia—the anarchy of the departmental system, the desire of each faculty member to "do his thing," the fear of doing anything in common—and beware of the "good men" fallacy; good ideas are what count. You will be blown away unless your educational banner is very good, very clear, and very firmly planted—unless you make very sure that every person you ask to join you understands and agrees.

From Jacqueline Grennan, who spent three months at our planning roundtable just as she was secularizing herself and Webster College, came another voice of experience: Avoid the intense, ingrown, incestuous, and smothering small community. Start big enough, with enough different programs, with enough variety of living and working relationships so that students and faculty are forced to confront the real world instead of falling into the mock heroics of utopia.

From David Riesman, just finishing his study of *The Academic Revolution,* came concern for the different types of students —the practical, career minded; the political, radical, and activist; those lost in search of themselves; the fraternity boys and sorority girls; the scientists and the humanists; the scholarly, and all the mixtures of these types. To be representative and healthy, you need all these and you need to serve them all, he said. Don't let the moral imperialism of the liberals, or radicals, or humanists, or educational experimenters run rough-shod over different but equally authentic experience and needs. And don't let the new amateur spirit prevail over the need for professional competence in an increasingly professional world.

And all of these and others pointed to another danger: the urgent is often the enemy of the important—so beware of an undue preoccupation with the contemporary. Don't let the urgencies of "relevance" overwhelm more important permanent concerns—for the adrenalin that flows in political action can prevent not only the study of history, but in any serious sense study itself.

The hardest initial choice was whether to accept the Hutchins-Barr-Buchanan challenge and rise one clear curricular banner to which others would be asked to rally. Since they knew that under their tutelage I had come to believe in the reading of great books as an essential part of liberal education, I sometimes suspected that they wanted me to take up their banner and simply carry on where the College at Chicago or St. John's College left off. Chicago after World War II was a golden time and Scott Buchanan will always be Socrates for me; it was all very catching, and wherever I go in the world I try to join a Socratic seminar around those linear things called books. That's the floating crap game to which I am addicted.

In addition, I had another medieval set of ideas. I liked the study, the practice and the teaching of law, and had—and have— the conviction that law as an undergraduate liberal art (not primarily as preprofessional training, but as a general study for any citizen) would provide a good lens through which to look at the body politic as a whole and at the problems of self-government. To which I added the hunch that the other ancient professions of medicine and theology, taken broadly to include psychiatry as well as physical medicine, and Eastern as well as Western religions, would be good as major undergraduate subjects unifying our knowledge about the mind, body, and soul.

A third set of notions about education-in-action I brought to college-making from the Peace Corps. There I had seen, as I said in my first statement on the college in November, 1966, "young Americans come alive and discover new capacities for action and service. Given real responsibility for real problems and challenged by crossing cultural frontiers, they learn to learn, and find they like it. . . . This is what ought to happen in college." We should seek to design, I wrote then, "a new curriculum for liberal arts education that prepares people to understand the world, to deal with its problems, and to live and work in it effectively." It would need to be "a school of the world" in the broadest sense: "not just the world of international relations, but the full twentieth-century world which students must go out into, which must now be seen as a whole, which can best be defined by its problems, including the problems of New York." Or, as Whitehead (1959) wrote in *The Aims of Education,* and as we later put on the cover of our catalogue:

> The tragedy of the world is that those who are imaginative have but slight experience, and those who are experienced have feeble imaginations. Fools act on imagination without knowledge; pedants act on knowledge without imagination. The task of a university is to weld together imagination and experience.

Did these ideas constitute a good and clear banner for a new college? Should I have insisted upon them as the touchstone for the selection of faculty and planning staff? That would have meant inflicting my own best educational experiences on others, my own moral imperialism. No one, of course, has any experience to inflict on others but his own, and Buchanan, Barr, and Hutchins urged me to have the courage of my convictions. The trouble was that I knew how bad my own education had been, notwithstanding their joint and several efforts. Moreover, those three men, along with their key colleagues like Alexander Meiklejohn, Mortimer Adler, and Mark Van Doren, had been designing and testing their educational platform for more than ten years before they raised their banner. Even so, Hutchins' College had been blown away, and the trouble with St. John's, as Buchanan himself said, was that what they had started in 1937 was a search for the true liberal college, yet the search seemed to have stopped with that first great books curriculum.

In any case, I decided that in order to start the search at Old Westbury with better minds than mine and to make it a continuing one, I would not impose my vision as the condition for collaboration, but would share the opportunity for innovation and creativity with the best colleagues I could find. So I assembled a planning staff of diverse men and women who accepted the general university mandate and added their own visions to mine; and we included students as well as faculty on that planning staff, so that the three immediate constituencies of a college—students, faculty, and administration—would be in dialogue from the beginning. Moreover, in order to make Old Westbury not a planned college, but a college that plans together in all of its parts, we decided to begin small and as soon as practical. We opted for organic growth.

For better and for worse, our fate seems to have been shaped by these original decisions. Even now in retrospect, knowing the price we have paid, I would probably make the same decisions—but I would take stronger measures to take into greater account the warnings given. I would do it again, but "set this down, set this down," as the poet would say: "It was a cold coming."

The "good man" theory only takes you so far, and that is not far enough. Men are not that good—nor women either—nor faculty nor students either. This is a time when consent everywhere is withering, and Old Westbury has been no exception. Our disagreements have been so fierce that they might have blown us up if we had started very big—with the 1,000 students originally planned. On the other hand our smallness has taken its toll: during the first year we had become the very intense and ingrown, and at times smothering community that Jacqueline Grennan warned against. Nor have we found the right formula for the relationship between utopia and reality. Organic growth creates its own realities, but tends also to create a little world of its own disconnected from the larger realities of the outside community or the world.

Our first priority right now, as I see it, is for us to overcome these tendencies and deal with the full range of our responsibilities as a State University College. Such a return to reality does not mean going back to the conventional bureaucratic path of development, for I doubt that the old dispensation can ever be a reality again. The old law of institution-building, by hierarchy, from the top down, and of academic institution-building, by department head down, is probably not appropriate for this age, or for the kind of college we want. But I can now see more clearly why for at least two or three thousand years this is the way men have generally gone about it. When you do it the organic way, assembling a small group of senior and junior faculty, possible future heads of academic divisions and assistant professors and students, all mixed up around a planning table, with the radical equality of a Socratic seminar minus Socrates, the ambiguity in relationships causes personal insecurities and tensions, especially when different roles and powers are later to be allocated. Moreover, the living organism so created, which has been in on everything, which has in fact been everything, inevitably fights the day when the nucleus is divided, when not everyone can be in on everything, when the whole becomes much greater than the first parts. I, for one, miscalculated how painful this would be; how much resistance, friction, and frustration this would cause.

Yet the course of organic growth, for all its inherent difficulties and the unnecessary difficulties we may have added, seems to me the most likely way to find an alternative to the departmentalism and giantism of American higher education, and to the alienation of the students. Against Albany's advice to begin with department heads and let them build their departments, I kept hearing John Gardner's countervailing words: The biggest problem in academia is the departmentalization that cuts up the body of knowledge and keeps us from seeing the world steady and whole.

The most important task is to find a better form of organization than departments. If departments ever get going at Old Westbury, he predicted, you will never be able to get rid of them. So start small, he urged—so small that departments don't make any sense —and in doing this you may discover the right alternative: you may rediscover the liberal college.

In starting small, with under a hundred students in September, 1968, two years ahead of schedule, we think we did discover a good alternative: constituent colleges, like those at Oxford and Cambridge in size and autonomy, except that unlike Oxford and Cambridge where the curriculum was settled two or three hundred years ago, each constituent college at Old Westbury will have the mandate of the college as a whole—to search for and design good and new forms of liberal education. "This plan," as we wrote in our catalogue,

> seeks to apply to Old Westbury the basic principle of federalism which American society has used in so many areas of government and industry—the federal system of competition and coordination already embodied in the structure of the State University of New York as a whole. This plan for a college of federated colleges . . . seeks to answer the complaints about the impersonality of a multiversity by combining the variety and large resources of a university with the unity and intensity of a small college.

> Each of the Old Westbury colleges will offer an academic program designed to provide a liberal education. These programs may vary from one another in teaching approach, educational emphasis or combination of subjects; but, in each, teaching and learning will be the first priority. The common question before the faculty and students of each college will be: What is the best curriculum for a college of liberal arts and science? These collegiate divisions will be small enough so that students and faculty can know each other; but they will not be self-contained communities. Students will generally spend at least half of their time in the particular college program they choose; they will be free in the other half of their time to work in the programs of the other colleges and will be encouraged to do so. . . .

> In calling for the formation of one constituent college after another over a number of years, and not giving unlimited life to any one college curriculum but rather exposing each to con-

tinuing criticism and review, the opportunity for innovation and creativity will be extended far beyond the period of initial planning. Through these "visions and revisions" Old Westbury will seek to give education the impetus and invigoration of a continuing experiment.

That is what our planning staff agreed to unanimously in 1967, after months of discussion and study of various models of cluster or constituent colleges, including special attention to Santa Cruz and Oxbridge. But then the question came, what will our first constituent college be? When will we declare it to be *one* constituent college and not the whole of Old Westbury? How and when do we create additional colleges?

Three times before the college opened we came to the brink of declaring our first program, faculty, and student body to be the first constituent college, and commissioning one or two men or small groups to begin planning the second and third colleges. But each time, after argument, we drew back and the majority of us concluded that dividing into separate colleges was premature; our resources were too thin, and it was too easy an escape from our disagreements. So we agreed to keep our arguments going around a common table and in one college. In the hot summer of 1968, before the new faculty and students came, Vice-Presidents Byron Youtz and Jerry Ziegler and I walked the fields and wondered whether we should make the division then; it was our last easy chance to do so, we realized, before the new and larger community would come with its inevitable vested interests and claim to control the future development of the college. But again we chose to wait until the time seemed riper—until our new colleagues came and our curricular ideas had further matured.

In February, 1969, after our first semester in which the educational differences among the first faculty seemed to be irreconcilable, it became clear to me and to Vice-Presidents Youtz and Ziegler, and to a majority of the faculty, that the time had come to divide into two or three constituent colleges. We did not want the first work-study program, focused on problems of race and poverty, to dominate the whole college. We took seriously our commitment to the state university, emphasized in our catalogue, which the university approved, that this urban affairs curriculum was only our *first* one, and that by 1970 a wide offering of liberal arts studies would be available, including programs in the natural sciences and other important traditional academic subjects.

And since our most important innovation in academic organization was likely to be the constituent college, why not proceed with that essential part of the Old Westbury experiment? This all seemed reasonable enough.

But the present's drive to control the future is an incalculable force, and is part of the price that you pay—that we have paid —for organic growth. I cannot adequately describe the passionate opposition by some faculty and many students to the proposed division into constituent colleges. We could not let the first group brought together around a particular set of educational ideas prevent the creation of the contrasting new programs that the whole concept of a "college of colleges" required. The faculty finally voted to go ahead with these constituent colleges, and after three turbulent months, including the sit-in by about a third of our students in May, in which this was a central issue, a majority of the students, including most of the sit-in students, seemed at last to have agreed.

There has been one good and important by-product of this process. As a necessary part of our new social contract, a constitution of the college has been drafted that establishes the constituent colleges as Old Westbury's major form of academic organization; that confirms the first two colleges (a School of Urban Affairs and a Disciplines School); that includes a general program for students not ready to choose any one constituent college (a program which Hutchins, Meiklejohn, Barr, and Buchanan might like); that creates an academic council representing faculty, students, and administration for the certification of future constituent colleges; that assures regular student participation on that and other legislative bodies without student domination; and that affirms the executive role of the administration and the predominant academic role of the faculty.

Looking back, I sometimes regret that we did not write the constitution and create the first constituent college before the first students and new faculty came. We would probably have had a smoother first year. But the constitution that is emerging should receive more consent and respect than one imposed by presidential or original faculty fiat. It embodies the concept of constituent colleges in a much stronger form than their prior establishment could possibly have done. It sets a novel and, I believe, promising pattern for academic governance. The confrontations of students, faculty, and administration may have been necessary to test and clarify the respective strength of each of these three essential constituencies of the federal kind of college we set out to create.

But I do not now want to underestimate the seriousness of some of the remaining disputes, for the shadow of confrontation and politicization still hangs over us. We all hoped that the heat of the first year would be converted into light, but this would not be a candid report if I did not note that the politics of our first year still cloud and block much real educational search and that this threatens to happen again.

The constitution can help, but no constitution can work if the disagreements among its constituencies are so deep as to cause a continuous civil war. And our disagreements may be that deep. As you have guessed, I have now come to the students.

In our catalogue we wrote boldly and optimistically two years ago:

> In creating this new college the State University sees the restlessness, curiosity and questioning of youth not as a spectre, but an opportunity. The turbulent, critical mood of today's students is a great occasion for education. Their complaints against the multiversity, their concern for relevance, their search for individual identity and their questioning of everything can lead to better teaching, more relevant courses, more disciplined and serious study, deeper personal understanding and greater involvement with public problems.

We did, even then, add a more sober paragraph:

> For both students and faculty the curriculum and the community of learning at Old Westbury will be demanding. Taking responsibility for one's own education and accepting partnership in a common venture will put pressure on each participant. The excitement of making a new college will not substitute for the attention required to master difficult arts or sciences. There will be disappointment for any who think they can change the world without understanding it, or understand it without study, or study without books. Contemporary studies will not sub-

stitute for the classics. Education-in-action, whether in the inner-city ghetto or suburbs of America or on the other side of the globe, should leave the actors thirsty for knowledge and theories to make sense of the experience.

But we miscalculated. Experience in the ghetto leaves sensitive and idealistic students thirsty not just for knowledge and theories but for more action. In criticizing a recent staement of mine that the college "will continue and expand its concern for, and commitment to understanding the local, national and international problems of race and poverty," a group of our sit-in veterans wrote in reply: "This college should be committed not only to 'understanding' these things but to *doing something about them*." One of the ways to do something, they think, is to establish the rule that half of our students, faculty and staff will henceforth be nonwhite—or as this latest manifesto puts it: "50 per cent representation of third world peoples at Old Westbury."

From that vocabulary you might think we recruited our first class largely from the SDS or black militants. We did recruit fourteen black and Puerto Rican students and three African or Asian students out of 85, or 20 per cent representation of "third world peoples," to use their description, probably the highest such proportion in any non-Negro American liberal arts college—and most young blacks are indeed relatively militant. But aside from one former regional organizer of SDS and a few others who were already active in the New Left, most of our students were relatively unpolitical, though very idealistic. They were drawn to the program of education-in-action, to experimental education (which to them meant primarily more urban or other contemporary, interdisciplinary studies, fewer requirements, and no grades), and to the idea of "full partnership." And at Old Westbury, or off-campus in the ghetto during our field program, they became radicalized.

When we fought all the way up to the chancellor to win approval for starting with this unconventional first program, we did not adequately take into account the special appeal it would have to a special student population. We thought the combination of great books with work on pressing current problems would discourage many mere activists and diversify the kinds of student who applied. Anyway, with a pool of ten applicants for every one place, we figured that we would be able to select the balanced and representative class Riesman had recommended and our admissions criteria had stressed.

We should have known better. From the first days of planning the college, our student colleagues had given us fair warning. After deciding that we would beg, borrow, and hire students right away to join us at the original planning table, we found ourselves, without much forethought, with three students on work-study terms from Antioch (kindly arranged by President Dixon, who advised us to see students as our chief ally and as the major force for educational reform), and four others from Berkeley, San Francisco State, Goddard, and Stony Brook (a dropout who had come knocking at our door). They were attractive, dedicated, idealistic, intense, impatient, intolerant, perfectionist, and otherwise radical or ready to be radical. They had been drawn by our rhetoric, and would accept no gap between it and reality. And they would accept no reality but our peculiar little community and their particular visions of the world.

Compounding this generational problem was the promise of "full partnership." In reading the university's 1966 Master Plan, I had noticed this intriguingly ambiguous phrase in the description of the new college; it was taken from an early memorandum on the college by Vice-Chancellor Frost, which was written in the aftermath of the explosion at Berkeley, at a time when the university was anxious to get ahead of the student revolution. Chancellor Gould had not wanted me even to see the memorandum because he wanted us to work on a clean slate. But there it was, in an official statement that had been formally submitted to the Governor and Legislature: Old Westbury would "admit students to full partnership in the academic world." With a lawyer's love of broad constitutional goals, like due process or freedom of speech or equal protection, I saw leverage in this idea of partnership and printed that excerpt from the Master Plan in all of our first documents, including finally the catalogue.

The words had leverage all right—with a vengeance. Opening Pandora's box might be a better description, for it brought down on us immediately all the furies of the would-be student revolution. (Though in defense it is fair to say that the box was

opened before we came along—by Berkeley and a worldwide cry
for participation—and could not have been easily closed in any
experimental college; and we may note that at the bottom of
Pandora's box, according to legend, after the other furies escaped,
there was Hope.)

From the beginning, most of the over-forty members of the
planning staff and I did our best to explain that partnership did
not mean the blurring of all separate powers and responsibilities,
including those of the faculty and president. We said we had in
mind a federal and republican system, with a strong student body,
a strong faculty, and a strong administration in continuing dialec-
tic. Power would not all percolate down from the president or the
chancellor, but neither would it all be shared equally, one-man-
one-vote.

But this is not what "full partnership" brought to mind to
our first seven students. Even though they were only going to be
with us for one term, and would not be around to live with the
consequences, they thought that all decisions should be made by
democratic vote, in which they would then outnumber the president
and the faculty together. When that did not happen to their satisfaction, though they did influence the shape of the first program
in major respects, they cried "betrayal," and accused us of
hypocrisy. When we said that the best of American history was the
story of the creative tension between the promises of the Constitution and their still inadequate fulfillment, they replied that this was
the worst of American history, and that they wanted no part in
that kind of apologetic liberalism. All this was moderated by the
large measure of consensus we reached on the first program and
the catalogue, and by the close friendships that developed while we
lived, argued, fought, sang, and danced together in those first six
fantastic months. "You can't fight so well against a president when
you call him by his first name," one of our students told a reporter.
Or as another student put it, leaving the president's home after a
friendly night: "I knew I shouldn't have come to dinner. It's going
to ruin our confrontation tomorrow."

So we decided to try a second group of student planners,
this time chosen for a summer workshop from the campuses of the
state university on special scholarships provided by Chancellor

Gould and announced through the regular campus student body
organizations. When those thirteen students arrived from colleges
like Geneseo, New Paltz, and Potsdam, we thought the voices of
moderation and practicality would at last be heard. But to our
amazement they seemed to be just as alienated from academia,
from scholarship, and from all forms of American authority as the
first group. "Just come to Potsdam," one of them kept saying as
proof of his general indictments. Their educational platform was
much the same—action now against injustice everywhere, personal
exploration of psyches, and the by-now familiar anarchy of no requirements, no evaluation, and "let everyone do his thing" (except
the president). When Chancellor Gould came to spend an after-
noon hearing their criticisms and proposals, they rested their case
primarily on the playing of Dylan's song, "You know something's
happening here but you don't know what it is, do you, Mr. Jones?"
And their response to the promise of "full partnership" was even
wilder: although they were only going to be with us for part of one
summer they thought they should have equal votes in all decision-
making.

     At that point no doubt we should have done something
drastic to diminish the undue expectations—like dropping the
phrase "full partnership" altogether, as the analytic philosopher
in our midst kept urging. But I was stubborn and believed that
further more explicit written clarifications and the logic of events
would suffice to show future students that we did not mean to
create at Old Westbury a majoritarian direct democracy whether
of the ancient Greek or the new SDS variety. And we should have
taken drastic action to diversify further our incoming group of
students to assure that in our first mix there would be some of the
more practical-minded or scholastically bent students. But we told
ourselves that the new students would probably be more representative, and that having already wrestled with the most radical spirit
of the new generation, we would be ready for whatever came.

     Then the first wave of our regular students came last sum-
mer, about a dozen students on work-study summer jobs. With
their generation's gay indifference to history and to prior contracts,
they said that all the arguments and agreements recorded in the
catalogue which they had read in applying to Old Westbury were

just other people's words, that this was to be *their* college. They demanded—unsuccessfully—that all further decision-making cease
until the full student body had assembled. They then wrote their
fellow students to hurry up and come, with sleeping bags, because
the "administrators" were trying to make decisions without them.

Then the rest of the eighty-five students came, and the first
night in our first community meeting someone claimed—to the ap-
plause of many—that the idea of full partnership had been betrayed
because the College Council and the administration had agreed
that, though all other social rules would be worked out by the
students, men and women should be assigned rooms on separate
corridors. When the same fellow used the "betrayal" argument
three times during the year I finally suggested that it could not
be betrayal when it kept happening—only a fool would keep being
betrayed all winter long—citing the woman who complained to
the judge that after being raped it was just rape, rape, rape, all
summer long.

There was one semi-conservative force, the nonwhite students who said they didn't want a degree of "G.G."—"Grooving
in the Grass"—which the middle-class whites seemed to seek. Instead they demanded hard courses in science, statistics, urban planning, social organization, and law. But on the political front, the
"Nonwhite Caucus," as it proclaimed itself, soon enlisted the support of a majority of the white students for the proposal of a 50
per cent quota for nonwhites; the student body voted to ask the
faculty to vote on this in a joint community meeting, one-man-
one-vote, and our series of confrontations began. Fortunately, the
majority of the faculty voted against submerging themselves in one
constituency with the students, and opposed the racial quota; and
I made it clear that as president I would veto it. That seemed like
a good step toward reality—and toward the necessary full and
separate identity and integrity of the faculty and administration.

In response, however, came the sit-in students' demand for
50 per cent votes in all decision-making bodies and their slogan,
"Power to the People." We have agreed in our draft constitution
on the formula of six faculty, five students, and two administration
members on legislative bodies, and on the president's authority to
veto committee decisions; and the lessons of the first year may lead

a majority to try to avoid further political confrontations. There seems at last to be a real thirst for study and educational search among most of our present students and faculty. But as the recent unsigned manifesto of an unknown number of militants makes clear, some intend to continue pressing for more student power, for their version of total participatory democracy, and for their kind of social action university. And no one can be sure that new students in later years will agree to honor the agreements of their predecessors.

So what am I complaining about? Isn't this partnership with continuing dialogue just what we asked for? Shouldn't there be some college in the United States where something like this is tried? Why not at Old Westbury?

If only curricular issues were at stake it might not be so bad. The work-study, urban problems program most of the students seem to want is probably a good one. Because of the sit-in we did not hold the intensive end-of-year evaluation of all parts of that program that we had planned. It combines theory and practice in a fresh way, seeking to integrate fieldwork and academic study to a degree that neither Antioch nor the Peace Corps has generally attempted. It is an imaginative response to the students' desire for relevance and to the college's mandate to "pay heed to the individual student and his concern with the modern world." It should no doubt be continued, extended, and improved—though there is no reason for it to grow beyond the four or five hundred student maximum we have set for the size of any one constituent college.

But the revolution of rising expectations among students at Old Westbury will not, at least not now, settle for that. Our first organic nucleus wants to make the whole college in its image, and much as I like and admire most of our first students, I think that would be a bad college. The moral imperialism of the so-called Movement is just the kind of thing Riesman warned us against. It tends toward a conformity as oppressive as any the nonconformists criticize. At Old Westbury it has already made it difficult for those students and teachers who differ. For example, the minority who oppose the 50 per cent nonwhite proposal are treated by some as pariahs.

A good college should always encourage and support the

most far-reaching study of politics, an essential liberal art, with the freest and fullest expression of opinion and public debate. It should encourage and support fieldwork and research in the most pressing public problems, no matter how controversial. But it should never surrender to or become an outpost for or an active agent of any particular political persuasion or any revolution but the fundamental one of liberal education. And that, as I see it, is the critical issue now at Old Westbury.

If the Movement or the would-be student revolution were really the wave of the future, then I would have to end on a dismal note. But all my political instincts tell me that the reverse is true, that the present wild form of student radicalism is going to subside, and without much repression, leaving the widespread general alienation of the young still to be understood and responded to. When the one thing the warring factions in the SDS can agree upon is Chairman Mao, whose last significant public appearance was floating down the Yangtse river like a stuffed puppet, and whose last great act was the unleashing of the Red Guard, then we should see how bankrupt the New Left is and we should recover our sense of humor. And neither the multi-purpose slogan "Kill the Pig" nor the armory of the Black Panthers will save them. The British Bobby at Hyde Park Corner has the right response: "All those who favor beheading the king, move aside and let the traffic pass." False revolutions need to be smoked out and punctured as much as false messiahs, and this one, like so many others in history, has overshot itself—overkill is the new word—and will now be, in fact is already being, repudiated by the common sense of the great mass of the American people.

So we had a hundred-people problem at Old Westbury— the problem of a hundred good people—and in 1969–70 with our new students we now have a 230-people problem. With all the ardor and naiveté of youth, most of them think they are in the avant-garde, but sadly, the one so many of this particular group have joined, like so many would-be avant-gardes, isn't going anywhere. It should not be too long before they face reality, it should not be too difficult for the majority at Old Westbury to face the reality that in a state university college the power does ultimately belong to the people—to the people of the state of New York.

Within that reality, our freedom to pursue utopia is very large. But we can blow this opportunity—we came close to blowing it already—if we do not now become the more diverse and representative college, the college of open and continuing search, the "college of colleges" we promised the university and the people of New York.

I said I was sad that this avant-garde isn't going anywhere, for we need great changes. We need the insights of youth. We need to understand and act on the sources of their alienation.

Two years ago I had high hopes that this new generation was coming like a giant Socrates to sting us from our pragmatic slumbers. Their sting had some effect, but I fear that they have caught too many of our vices: the anarchy and the violence in the modern American soul. As the son accused by his father of grievous wrongdoing replied: "Dad, where did I go wrong? Was it heredity or environment?"

But you see, I suffered too from too high expectations, and I do not want to swing too far down now. Far better the discontent than complacency. I am told that the turbulence at our college comes from the fact that we lack the oil of apathy that keeps most faculties and colleges going. The spirit of our students, unlike nearby ones who were breaking windows and burning buildings while our students were asking for full partnership, went beyond alienation. They are not, not even the most extreme cutting edge, the great slouching beast of Yeats's *Second Coming;* we are not going to be swept aside by the blood-dimmed tide. The center, bad as it is, is going to hold, and so are our colleges and universities, bad as they are. There is world enough and time. It is earlier than we think. But we cannot just say No—though sometimes that is the most immediate thing to say. We must say Yes. In the end it is good ideas that count, and they are what we need now.

In September 1968 I opened our little college with Marvell's *To His Coy Mistress.* We would roll all our strength and all our sweetness into one ball and make the sun run. I ended the year reading Eliot's *Journey of the Magi.* That winter was the worst time for a trip like ours. Was it a birth or a death?

During the sit-in I suddenly realized that the metaphor in the back of my mind for all this was much less elegant. I remembered the many months in 1944 when I was in the Air Force in Selma, Alabama, spending weekends on a horse in the country, riding with a veterinarian friend. Occasionally he would help a cow give birth to a calf. Sometimes the delivery was easy and a beautiful calf would emerge smoothly. Sometimes my friend had to give the cow a lot of help, and even cut her some. Once my friend had to get ropes up inside around the calf and we had to pull and tug for a long, long time. The calf is dead, he finally told me, but we have to get it out to save the cow. At last we did, and we saved the cow.

Need I tell you that the nickname for the College at Old Westbury is C.O.W.—in fact SUNYCOW? At times I have feared that our first effort would be stillborn, and that our job was to save the college. But our first program and even the idea of partnership, somewhat bloodied, is alive and kicking. This presents any founding father with a psychological test. One kind of parent looks at his newborn, especially a brain-child, and says, "Oh, this is not what I had in mind, not at all, throw this miserable thing out and let's start again." The other kind says, "It isn't quite what I hoped for, but life is precious, any life, and full of wonderful surprises. Let's nurture this little creature; let's help it become everything it is capable of becoming."

So you see I do think we have had a birth at Old Westbury. Having chosen the organic way, I hope we will continue to opt for life.

Chapter 9

Cooperation Among Private Colleges

Clifford T. Stewart

H. R. Kells

To what degree can a cluster (or group) of intimately, but voluntarily, associated small private colleges achieve economic and academic advantages specifically through their cooperation? To answer this question, two studies of The Claremont Colleges in Claremont, California, were conducted and reported in considerable detail during the period 1966–68 as part of a larger set of investigations into collegiate cooperative arrangements entitled The Claremont Studies in Cooperation (Kells, 1967, 1968; Kells and Stewart, 1968a, 1968b; Stewart, 1967; Stewart and Hartley, 1968).

The specific foci of this chapter, cost comparisons between cluster and non-cluster colleges, and the extent of academic cooperative arrangements at an established, multicollege, voluntary cluster college group, are two of the most important forces propelling the movement of closer cooperation between colleges. Many colleges, particularly small, isolated, private colleges, are in financial difficulty and are isolated intellectually. Since the cluster or coordinate college arrangement is seen as at least a partial answer to these problems, it should be possible to demonstrate the validity of this assumption by examining a successful cluster of private colleges. The investigation of cost savings of various kinds at The Claremont Colleges, a group whose cooperative ventures have been motivated chiefly by the intellectual advantages of the small college within the university-like setting rather than by the hope of substantial cost savings, should nonetheless provide ample evidence that such savings are attainable. In like manner, the existence of an array of joint or complimentary academic interactions at a group of relatively affluent, self-sufficient colleges should indicate that colleges which "need" one another badly can surely achieve similar results. Colleges with sufficient "need," of course, often consider corporate mergers with other such or stronger colleges in order to achieve economic viability, academic adequacy, or coeducational opportunities. However, the outright merger brings a substantial or complete loss of identity and of opportunity for the maintenance of differences in educational approach of the former constituent units. Consequently, many college trustees, administrators, and faculty study committees are interested in determining whether economic and intellectual advantages can be achieved through an arrangement which preserves institutional identity, a degree of institutional autonomy, and the potential for educational difference and change which is consistent with the prerogatives of a distinct collegiate faculty.

The Claremont Colleges began their movement into group existence in the 1920s. In 1919, when Pomona College was thirty-two years old and had an enrollment of 700 students, the board of trustees of that college adopted a resolution providing that enrollment would not be permitted to exceed this number. Their desire to operate as a small college was being challenged by a dramatically increasing number of qualified applicants. President James A. Blaisdell proposed that a group system be established to preserve the close relationship among students and between students and faculty while permitting more comprehensive facilities to be built for the use of the group members. The idea is best expressed in his own words (in Kells, 1967, p. 21):

> My own very deep hope is that instead of one great, undifferentiated university, we might have a group of institutions divided into small colleges—somewhat on the Oxford type—around a library and other utilities which they would use in common. In this way I should hope to preserve the inestimable personal values of the small college while securing the facilities of the great university.

In 1925, what is now Claremont University Center was incorporated in order to offer graduate work and to otherwise serve the interests of the various colleges. This agency administers the joint (or central) services for the group of colleges. In 1926 Scripps College was incorporated; in 1946, Claremont Men's College; in 1955, Harvey Mudd College; and in 1963, Pitzer College.

Each college, therefore, was established as a separate, independent institution, each with its own faculty, board of trustees, president, students, and academic programs. Pomona was and remains a coeducational general liberal arts college currently enrolling 1,300 students; Scripps, with 550 women, emphasizes the humanities; and Claremont Men's College, with 800 men, stresses economics, political science, and public affairs. Harvey Mudd offers principally science and engineering courses for its 360 students, most of whom are men. Pitzer, with 600 women, emphasizes the social and behavioral sciences; and Claremont Graduate School, with about 900 students, as the educational entity of Claremont University Center, offers master's degrees in seventeen fields and doctorates in thirteen.

In 1965, with funds provided under a Ford Foundation Challenge Grant, The Claremont Colleges established an Office of Institutional Research, the purpose of which is to continually ex-

amine the extent of cooperation between the colleges and to provide the documentation and analyses which point to potential
additional cooperative ventures. The early efforts of this office were
concerned with the extent of academic and other cooperative arrangements in Claremont. A summary of cooperative arrangements
at Claremont is presented in Table 10. There are twenty-five activities in which all of The Claremont Colleges cooperate and another
nine in which combinations of two, three, four, or five cooperate.

The greatest evidence of academic cooperation in Claremont
is the degree of joint planning of courses and programs among the
colleges and the resultant student cross-registration or registration
in a college other than the student's own college.

The purpose of permitting course registrations in other
colleges is to make available to the student as wide a range of
courses as possible without burdening the individual colleges with
the total cost. As mentioned before, some of The Claremont Colleges have specific curricular emphases, whereas others are broadly
based liberal arts colleges. None of the colleges attempt to maintain
program depth in all fields. Student cross-registration, then, is a
major mechanism whereby academic cooperation occurs in Claremont.

Three types of courses are involved in the cooperative
activities of the colleges. First, there are the regular courses offered
by each college, and most of these are open to students from all of
the other colleges. Second, there are joint programs and courses
that by design involve students from several colleges. For example,
the colleges offer a program in classics, but no one college wishes
to bear the full expense of a university-size classics department.
The four colleges with classics departments therefore cooperate to
offer a full program in classics to students in all the colleges.

As another example, three of the colleges with a combined
enrollment of 1,900 have formed a joint science department. None
of the three colleges emphasizes the natural sciences and therefore
have combined their resources to provide science offerings for their
students. Eleven faculty members on joint appointment with the
three colleges make up the science faculty. A joint science building
contains the various classrooms, laboratories and equipment, and
faculty offices. The two undergraduate colleges not involved in

Table 10

Cooperative Ventures and Joint Facilities
of The Claremont Colleges[a]

Involving all six colleges:

1. Library
2. Business Office
3. Office of the Chaplain
4. Service Shops
5. Bridges Auditorium
6. Telephone Service
7. Health Service and Infirmary
8. Psychological Clinic and Counseling Center
9. Campus Security
10. Garrison Theater
11. Faculty House
12. Office of the Provost
13. Print Shop and Addressograph
14. Challenge Campaign
15. Cross Registration of Courses
16. Faculty Exchange
17. Office of Institutional Research
18. Computer Center
19. Human Resources Institute
20. Bookstore
21. Development Office
22. Purchasing
23. Personnel Office
24. Joint Campus Plans Office
25. Student Newspaper

Involving the number of colleges indicated:

26. United Council (undergraduate students)	5
27. Classics	4
28. Drama and Music	4
29. Joint Science Program	3
30. Language Lab	3
31. Forensics	3
32. ROTC	2
33. Admissions	2
34. Physical Education	2

[a] Does not include cooperative efforts with colleges outside of Claremont.

this program each offer a full range of courses in the natural sciences. The joint science program has been formalized in an agreement which specifies the role of each college in appointment of faculty, financial responsibility, and so on.

Included in this category of joint programs and courses are less formal arrangements for selected courses in mathematics or sociology, as examples. These courses are offered jointly even though there are no overall joint programs in these areas. The faculties of the various colleges in certain disciplines get together and decide on courses to be offered jointly. Courses chosen are those which should be offered in the program but which one college would have difficulty filling each semester. Such courses may be at elementary, intermediate, or advanced levels.

A third category of courses consists of those taught by full-time members of the Claremont Graduate School faculty for undergraduate students. These are called intercollegiate courses and are taught in a variety of subject areas. For the most recently completed semester (Spring 1969), there were 2,281 cross-registrations in regular courses (14 per cent of all registrations). Each semester some 30–40 per cent of the students take one or more courses off campus, and over a four-year period, 80–90 per cent of the students register in off-campus courses.

Regulations pertaining to cross-registration have become more and more liberal over the past several years in response to student requests. Some students, however, take no off-campus classes; others, one or two during the four years; while some take up to half of their courses during their junior or senior year off-campus, depending on courses available in their home college, major field of study, desired electives, preferred professors, and other factors.

How does this academic cooperation work? What does it accomplish? It accomplishes its main goal of providing a wide range of course offerings and sufficient depth in the various fields to students in all the colleges. Students may take these courses as part of their major or may use them as elective subjects. It also gives the students the opportunity to choose professors from other colleges and to be in classes with students from other colleges. A student registers on his own campus for all the courses he wishes to take in any of the Claremont colleges.

Are there any problems? There are many. Curriculum planning can become quite a problem since it may involve two to six colleges. Each college is free to develop its own curriculum and this, in fact, is what happens. However, there is usually a great deal of coordination among the deans and the faculties of the colleges in their continuing efforts to use available and new resources in the most efficient way. When a new course is to be added in any college or when a new faculty member is to be hired, this information becomes available to all of the academic deans and to the faculty members in the appropriate areas. This usually, but not always, eliminates duplication of courses and the hiring by several colleges of faculty members with the same specialties within disciplines. There are problems of coordination among the faculties of the various colleges concerning who will teach what the following semester, who will be on sabbatical the following semester or year, and who will replace them. All of this requires a great deal of time, but it provides an automatic and constant review of the curricula of the various colleges. The deans and the faculty are also constantly aware of the make-up of faculty in the various colleges and are therefore in a better position to make decisions concerning courses and staffing.

In certain laboratory courses, courses in art instruction, or certain of the language courses, there are a limited number of spaces or facilities, which determine the upper limit of class size. Therefore, registration must be limited in such courses and this usually means that it is the students from other colleges who are denied registration in these courses. Fortunately these limitations do not affect more than a few students each semester. If the problem becomes more serious, then a different system of registration or a different distribution of course offerings may be required.

As in any college or university, courses occasionally become too large. This is potentially quite a problem at The Claremont Colleges since students register for all their courses (including those offered by other colleges) on their home campus. Therefore, class sizes are not fully known until some time after registration on all campuses has been completed. Since there are generally no limitations placed on class size, it sometimes becomes necessary to teach large sections. These sections are divided into smaller ones when faculty are available to teach them.

The newest Claremont college, Pitzer, opened in 1964 but is able to "hold its own" in cross-registration because of its special emphasis. Pitzer students are able to take advantage of the wide variety of course offerings at the other colleges, while enrollments from other colleges at Pitzer are predominantly in anthropology and sociology courses. This shows that a new college can allow its students to register in other colleges for courses it does not offer and, at the same time, bring students from other colleges into strong programs in particular fields. This is possible because Pitzer has concentrated to some extent on developing programs not emphasized by the other colleges. For example, only one of the other colleges offers work in anthropology. A strong program in this area is now available because Pitzer has planned this program with Pomona College and has committed its resources to securing excellent faculty in, among other areas, anthropology and the related fields of sociology and psychology. Thus, this new, small college can attract good faculty because there are opportunities for them to teach students of several undergraduate colleges and to teach, in some fields, at the graduate school. The students, of course, are highly in favor of cross-registration, not only because it gives them the opportunity to take courses not available on their own campus, but because it provides the opportunity for interaction with students and faculty of the other colleges.

Some colleges send far more students to courses on other campuses than they teach in return. This imbalance is not paid for, but there is an effort made for the next semester or year to achieve a better balance between colleges through adding appropriate courses at "debtor" colleges.

In summary, regarding the extent of academic cooperation at Claremont, it is probably accurate to say that although many Claremont trustees and administrators would like to see more joint program planning, more joint use of facilities, and more consultation on faculty appointments, the record of substantial academic interchange, joint planning, and student enthusiasm for the whole idea should suffice to demonstrate that a desired level of academic interdependence and complementarity can be achieved with mutual respect between collegiate faculties. One must grant that until now the Claremont cooperativeness has been somewhat assured by the fact that the group has spawned and carefully built its own colleges. But what about existing colleges which move to adjacent arrangements with all of the potential problems of strangeness, lack of understanding, and potential academic aloofness? This will be the next venture at Claremont. The group sold twenty acres of adjacent land to Immaculate Heart College in 1965 and invited this innovative, Catholic girls' college to become "a good neighbor." Although it will not become a member of The Claremont Colleges, Immaculate Heart will join in quite a number of academic cooperative ventures with member colleges, and will purchase some joint services from the group. It can be reported already that a joint natural science facility will be constructed by Immaculate Heart and Harvey Mudd Colleges, and the Immaculate Heart faculty has agreed to drop some Master's programs in favor of participating in existing Claremont Graduate School programs. Some present IHC graduate programs will become the only programs in those fields in Claremont. These are remarkable efforts which indicate that additional cooperation is possible between the schools when IHC arrives in Claremont in 1971.

In order to address the question of operating economies, it was felt that comparisons should be made between the cost picture for certain joint services at Claremont and carefully selected institutions elsewhere. The project was supported by a grant from The ESSO Education Foundation and involved four of the Claremont colleges (Claremont Men's College, Harvey Mudd College, Pomona College, and Scripps College) and eighteen other colleges, subgroups of which were used as comparison groups for the four Claremont colleges. Pitzer College and the Claremont Graduate School were not included in the study since the former admitted its first students in 1964 and a group of comparison institutions could not be found. CGS differs organizationally from most graduate schools and did not, for the three-year period covered, participate in all the cooperative functions studied. Cost data for the Claremont group as a whole did include the Pitzer and Claremont Graduate School information.

The project was initiated by compiling a list of some fifty possible comparison colleges. Each college in the list was chosen because of its similarity to one of the four Claremont colleges in the study. Factors considered were enrollment, annual expenditures, academic reputation, selectivity of admissions processes, faculty compensation level, assets, endowment, tuition, type of student body, and curricular emphasis. Of course, no two colleges are exactly comparable with respect to all of the variables mentioned, but the colleges were matched as closely as possible and eighteen were finally selected for use in the study. For Harvey Mudd College, only two colleges were satisfactory for comparison purposes. For each of the other Claremont colleges, five colleges were chosen for the comparison group. For overall comparisons, an Ivy League school was matched to the total Claremont group on the variables mentioned.

Although an attempt was made to measure the level of service received as well as cost, no judgments were made concerning the quality of some of the particular services, for example, that received at a college infirmary, or of the quality of the holdings of or the staff services rendered through the library. Some judgments of this type were, however, implicit in the selection of the institutions to be included in the study.

Various documents from the eighteen comparison colleges were studied further, with special attention being given to annual financial reports. Because of the arcane and seemingly infinite variety of techniques of accounting for monies received and spent, each comparison college was visited by one of the investigators to go over the data with the chief financial officer as well as to discuss appropriate areas under study with other college staff members as required. The decision concerning the specific function or activities to include in each category (library, health services, and so on) was reached after much discussion with those persons. Their judgment of the best way to distribute costs in each case for their own college, based on the distribution of personnel time and the functions performed by individuals and offices, identified costs more accurately than otherwise would have been possible.

All of the comparisons in the study are based on a three-year average (1964–65 through 1966–67) unless otherwise noted.

Colleges in the comparison group for Pomona are referred to as "Coed Colleges," for Scripps as "Women's Colleges," for Claremont Men's (CMC) as "Men's Colleges," and for Harvey Mudd (HMC) as "Engineering Colleges." "The Claremont Colleges" (CC's) refers to all five undergraduate colleges plus the Claremont Graduate School, and its comparison is referred to as "Ivy."

Each joint service area included in the study is considered separately. The first service to consider is the library. Costs of college libraries can be divided into two categories: operation of the library (referred to as "costs" in this report), and book purchases (referred to as "expenditures for books"). The results of the study indicated that the cost per student in the comparison colleges decreases as the size of the student body increases, at least up to about 1,000. The trend then reverses and moves upward to that of the Coed Colleges and Ivy (see Figure 13). Scripps College supports

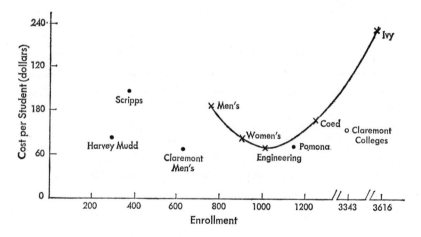

FIGURE 13. Cost of operation of the library per student plotted against enrollment.

a library of its own as well as a share of the central library and therefore has higher per student costs than the other Claremont colleges.

It is important to examine what resources and services are provided for the costs referred to above. One measure of the resources available to the students is the number of volumes per student (books, micro editions, bound journals and serials, excluding documents). For services available, two that can be measured fairly objectively are the number of volumes circulated per student and hours the library is open per year.

When volumes per student are plotted against enrollment, the same pattern as seen in Figure 13 emerges.

The service measure of hours open per year shows a fairly strong positive relationship to cost per student, but there is no relationship between cost per student and volumes circulated per student. We could reasonably expect a relationship between these latter two since number of volumes circulated per student is a service measure, that is, reflects activity level for the library staff. However, the number of volumes circulated is affected by a number of such factors as adequacy of reading rooms in the library, circulation policy, whether stacks are open or closed, reserve book policy, size and adequacy of the library collection, as well as nature of the student body. It is interesting to note that no relationship was found between the number of volumes circulated per student and either the number of volumes per student or the number of students.

As can be seen in Figure 13, The Claremont Colleges' composite cost for the operation of the library is at about the midpoint of the comparison colleges' costs. This also holds for the variables of volumes per student, volumes circulated per student and hours open per year. Whereas the number of volumes per student overall for the CC's is about average, the total number of volumes available is larger than for most colleges the size of individual Claremont colleges; that is, each student at HMC, Scripps, and so on, has access to a wider variety of volumes than is true of students in most colleges with enrollments of 300–1,200.

Turning now to expenditures for books, the pattern for comparison institutions is one of decreasing per student expenditures as enrollment increases up beyond 1,000; then the trend reverses (the same pattern, again, as shown in Figure 13). In summary, the library costs of the *individual* Claremont colleges are lower than those of the individual comparison institutions, all of which of course do not have access to the resources and services available to The Claremont Colleges.

Considering the individual colleges, Scripps and HMC show higher per student costs than their comparison groups but have only one-half and one-third the enrollment respectively. Pomona and CMC are slightly smaller than their comparison groups, but show less per student costs. Scripps, HMC, and CMC costs fall well below the cost line of comparison institutions. Since each college in the cluster derives some advantage of size from the group, per student costs decrease at lower enrollment levels for the individual cluster colleges.

The per student costs and overall costs tend to parallel pretty well the measures of resources and services, showing generally that "you get what you pay for." From the point of view of each individual college in the cluster, however, it is at the service level of the group for the per student cost of the group, thereby achieving a cost advantage compared to individual operation. Although The Claremont Colleges overall demonstrated a lower group cost for library services than did its group comparator, Ivy, one would normally expect that the Claremont group costs would not be substantially more favorable than the costs in most universities of the same size.

A word should be said about the increase in per student costs when colleges exceed a certain size. Again looking at Figure 13, the per student costs are seen to increase when enrollment exceeds approximately 1,000 to 1,100. Perhaps when libraries reach a certain size, increasing emphasis is placed on special collections, rare books and out-of-print editions. This would increase the cost of book purchases per volume while lowering the volumes per student and very likely increasing the cost per student. This same type of reversal of cost per student for the larger colleges will be noted in some of the other areas studied.

The second joint service to consider is the business office. The business office for The Claremont Colleges charges for services on the basis of a formula which weights equally total assets, endowment, tuition and fees income, and total annual expenditures of each of the colleges involved. These items, which overlap considerably, are believed by the presidents and treasurer to represent fairly accurately the costs incurred by the business office for handling the financial affairs of each college. The amounts of these four items are added together for each college and that total, as a percentage of the totals of all the colleges, represents the individual college's share of the business office expense (with some extra charges being made for handling special funds such as trust deed loans). The amount paid by each Claremont college was considered in this study to be the cost of operation of the business office for that college.

For all comparison colleges included in this study, the same four factors were used to compute the number of dollars handled by the business office for the college. When the cost per thousand dollars handled is plotted against total dollars handled, all of the comparison colleges fall into a pattern of decreasing unit costs with increasing volume of money handled. This relationship is stronger than that between cost per thousand dollars and enrollment; that is, size of college seems to be less related to this cost than is the activity level.

Each Claremont college and The Claremont Colleges as a group show lower costs than any of the comparison groups. Three of the four are quite low in terms of dollars handled, but this does not get translated into higher costs, probably because they are part of a larger business operation. There may be some reason to examine the rationale for the method of computing charges for business office services within The Claremont Colleges (for example, "Does it cost as much to handle $1000 of endowment as it does to handle $1000 of tuition and fees?"); nevertheless, overall, the central operation appears to have a financial advantage over the individually operated college business offices of comparison institutions.

The third area of joint services to consider is health and medical services. At The Claremont Colleges, records of treatment are not separated by colleges and therefore information concerning the individual colleges is not available for comparison, but that for the group can be ascertained and compared. One of the comparison engineering colleges had no health services and that group was, therefore, omitted from this study. Ivy was also eliminated from the comparisons because costs and services for this area could not be clearly identified at that institution.

The cost per student for health services for the various

groups of colleges ranged from thirty to forty dollars. The larger colleges (Coed and CC's) had lower unit costs than the smaller colleges (Men's and Women's). The cost per visit to the health service varied from a low of $4.73 (Coed colleges) to $6.46 (Claremont Colleges), $7.11 (Men's colleges) and $8.49 (Women's colleges). On this measure the colleges fall in the same order as on cost per student.

Students typically pay for health services on a per student basis (health fee) rather than by the visit, and on this basis (cost per student) the larger numbers (enrollments) correlate with lower unit costs. In the case of The Claremont Colleges, this low cost is associated with high service in terms of doctor duty hours per student.

For health services then, it seems that a larger combined center such as is available at The Claremont Colleges does provide cost savings and can present a more favorable situation than that at most individual colleges.

A fourth joint services area to be considered is the psychological clinic and counseling center. Of the eighteen comparison colleges in this study, only eleven had psychological services. Seven of the nine colleges with enrolments over 1,000 had such services, but only four of the nine with enrollments under 1,000 had them. There was no relation between total enrollment and the amount of money spent for the services except that The Claremont Colleges and Ivy, with by far the largest enrollments, spent considerably more for psychological services. The cost per student tended to decrease as enrollment increased up through 1,250, with a reversal taking place for The Claremont Colleges and Ivy.

Given the wide range of services available in the various colleges and the limited information concerning costs, no conclusions can be drawn regarding cost advantages to cluster or non-cluster colleges. Some speculation is possible, however, based on the experience of the eighteen comparison colleges. For example, it is unlikely that Harvey Mudd College, with less than 300 students, would have psychological services of any kind if it were not part of a cluster of colleges. Scripps and CMC would individually have about a 50 per cent chance of having such services. Pomona, as a separate, independent college, very likely would have a psychological clinic and counseling center which would offer fewer services than are now available to the students and which would cost slightly less per student.

Maintenance and repair constitutes a fifth area of joint services. For the Men's, Women's, and Engineering colleges, the situation observed was clearly a decrease in per student costs as enrollment increases. The Coed Colleges and Ivy, with the largest enrollments, show a reversal of the trend. This is probably the result of the need to maintain at the larger colleges large auditoriums, campus centers, and other facilities not usually found on smaller college campuses. Although student body size may generally reflect the amount of maintenance activity to be carried out, it would be more accurate in this case, to relate maintenance costs directly to square footage of buildings maintained and number of acres maintained. Acreage figures were uniformly available but information concerning total square footage of college buildings maintained was, with few exceptions, unavailable. Acreage figures alone are not helpful since colleges that have approximately the same number of students and buildings vary considerably in acreage. Concerning maintenance, there was insufficient information available to determine any cost advantage for cluster or non-cluster operation.

With respect to the colleges and the joint service areas included in this study, it appears that for some of them (library, business office, health services) there are advantages in a central operation. These advantages include cost benefits or economies as well as increased resources, in terms of both quantity and variety of services available. The advantages derived from the combined or central operation in the cluster college result from the individual small colleges having the size advantage of the group which permits unit costs to decrease at lower enrollment levels. Individual independent colleges, large or small, receive only what they can individually support.

This brief look at cost comparisons at one cluster group and eighteen non-cluster colleges indicates that a much clearer picture of the operations of both types of colleges is needed. More extensive studies need to be conducted in this area to include more clusters of colleges, a wider range of independent (non-cluster) colleges, plus state and church-related institutions. More meaningful cost and service measures must be developed. Some of the measures used here may prove to be adequate for some purposes or may help to point the way to much needed operational definitions for use in cost-service comparisons.

Despite the obvious need for more work on the questions of the extent of and conditions most suitable for academic cooperation between cluster colleges, and the presently achieved and potential cost savings possible through group action, it is safe to say that the Claremont experiences to date have demonstrated that voluntarily associated, privately controlled cluster colleges can work cooperatively to achieve an academic community and level of economy needed by many of the isolated, faltering colleges in our country today. Further work is needed and other types of cooperative ventures may bring even greater advantages in some situations, but surely the Claremont experience should be heartening to many.

Chapter 10

Problems Created and Resolved

Jerry G. Gaff

Insight into the nature of an organization may be obtained by examining its problems as well as noting its successes. Although cluster colleges seem to have enjoyed at least short term success, they also have met with difficulties. This chapter explores several of the problems which cluster colleges have encountered, especially those problems which seem endemic to these schools. The problems fall into three general categories: those stemming from their developmental stage, those surrounding the implementation of their plans, and those emanating from their own innovations.

One of the most important things to be said about cluster colleges is that the nature and quality of life on their campuses change over time. During their early years most cluster colleges are characterized by a great deal of enthusiasm and optimism. Everyone is excited about the new venture and a spirit of innovation fills the air. In a study of experimental colleges, Watson (1964, p. 97) has noted:

> Any new experimental school is a kind of utopian project. Its organizers seldom wish to advance a limited reform—they plan to introduce a new integrated whole. Each sets out to design the best combinations of the many good features of schools known to the founders. The new school is a dream come true.

The innovative spirit found on most campuses can perhaps be labeled utopian. The schools have embodied the vision of the early planners, and that vision has lured faculty and students with its cogent criticisms of the status quo, with its contemporary and creative alternative structures, and with its promises of offering a better educational world.

In order to use the term *utopian* as an analytic tool to understand the spirit of this new school, an ideal type will be created.[1] This ideal type will contain the major features of utopianism, and although it will not accurately describe any single school, it may be useful as an intellectual device for understanding qualities of utopianism wherever it occurs. The concept contains several distinct but interrelated dimensions:

A utopia is based on widespread and deeply felt dissatisfaction with the contemporary scene; the current disorders are thought to be so severe that they cannot be overcome by piecemeal adjustments. The evils necessitate an entirely new way of life.

The new design calls for the solution of the present evils by adopting entirely new structures. Though the innovators have had no experience with their proposed revisions, they assume that their own moral order will be far better than the present system.

The utopia at its best is a work of art. The various threads of the design are woven tightly together, each strand blending with the rest and each reinforcing the entire fabric. This holistic structure

[1] The previous work of Goodwin Watson (1964; 1966) was helpful to the author in refining this ideal type, although most of the ideas presented here have been developed independently of his work.

tends to resist change, for a change in any part threatens to undermine the entire enterprise.

The utopia on paper is an abstract of the "perfect order." In its Platonic form, the plan tends to assume perfect motivation of all individuals. Naturally, the ideal may suffer some distortion as it is translated into reality.

The new creation, being in opposition to the established order, must not risk contamination; it must be sharply set apart from the corruption around it. Outsiders tend to be viewed with scorn or contempt, occasionally mixed with pity, and they are regarded by loyalists within the protective confines of the isolated colony as lacking their own purity of heart.

In direct proportion to its rejection of those without, the utopia succeeds in uniting those within. The internal cohesiveness is gained in large measure from its rejection of those without.

The high moral aims of the new organization generate the commitment needed to achieve them; the new faith welds its members together and directs their common efforts toward the realization of the common goals. Vast amounts of potential energy are released, and the utopians can accomplish many of their high purposes.

Life in a utopia is amazingly rewarding. As utopians drive themselves to achieve their moral aims, they obtain great human fulfillment. They receive not only happiness but perhaps the greatest rewards of all; a deep feeling of personal worth and a sense of pride in their work, work which is assumed to be a contribution to the betterment of mankind.

Because they live in an ideal world, utopians fail to notice facts which tend to disconfirm their beliefs. When deviations within the group become so gross as to command attention, the evils may be attributed to weaknesses of individuals rather than to any deficiency in the system. Because the unfaithful represent a threat to the entire community, they may be treated harshly and often banished from the circle of the elect.

In a utopia individuals are not inclined to question their purposes. Nor is there any need to obtain knowledge about the consequences of those purposes or of the structures which they dictate. Those purposes and practices are self-justifying—they are matters to be accepted on faith. To question those bases of the moral order or even to insist on obtaining empirical knowledge about them constitutes heresy.

Because the original design cannot be implemented exactly as conceived, because even the best plan fails to account for every contingency, because there are unanticipated consequences, and because utopians tend to be hostile to empirical knowledge, preferring rather to solve their problems simply by re-proclaiming their first principles, the history of most utopian settlements has not been a happy one.

Deferring for a moment the application of this analytic typology to the cluster colleges, it must be pointed out that utopian thinking abounds in the literature on higher education. Statements by militant students on many campuses, books by outspoken critics like Goodman (1964), articles by competent researchers like Katz and Sanford (1965), and government publications by thoughtful men like Hatch (1960) all document a growing list of evils in the present educational machinery and make numerous proposals, practically all untried by them, to overhaul the existing equipment. These national utopians tend to assume that all will be well in higher education if only their entirely reasonable proposals calling for a new grading system, more independent study, less emphasis on collegiate fun-type activities, a greater emphasis on the interrelatedness of knowledge, smaller educational units, more teacher-student contact, and the like would be implemented. Because American higher education has been so often cut out of the same mold, few have had any substantial experience with these proposals; since they lack detailed knowledge about their most reasonable alternative plans, even the most rational of men may be made into utopians. Their proposals often are advanced with hopes and sometimes with a fervor which belies their idealism. In the wake of the recent burgeoning national discussion concerning the state of higher education, the cluster college planners have been able to draw upon many of these largely untried proposals, blend them together, and design a whole college in which these ideas could be given a full and fair trial.

While it is possible to affirm with Watson that "any new experimental school is a kind of utopian project," cluster colleges tend to become more utopian than most. Because they are semi-autonomous colleges located on a campus with other, often established and conventional, schools, the pioneers not only struggle to eliminate the abstract problems of the conventional system but tend to concretize those problems by pointing to them in the rest of the university. Erikson's concept of an identity crisis, although meant to refer to individuals, offers utility in describing this institutional phenomenon. A new cluster college as a fledgling school must be concerned with creating an institutional identity. One of the ways a positive identity can be created according to Erikson (1962, p. 102) is first to form a negative identity, that is, an image of what one would not like to be under any circumstance. Thus, a cluster college can establish its own identity by creating an image of inadequate undergraduate education, by assuming it abounds at colleges throughout the country, and by concretizing that symbolic evil in more traditional portions of the university. After making the neighboring colleges into a negative identity, the cluster college's reformism within the structure of a collegiate university does contribute to its utopianism. The negative identity phenomenon is more widespread when a single small subcollege is appended to a long-established larger university; it appears to be less common at universities composed entirely of similarly sized colleges. In the latter situations the all-university departments are the chief adversaries of cluster colleges rather than other colleges.

A brief recounting of life during the formative years of one new college will illustrate this utopian mentality. The purposes of the school were expounded repeatedly by the provost in speeches which blended the style of Protestant evangelism with the contents of persuasive educational philosophy. These ideals, echoed by many, were a call to arms. The faculty responded by devoting great attention to creative structuring of their courses and to filling them with relevant content. Their frequent and enthusiastic contact with students in a variety of academic and nonacademic situations, their involvement in independent study projects, and their frequent, lengthy, and often intense faculty meetings in which they conscientiously endeavored to make policies which met the needs of the students were visible indices of their commitment. Indeed, their involvement did not cease at the edge of the campus; faculty members often met socially as well, and more often than not, their conversations centered on the new school.

Students too responded to the clarion call. The promise of being somehow better educated than students in other colleges motivated them to accept the challenge of the core curriculum, to endure daily classes with the added burden of seminar participation, and to pursue the heavy reading and writing assignments. Almost unmercifully they structured, fractured, and restructured their minds and their selves in a never-ending cycle as they encountered new knowledge and new people and as they searched for the relevance of these encounters for their own lives.

The entire community was brought together weekly by the collective ritual of the all-college dinner and program. In addition, there were periodic formal gatherings of the school as in annual faculty research lectures and the yearly awards banquet. Informally there were frequent town meetings of most of the group to thrash out common problems and an occasional off-campus retreat in which significant portions of both faculty and students discussed matters of concern to the entire community.

During the time the utopian mentality prevailed, the faculty and students tended to see themselves, in the words of one professor, "as rebels against an imagined monolithic status quo." Most were only vaguely cognizant of the historic innovations of Gilman at Johns Hopkins, Eliot at Harvard, Meiklejohn at Wisconsin, or Hutchins at Chicago; the more recent efforts at Reed, Antioch, or Sarah Lawrence; or the contemporary experiments at schools like New College in Florida, Florida Presbyterian College, or other cluster colleges. This relative isolation from the historical developments, from the contemporary reform movements, and even from the life on the "other side of the campus" produced a collegiocentric view. The new cluster college and it alone was engaged in a pioneering struggle against mighty odds to overcome the inertia of tradition, to rejuvenate the local campus, and to renew the increasingly important institution of higher education throughout the land. Although this account is taken from one school, there is abundant impressionistic and anecdotal evidence that it is typical of the early years of most of the cluster colleges in this study.

This utopian spirit has definite utility in establishing a new school. It simplifies a most complex state of educational affairs, identifies the evils, promises a minor apocalypse, and mobilizes people to innovate. And to a considerable extent it functions as a "self-fulfilling prophecy." Other things being equal, the initial success of many of these schools, as evidenced in some of the statistical data reported earlier, may be proportional to the degree of their utopian mentality.

Despite the fact that participants of a utopian colony prefer to live in their faith world, the real world eventually presses upon them. Inevitably they gain experience, both good and bad, expected and unexpected, with the consequences of their creation. Knowledge of the effects of their venture destroys the previous myths. Maturity and experience mellow participants, and the college slowly changes.

Watson (1966) has observed that many experimental colleges have collapsed after their utopian adventure spent itself. New College at Columbia, Black Mountain, and the Experimental College at Wisconsin all lasted about seven years; they fell during their post-utopian period after they had made excellent records in their early years. One of the subcolleges has been phased out of existence before graduating its first class by being reassimilated into the larger and older portion of the school and a few others appear to be resting on a weak foundation. Some of the reasons for the short lifespan of schools following periods of radical innovation may be discerned by looking at the stresses created during the utopian phase, for the chief task of the post-utopian stage is to correct the excesses of the early years in the light of knowledge about their consequences. Again in order to highlight these problems an ideal type of post-utopian stage of development will be constructed and a few observations will show how the post-utopian tensions affect life at some cluster colleges. Again this is a logically interrelated series of fairly extreme statements which should not be taken for an accurate description of any one or all cluster colleges.

One of the most pressing problems of the post-utopian stage is to maintain continuity in the face of a turnover of participants. Watson (1966, p. 5) notes:

> A typical formation in the experimental college faculty is a core group consisting of the Founding Father (or Fathers)

surrounded by an inner circle of close admirers and collabora-
tors. Further from this core are numerous additions and newcomers needed for institutional operation, but to whom the
original vision has not been well communicated.

This formation poses two problems of continuity—the replacement
of the leader and the addition or replacement of faculty.

The community is placed under considerable stress when
its leader takes his charisma and leaves their midst. He symbolizes
the new venture, and they have come to be dependent upon him in
numerous often recognized ways for leadership; his departure
leaves a void and considerable insecurity within the group. And,
of course, it is always impossible to find an entirely suitable replacement for the innovative leader; his successor inevitably pales
from the contrast for a period of time. One of the reasons the successor has difficulty succeeding the founder is that he is usually a
quite different kind of person; he is a manager of an established
enterprise and not a visionary leading his flock to a promised land.

The followers too pose a problem of continuity. As the college expands or as some of the original cast are replaced, the new
faculty may be less committed to the kind of school they find. The
ideals may not be so well communicated, the purposes can never
have the same driving power, and the rationale behind some of the
practices is never entirely clear to the newcomers. And the new
faculty will certainly have ideas of their own which they would like
to impose upon what they assume to be an experimental school;
though these new ideas are to be expected and though they may be
actual improvements, they may pose threats to the veterans of the
school. In this situation the original faculty, the wild-eyed radicals
of the recent past, may be suddenly transformed into beleaguered
conservatives, vigorous defenders of their own *status quo*. For some
period of time an innovative program may tend to be seen as
poured in concrete, it may be even more impervious to change than
a less innovative school.

The purposes of the college increasingly lack their previous
motivational power. The new leader, having a more administrative
bent, is less inclined to espouse the ideals and to use them as a call
to arms. The faculty, like the barnyard creatures of *Animal Farm,*
find it increasingly difficult to recall exactly what the first principles

were; under the most reasonable questioning of the new faculty members and new students, they may be hard put to justify some practices. When the ideals are mentioned, they lack their original motivation power. Because both faculty and students have had some experience with these purposes and structures, they lack the moral purity they possessed when they were first sounded. Some participants even may think that those who proclaim the original institutional ideals are hypocritical; for them the resounding purposes actually turn them against the school.

The community is slowly transformed from a sparkling new order to a continuing organization. The thrill of creating a new institution cannot be matched by the effort of managing the not-quite-so-new system. Here the excesses of the earlier era, especially the heavy work load of the faculty, become serious. While the faculty could willingly endure the pressures of intense student-oriented teaching during the period of utopian idealism, they certainly will not do so in the light of the post-utopian realism. Their professional sacrifices, though tolerable during an earlier era, are less and less defensible. The institution learns that if its innovations are to work the way they were envisioned, they will be costly, more costly than imagined during the heydays of the revolution.

The illusions of the earlier day lead to a certain amount of disillusionment. The original hopes could never have been entirely fulfilled; the new venture could never be so radically different from all other institutions as the founders dared to dream. Inevitably, the day of reckoning must come. As evidence shows that the new school is only partially successful in realizing their hopes, as the school is seen to be more like other colleges, and as its innovations become institutions, the faculty members ask, "Was it all worth it?" The answer can only be, "partially," for the utopian dreams are never entirely within reach. Often this realistic assessment leads to an element of self-pity for the personal sacrifices the utopians had made earlier and perhaps even to some resentment over what some may come to regard as their previous folly.

The group becomes more fragmented. The failure of the ideals to unify the group, the increased feeling that the group is not so radically different as it had once imagined, the retreat into greater privatism by the previously over-involved faculty, and the modification of the original vision as a result of knowledge gained, all tend to destroy the intense cohesiveness of the earlier period. This very fragmentation may, if extensive and prolonged, accelerate a decline from the earlier society and create a vicious circle which may reduce the college to the very traditionalism against which it originally rebelled.

The society may lose support from the outside. If the experiment occurs in a college embedded within a larger institution, the university may devote both attention and financial aid to the new program for a period of time until it can stand on its own. But the central university administration may see evidence during the utopian phase that the college has established itself and may attempt to reduce financial and other types of support at precisely the time it is most needed, that is, when the psychic rewards of the utopian period no longer suffice. By this action the university may unwittingly weaken the school at the peak of its achievement.

Also, the more powerful elements of the university may have absorbed all of the criticism from the upstart school they could tolerate, and those factions may find the college in the post-utopian stage more vulnerable internally and less staunchly defended by the all-university administration. Hence, they may be able to bring their power to bear to further intensify the pressures on the cluster college at a critical stage in its history.

As this typology suggests, the problems of the college in the post-utopian stage of development are largely those of correcting the excesses of the utopian phase. While the utopian spirit fosters the successful creation of a radically innovative college, it creates the basic problems of the succeeding historical stage. Utopianism may help establish a college, but as other schools have learned, this spirit may be harmful to its longevity.

A second set of problems faced by cluster colleges is that of trying to create an operational intellectual community which approximates their idealized image of that concept. When a new college is announced, especially if it is to be an innovative one, it tends to attract faculty and students who are dissatisfied with usual procedures and who see an opportunity to help make a college in their own image. There are inevitably unarticulated differences among the members of the group, and as hard decisions about policy matters must be made, disagreements result. These differences may be intensified by the heightened level of expectation each person has and by the contrast with the earlier perceived consensus among participants. More is needed to unite a community than opposition to the conventional procedures, and positive actions make a certain amount of divisiveness. For example, one subcollege found its faculty divided into two camps, each committed to different views about the way an innovative college should be run. The conflict became so severe that college faculty meetings had to be eliminated and business was conducted through meetings of divisions.

Some cluster colleges have discovered that it is particularly difficult to build an undergraduate college in those places it is most needed, that is, in universities dominated by research and graduate training. Faculty of cluster colleges in these settings often have dual appointments in both the colleges and an all-university department; sometimes they are merely "loaned out" to a cluster college. These arrangements tend to remove the faculty from the orbit of the college and to prevent their total involvement in the life of the college, for such part-time professors may have to teach courses, supervise graduate students, and continue to take part in the politics of their department. The difficulties inherent in making a successful subcollege are aggravated by the reward structure of these universities. Typically, faculty who primarily teach undergraduates in these universities are less likely than their colleagues to receive promotions or salary increases, and such practices are a threat to the concept of cluster colleges. Even in the universities where the reward structure does support faculty who teach in subcolleges, faculty members may feel the need to continue to engage in research and scholarly activities to ensure their professional mobility. All of these pressures militate against the establishment of subcolleges in the largest and most prestigious universities.

One of the primary ways a subcollege attempts to build an intellectual community is through a common core curriculum. Yet some schools have found it difficult to maintain an effective core curriculum. Sometimes students find it too confining, faculty disagree about the appropriate content, and personal rivalries or conflicts develop among the teaching faculty. These may be some of the reasons why one university with three subcolleges witnessed a decrease in the number of core courses in each successive college from six to four to three; then within two years the third college eliminated even those three.

If it is difficult to effect a community, it is also difficult to effect the kinds of significant innovations to which cluster colleges aspire. This is so for several reasons. First, a subcollege appended to an existing college must be granted some independence from the prevailing rules, procedures, and conventions of the university if it is to make any significant break with the past; some schools have been denied such autonomy. For example, some subcolleges must gain permission to add or alter courses from all-university curriculum committees, adhere to existing policies, and enforce university-wide student rules and regulations. To the extent that colleges are locked into existing procedures, they have little freedom to initiate important innovations.

Other cluster colleges seem to have autonomy, but they fail to implement innovations either because their planners were satisfied with conventional ways or because they lack the imagination or courage to do anything different. Just tinkering with a grading procedure or adding a few problem-centered courses cannot be regarded as very daring or significant innovations, yet that is about all that some cluster colleges which claim to be innovative have attempted.

But even after a school is once launched on a course of making substantive innovations, it often has trouble finding faculty members who are committed to those changes. In addition to being committed primarily to the teaching of undergraduates, faculty are needed who are competent and interested in interdisciplinary teaching, knowledgeable about practical social problems, willing to interact frequently and personally with students, and able to take some responsibility for administering their school. These are difficult requirements to fill during an age in which so many professors are interested in teaching graduate students, specialists in an academic subdiscipline, separated from societal problems, removed from students, and unconcerned with the governance of their schools. Accordingly, cluster colleges tend to seek out the mavericks of the profession. Some schools have looked for this type of professor in the few interdisciplinary graduate programs such as those offered by the Committees at Chicago, the Doctor or Social Science program at Syracuse, and the Department of Social Relations at Harvard. Others have taken a number of faculty from the ranks of the Peace Corps or other social action programs. More have recruited young faculty, those not yet fully socialized to the values of the profession. But occasionally a school will find itself with an innovative program on paper only to end up with a significant portion of its staff unwilling or unable to support it.

The various pressures which make it difficult for a school to build a community and to effect innovation also interfere with the plan to promote structured diversity on the campus. If a sub-unit of a larger whole is not able to deviate markedly from established routine, it cannot provide a significantly different environment. However, even rhetoric about building a different climate may be enough to attract a distinctive kind of student and faculty and their very presence may make the subcollege a qualitatively different place. It is problematic, however, how long such distinctiveness can be maintained if the rhetoric is not supported by actual practice.

One of the most serious problems in implementing a cluster college program is lack of funds. Notwithstanding the fact that sub-colleges can effect operating economies by tapping into the central services of the university and that federated colleges can save money while extending their resources, cluster college programs are expensive to operate. Their emphasis on close human relationships and individual instruction requires that they have a low faculty-student ratio, and in a period of academic inflation this means an expensive program. Unfortunately, trustees of some schools have required subcolleges to operate at the same level of expenditure as more conventional portions of the school. Despite the fact that they are attempting to do more than traditional schools in the same system by providing a vital undergraduate education while still serving research, graduate training, and social service needs, they are allotted no more funds with which to do those tasks.

Furthermore, some cluster colleges have run headlong into the fantastic though widespread economic assumption that it costs many times more to educate an advanced graduate student than a beginning freshman student. According to this principle, a campus with a large proportion of graduate students is entitled to a larger share of the system's budget than is a campus with a predominantly undergraduate student body. One campus with an undergraduate program organized around subcolleges found itself trapped by this reasoning and had to expand its graduate program simply to justify the number of faculty members it had. Doubtless this act will ultimately shift the emphasis from undergraduate to graduate education and undermine the ideal if not the reality of the colleges. Another campus was even worse off, for it discovered its graduate programs to be less popular than it had hoped. Thus, it could not add the relatively few graduate students which would have justified its number of faculty, and it had to admit many more undergraduates to justify its budget. This act increased the student-faculty ratio, and made instruction far more impersonal than the school had intended.

Several universities have discovered that cluster colleges are more expensive to operate than they had originally realized. Sometimes the private and small or moderate-sized universities found their already limited budgets became even more strained. Their problems sometimes have been increased because cluster colleges have not attracted enough students. This limited enrollment has been a problem especially for radically innovative subcolleges which have been attached to quite conventional and small schools. Such universities may not attract a sufficiently large or diverse group of students to allow the subcollege to operate at full capacity. Already one subcollege has been reassimilated into the parent school at least partly for financial reasons, and others have encountered more difficulty than they expected.

Even if cluster colleges are able to implement their programs reasonably well, they encounter other problems. Typically, the defects of an organization mirror its strengths. Thus it is that some of the most serious problems of cluster colleges derive from those very features which planners have purposely implemented to make them distinctive. The collegiate structure and the internal innovations adopted by these schools not only help alleviate some of the most serious difficulties facing contemporary colleges, but they produce their own special difficulties.

Most cluster colleges appear to have fostered a sense of

community, individualized instruction, and warm student-faculty relationships. However, the personal approach is responsible for some of their most serious problems. The emphasis upon a more personal approach to education has led in several of these schools to an inordinate concern with the human psyche, analysis of human encounters, and introspection. While all of these concerns are valuable and an important part of the educational experience, occasionally they have become extreme within the context of a whole college environment which values and emphasizes such matters. This extreme preoccupation with existential concerns tends to make a school into a cloistered college, one which leads students to focus excessively upon their own inner worlds. Martin (1968, p. 97) has observed that some students ". . . follow up the college's commitment to social and political analysis and the concomitant sensitivity to human relations with a relentless introspection that peels off the layers of the human psyche until its is raw and bleeding or until nothing is left."

Cluster colleges typically attempt to build a community as well as make education relevant to the needs of each student, but several have learned that these purposes are fundamentally antithetical. Students have taken up the call for personal relevance, and often this means experimentation with sex, alcohol, and marijuana and other drugs. Understandably some of these activities have led them into contact with the local police; and police raids have created more tension and conflict within the group. While most members of cluster colleges are quite permissive, the disruption of study and the involvement of the school in a public scandal have created deep dissension in more than one college. Those who favor "relevance" argue that each individual should be allowed to do his own thing regardless of the effects upon the rest of the group, while those who favor "community" argue for some minimal standards to which all members should adhere. For example, students in one school became so split over the widespread drug use that the sense of community was destroyed. Understandably, the divisiveness carried over into the classroom, interfered with seminar discussions, and impeded the academic program.

In addition, cluster colleges have had more than their share of college-wide crises. Their small size, the speed with which both information and rumors travel, and the widely shared concerns occasionally escalate a personal problem into a college crisis. Some schools have learned that in a close community the problems of one person come to be shared with others and may dominate the college for a period of time.

Cluster colleges have been critical of bureaucracy with its abundance of rules and regulations and have tried to replace it with a more personal approach. But they have discovered that there are problems with this approach too. When few rules exist, they tend to be made up after the fact, and regulations may be applied differentially to different individuals because of their unique circumstances. This procedure opens the way for capriciousness and permits factors extraneous to the germane issues to influence decisions concerning students. For example, one faculty sits as a group after each term to discuss what should be done with students who appear not to be doing well. Each member tells what he can about why a student is doing poorly, what might be done to help him improve, and what action the college should take to assist him. The professors are sincere, dedicated to the students' welfare, and willing to spend all necessary time to arrive at the best decision. It appears ideal. But in fact the criteria used in dismissing a student are not uniform, and new, perhaps arbitrary, criteria may be devised on the spur of the moment. Cluster colleges have learned that when "rule by law" is replaced by "rule by people," problems are created by the arbitrary and capricious decisions of even concerned and dedicated people. However, since these schools have attempted to provide education with a personal touch, it should be no surprise that some of their greatest problems center around personalities.

The cluster college has been shown to be a vehicle for innovation. Most of the new schools have adopted at least some new ideas, different structures, or particular practices which set them off from other schools in both the local and national context. While there is considerable variation among the schools, cluster colleges as a group are fairly innovative, in deed as well as in word.

But being innovative has led to several problems. An experimental college is one that dares to be different, but being different creates insecurity. This insecurity is expressed in a number of ways. Students wonder whether they will be as well prepared as they would have been if they had gone to a more traditional school or whether their degrees will mean as much; faculty worry about their own future job possibilities as they devote more time and energy to teaching than to research; administrators are concerned about how well their school will compare with others in terms of conventional criteria of excellence such as student test scores, scholarship winners, or graduate school admissions. In these ways the college may become an extension of the self for many of the participants. In some instances the school experiences a hardening of the innovations; it fixes upon its program as an experiment to end all experiments. Other schools launch a new program, try it for a short period of time, and in a short time completely revise that program in favor of some newer idea. Both the resistance to further change and the flitting from innovation to innovation represent alternative responses to the insecurity which characterizes young, unproven cluster colleges. And of course such tinkering contributes further to the insecurity of the participants.

When the schools are successful in producing a distinctive milieu, it may cause a kind of culture shock when freshmen arrive. For example, students long nurtured on structured education may find it difficult to cope with independent study, ungraded courses, and few social rules. Even when they know intellectually what to expect, they must learn existentially to work effectively in this very different kind of environment. In addition, there may be a reverse culture shock when they leave. Graduates thoroughly imbued with liberal intellectual biases are often unwilling or unequipped to work in the business world. If they elect to enter graduate or professional school, they frequently find these more conventionally structured places uninspiring. Playing the grading game, restricting their ideas within disciplinary boundaries, and listening to lectures alienates many cluster college graduates from graduate school; after their exciting undergraduate experience, graduate schools may be a drag. In either event, students must undergo a "debriefing" and relearn to get along in the "real" world again when they have the protective confines of cluster colleges.

The innovations have not been panaceas. As has been pointed out in several passages in this book, organizational arrangements which have been adopted to solve some problems create other, often unanticipated, problems. It should be no surprise that innovations designed to make education more personal create personal problems, that attempts to make education more flexible cause problems about coping in an unstructured environment, or that efforts to create diversity produce problems about differentness. But these have been surprises to some who have assumed that their own newly designed college will be that long-sought, perfect educational world.

In most instances where the collegiate structure has been employed it has led to real differences among the several schools. Especially where subcolleges are appended to an established university, they generally have created a distinctive image, attracted a special breed of student and faculty, and established a particular subculture within the university. To this extent the collegiate pattern appears to better meet the needs of a heterogeneous student body than the monolithic university.

But this very diversity produces several serious problems. Perhaps the most unsettling of all the problems is the discovery that pluralism often leads to conflict between the several schools. In federated colleges, especially where there are marked disparities in size, wealth, or quality of program, there may be inordinate concern over the relative status and power of each school in the group. In subcolleges the concerns are similar. For example, subcolleges located on existing campuses have been able to attract students who are both brighter and have more of an intellectual orientation than students on the main campus. This fact is probably the result of their smaller size, more limited mission, sharper image, and greater promise of free and intellectually stimulating atmosphere. Whatever its cause, one of the effects of this kind of diversity is to create pride on the part of the subcollege and jealousy on the part of those in the parent institution; both are feelings which tend to produce disharmony between the schools.

Subcolleges also usually attract a different breed of faculty member than is found in the conventional departments of the university, but a sound perceptual phenomenon accentuates whatever differences exist. Faculty in some subcolleges have come to see their colleagues elsewhere as stuffy, conventional, and irrelevant, while faculty in some established portions have come to see their colleagues in subcolleges as permissive, activist, and radical; each group tends to think the other has perverted the quality of education. Each group tends to absolutize its own particular view of students and faculty whose interests are dissonant with its structures. Several of the planners of new schools have been surprised at the criticism from some of the faculty, shocked at the "hippie" element within the schools, hurt by attacks by some student activists, or disappointed by the indiscreet use of sex or drugs. The primary architect of one school, for example, actually thought it would have no dropout problem. It was thought that if students were having academic difficulty they would be easily detected by their teachers in the normal course of their discussions, and both would work to correct their deficiency; planners could not conceive that students would voluntarily leave such a stimulating environment. Subsequently, the high dropout rate became a serious problem at that college. No single plan has yet successfully met the needs of all students.

These then are some of the problems faced by cluster colleges as they attempt to implement, cope with, and mature with their new form of organization. The problems are not unique to cluster colleges and not all cluster colleges face each of them, but they are widespread in these schools. The existence of problems should not be regarded as evidence against cluster colleges. Rather, knowledge about the kinds of difficulties an organization faces should provide insights about the nature of that organization. Since all schools have problems, perhaps one way to assess the effectiveness of a school is by the quality of the problems it creates. And the problems associated with the task of effecting significant innovations in colleges and universities are significant educational problems.

While cluster colleges have created new problems, they also have provided at least tentative solutions to some of the most serious problems facing American higher education today. As Kerr has said in the prologue quotation, "the improvement of undergraduate instruction will require the solution of many sub-problems," and cluster colleges have attempted some of those solutions:

The problem of giving adequate recognition to the teaching skills of the faculty can be resolved by creating colleges specially designed to provide an undergraduate education, attracting faculty members who are committed to this mission, creating a setting in which the effectiveness of teachers can be known by their colleagues, and giving provosts of the college a hand in deciding whether and how to reward professors.

The problem of creating a curriculum which serves the needs of students and faculty members can be resolved by offering a variety of curricula, bringing the disciplines to bear on an analysis of contemporary social problems, and by encouraging cross-disciplinary inquiry—all of the while allowing the usual curricula to continue to exist.

The problem of preparing the generalist in an age of specialization can be resolved by adopting core courses, encouraging students to go beyond the usual disciplinary categories, allowing students to supplement their academic learning with off-campus experiences, and requiring students to write integrative examinations or senior theses.

The problem of the student as an individual in the mass student body can be resolved by establishing small subcolleges on large campuses, individualizing instruction, and bringing him into closer contact with his teachers.

The problem of making the university seem smaller as it grows larger can be resolved by adding whole colleges rather than incorporating growth within existing structures. The problem of increasing the range of contact between faculty and students can be resolved by creating "living and learning" environments in which student experiences can enter the classroom and the intellectual context of the classroom can permeate student experiences.

The problem of raising educational policy to the forefront of faculty concerns can be resolved by articulating alternatives to the conventional practices, encouraging faculty members to try out the new teaching methods, and devising ways of sharing authority for policy decisions. These solutions are not likely to be final, but they are at least provisional solutions to the problems which Kerr and others have identified.

Furthermore, the best available evidence from the disciplined inquiries contained in this volume suggests that these solutions are viable.

The chapters by Newcomb and his associates and by Gaff have shown that subcolleges do foster a greater sense of community, encourage closer student-faculty relationships, and provide greater individual attention than do larger and undifferentiated portions of the same school. Cluster colleges do appear to be vehicles of innovation; Martin and Wilkinson have shown that faculty members are more favorable toward and knowledgeable about innovations, while Heist and Bilorusky have shown that students attracted to subcolleges are more supportive of flexible and individualized education than are students in other portions of the same university. The innovations have collectively produced the kind of intellectually stimulating and personally enriching environment planners desired, at least in the two schools studied by Newcomb and his associates and by Gaff. In addition, cluster colleges do provide structured diversity on a single large campus, as shown in various ways by all of the reports. The diversity within the entire campus is paralleled by a homeogeneity within the cluster colleges. Heist and Bilorusky have shown that homogeneity among students is the result of selective recruitment of freshmen, while Newcomb and associates have suggested that the cluster college experience may accentuate initial tendencies toward value similarity. Martin and Wilkinson have demonstrated that a similarity of values among faculty and students exists in cluster colleges. Evidence supplied by Stewart and Kells shows that a clustering of small colleges does extend the range of academic resources available to any one school, and that cooperative arrangements in a variety of central services and facilities provide both economic advantages and better services to all parties. Collectively, this assembled research gives impressive empirical support to the cluster college concept.

But to be perfectly clear about these results, they *do not* prove that the cluster college is superior to either the undifferentiated large university or the independent small college. This is so for several reasons. First, while the generally favorable results presented in the five research reports are valid, they fail to tell the whole story of cluster college life. To be sure, cluster colleges do appear to be generally successful, but they cannot be regarded as an unqualified success or as equally successful in all places. Wofford and Gaff have discussed a few of their problems and a balanced study must acknowledge these difficulties. Second, systematic research has been conducted on only a sampling of existing cluster colleges, and there is no certainty that such favorable results as presented in this volume are generalizable to all other settings. Indeed, there are important reasons to think that they may not be. For example, there are important differences between subcolleges and federated colleges, between subcolleges at research-oriented large universities and at teaching-oriented small colleges, and between single cluster colleges on a campus and multiple colleges. Third, it is not known what the short-term or long-term effects of these various educational programs are on their students. The projects headed by Heist and by Newcomb both are designed to learn how students change during their college careers, but neither of them has been completed yet. Of course, the long-term effects of college five, ten, or twenty years after students graduate are impossible to know at this time. The ultimate criteria—desirable changes produced in students, the persistence of these changes throughout life, and their long-term benefits to the person and to society—require years to apply systematically to a school, and information about the way cluster colleges measure up on them will be lacking for some time to come. Fourth, little is known about *why* the empirical results were obtained. Is it because of the fact of clustering or does the kind of clustering arrangement make a difference? What are the effects of cluster college size, the number of colleges at a single university, or the kind of procedures they adopt? Or perhaps the critical variables are not even these structural ones, which have been emphasized throughout this volume; perhaps process variables, the way structures are used, are more important. Or perhaps the favorable results were obtained only because of a self-fulfilling prophecy rather than because of the cluster college organization or the internal innovations these schools have adopted. Until some of these questions are answered more satisfactorily, understanding of the effects of cluster colleges will remain clouded. Finally, the studies reported here focus more upon cluster colleges than the total university context of which they are a part. Little is known, for example, about the impact of a cluster college upon the rest of the university. It may be that the grouping of students and faculty with similar interests may have deleterious effects caused by removing them from interaction with their peers in other colleges.

And yet when all is said and done—when one takes an overview of the results and limitations of the existing desciplined inquiry; when one assesses the experiences of students, faculty, and administrators; and when one looks at the problems both resolved and created—the cluster college concept emerges as a promising mechanism by which to place undergraduate liberal education once again at the center of the House of Intellect.

Bibliography

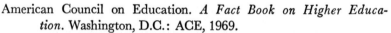

American Council on Education. *A Fact Book on Higher Education*. Washington, D.C.: ACE, 1969.

BELL, D. *The Reforming of General Education*. New York: Columbia University Press, 1966.

BENEZET, L. "College Groups and the Claremont Example." In L. Wilson (Ed.), *Emerging Patterns in American Higher Education*. Washington, D.C.: American Council on Education, 1965, pp. 199–202.

BOYAN, N. J. "Educational research and educational policy." Invited address at annual meeting of the American Educational Research Association, Los Angeles, February, 1969.

BRICK, M., AND MCGRATH, E. *Innovations in Liberal Arts Colleges*. New York: Teachers College, Institute of Higher Education, 1969 (Mimeographed).

BURNS, R. E. Speech delivered at College of the Pacific, 1959.

CLARK, B. R. "The New University," *American Behavioral Scientist*, May–June, 1968, pp. 1–4.

CLARK, B. R., AND TROW, M. "The Organizational Context." In T. M. Newcomb and E. K. Wilson (Eds.), *College Peer Groups: Problems and Prospects for Research*. Chicago: Aldine, 1966, pp. 17–70.

CRONBACH, L. J., AND SUPPES, P. (Eds.) *Disciplined Inquiry for Education,* cited in Boyan, N. J. "Educational Research and Educational Policy." Invited address at annual meeting of the American Educational Research Association, Los Angeles, February, 1969.

DARLEY, J. *Prediction and Performance.* Berkeley: Center for Research and Development in Higher Education, 1961.

DRESSEL, P. L. *Evaluation in Higher Education.* Boston: Houghton Mifflin, 1961.

ERIKSON, E. *Young Man Luther.* New York: Norton, 1962.

FELDMAN, K. A., AND NEWCOMB, T. M. *The Impact of College on Students.* San Francisco: Jossey-Bass, 1969.

GAFF, J. G. *Innovations and Consequences: A Study of Raymond College, University of the Pacific.* Stockton, Calif.: University of the Pacific. Final report to U.S. Office of Education for research project No. 6-1257, 1967.

GAFF, J. G. "Innovation and Evaluation: A Case Study," *Educational Record,* Summer 1969, pp. 290–299.

GOODMAN, P. *The Community of Scholars.* New York: Random House, 1964.

GRANT, W. V. "Number and Size of Institutions of Higher Education," *American Education,* August–September, 1969.

HATCH, W. *The Experimental College.* New Dimensions in Higher Education No. 3. Washington, D.C.: U.S. Government Printing Office, 1960.

HEIST, P. "Diversity in College Student Characteristics," *Journal of Educational Sociology,* 1960, pp. 279–81.

HEIST, P., AND YONGE, G. *Manual for the Omnibus Personality Inventory.* New York: Psychological Corporation, 1968.

HOWARD, L. C. "Is Higher Education Ready for the Negro?" In L. C. Howard (Ed.), *Interinstitutional Cooperation in Higher Education.* Proceedings of a conference at Wingspread, Racine, Wisconsin, March 3–4, 1967.

JENCKS, C., AND RIESMAN, D. "Patterns of Residential Education: A Case Study of Harvard." In N. Sanford (Ed.), *The American College.* New York: Wiley, 1962, pp. 731–73.

JOHNSON, E. L. "New Collegiate Options through Joint Action," *Liberal Education,* March, 1968, pp. 80–87.

KATZ, J., AND SANFORD, N. "Causes of the Student Revolution," *Saturday Review,* December 18, 1965, pp. 64–79.

KELLS, H. R. (Ed.) *The Cluster College Concept.* Reference book of contributed materials for the invitational conference on the cluster college concept at the Claremont Colleges, March 30–31, 1967.

KELLS, H. R. "A Significant Problem Deserving Study: The Cluster Colleges." In proceedings of the Eighth Annual Forum on Institutional Research, 1968, pp. 97–100.

KELLS, H. R., AND STEWART, C. T. "The Conference on the Cluster College Concept: Summary of the Working Sessions," *Journal of Higher Education,* April, 1968, pp. 359–363. (a)

KELLS, H. R., AND STEWART, C. T. "The Intercollegiate Program of Graduate Studies," *Journal of General Education,* 1968, *20* (1), 1–12. (b)

KERR, C. *The Uses of the University.* New York: Harper, 1963.

KULIK, J. A., AND REVELLE, W. R. "Hierarchical Clustering of Personality Variables." Unpublished manuscript. Ann Arbor: University of Michigan, 1969.

LAZARSFELD, P. F., AND THIELENS, W., JR. *The Academic Mind.* Glencoe, Ill.: Free Press, 1958.

Livingston College. Undated draft of the catalogue.

MARTIN, W. B. "Has the Revolution a Future?" Speech given at Raymond College, University of the Pacific, September 8, 1965.

MARTIN, W. B. "The Problem of Size," *Journal of Higher Education,* March, 1967, pp. 144–52.

MARTIN, W. B. *Alternative to Irrelevance.* Nashville: Abingdon, 1968.

MARTIN, W. B. *Conformity: Standards and Change in Higher Education.* San Francisco: Jossey-Bass, 1969. (a)

MARTIN, W. B. *Institutional Character in Colleges and Universities: The Interaction of Ideology, Organization, and Innovation.* Berkeley: Center for Research and Development in Higher Education, 1969 (Mimeographed). (b)

MASON, B. B. "Research on Students." Stockton: University of the Pacific, in progress.

MCCONNELL, T. R., AND HEIST, P. "The Diverse College Student Population." In N. Sanford (Ed.), *The American College.* New York: Wiley, 1962, pp. 225–52.

MCCOY, P. C. "The Forms of Interinstitutional Cooperation," *Liberal Education,* March, 1968, pp. 30–40.

MCFEE, A. "The Relation of Selected Factors to Students' Perception of a College Environment." Unpublished Master's Thesis, Syracuse University, 1959.

MCFEE, A. "The Relation of Students' Needs to Their Perception of a

College Environment," *Journal of Educational Psychology,*
1961, *52,* 25–29.

MCHENRY, D. E. "Small College Program for a Large University,"
College and University Business, July, 1964, pp. 31–33.

MERTON, R. "Manifest and Latent Functions." In *Social Theory and
Social Structure.* New York: Free Press, 1957.

MILLER, P. S. "Clearing the Way for Innovation," *Educational Record,*
Spring, 1967, pp. 138–43.

MOORE, R. S. "Cooperation in Higher Education." In L. S. Howard
(Ed.), *Interinstitutional Cooperation in Higher Education.*
Proceedings of a conference at Wingspread, Racine, Wiscon-
sin, March 3–4, 1967.

Nasson College. *Nasson College Bulletin: The New Division Catalogue
Issue,* NC, 1967–68.

NEVILLE, H. R. "The Individual in the Large University." Speech
delivered to National Association of State Universities and
Land-Grant Colleges, Columbus, Ohio, November 12–15, 1967.

NEWCOMB, T. M. "The General Nature of Peer Group Influence." In
T. M. Newcomb and E. K. Wilson, *College Peer Groups.*
Chicago: Aldine, 1966, pp. 2–16.

NEWCOMB, T. M., BROWN, D. R., KULIK, J. A., REIMER, D. J., AND RE-
VELLE, W. R. "A Small Residential Community Compared with
Three Control Populations." Unpublished manuscript. Ann
Arbor: University of Michigan, 1969.

Office of the Academic Vice-President. Memo concerning "A Possible
Academic Reorganization at Wesleyan," Wesleyan University,
November 10, 1967.

OLSON, L. A. "Residential Colleges in a Large University." In Proceedings of the Eighth Annual Forum on Institutional Research,
1968, pp. 87–90.

OLSON, L. A. "An Alternative Model: The Residential College." Paper
read at annual meeting of the American Personnel and Guidance Association, 1969.

PACE, C. R. *College and University Environment Scales: Preliminary
Technical Manual.* Princeton: Educational Testing Service,
1963.

PACE, C. R. *CUES Technical Manual—Revised.* Princeton: Educational Testing Service, 1969.

PACE, C. R., AND STERN, G. G. "An Approach to the Measurement of
Psychological Characteristics of College Environments," *Journal of Educational Psychology,* 1958, *49,* 269–77.

PATTILLO, M. M., AND MACKENZIE, D. M. *Eight Hundred Colleges Face the Future*. St. Louis: Danforth Commission on Church Colleges and Universities, 1965.

PUTNAM, F. W. "Interinstitutional Cooperation in the Natural Sciences," *Liberal Education*, March, 1968, pp. 41–53.

RADCLIFFE-MAUD, LORD. "Oxford and the Collegiate University Idea," *Journal of Higher Education*, 1967, pp. 11–22.

Raymond College. *Liberal Education and the Raymond Program*. Raymond College, 1963.

Residential College, University of Michigan. *The Residential College Announcement*. Ann Arbor: University of Michigan, 1967–68.

Select Committee on Education. *Education at Berkeley*. Berkeley: University of California, 1966.

SPURR, S. H. "Organization of the Liberal Arts in the Large University," *Journal of Higher Education*, 1968, pp. 11–22.

STERN, G. G. *Scoring Instructions and College Norms: Activities Index, College Characteristics Index*. Syracuse, N.Y.: Psychological Research Center, Syracuse University, 1963.

STEWART, C. T. *Studies of Cooperation in the Claremont Colleges: Academic Cooperation*. In Proceedings of the Seventh Annual Forum on Institutional Research, 1967, pp. 125–31.

STEWART, C. T., AND HARTLEY, J. E. *Financial Aspects of Interinstitutional Cooperation: Unit Costs in Cluster and Non-Cluster Colleges*. Claremont, Calif.: The Claremont Colleges, 1968.

SUMNER, W. G. "The Absurd Effort to Make the World Over." In A. G. Keller and M. R. Davie, *Essays of William Graham Sumner*. New Haven: Yale University Press, 1934.

TAYLOR, H. Letter cited in Select Committee on Education, *Education at Berkeley*, 1966, pp. 44–45.

TAYLOR, H. *Students Without Teachers: The Crisis in the University*. New York: McGraw-Hill, 1969.

TROW, M. "Undergraduate Teaching at Large State Universities," *Educational Record*, Summer, 1966, pp. 303–19.

TUSSMAN, J. *Experiment at Berkeley*. New York: Oxford, 1969.

University of California, Santa Cruz. *Undergraduate and Graduate Bulletin*, 1966–67.

WATSON, G. "Utopia and Rebellion: The New College Experiment." In M. Miles (Ed.) *Innovation in Education*. New York: Teachers College Press, 1964, pp. 97–115.

WATSON, G. "Some Notes on Experimental Colleges in America." Paper read at conference on Innovation in Higher Education sponsored by the Union for Research and Experimentation in Higher Education at Magnolia, Mass., May, 1966.

WISE, G. "Integrative Education for a Dis-Integrated World," *Teachers College Record*, March, 1966, pp. 391–401.

WHITEHEAD, A. N. *The Aims of Education.* New York: Macmillan, 1959.

Index

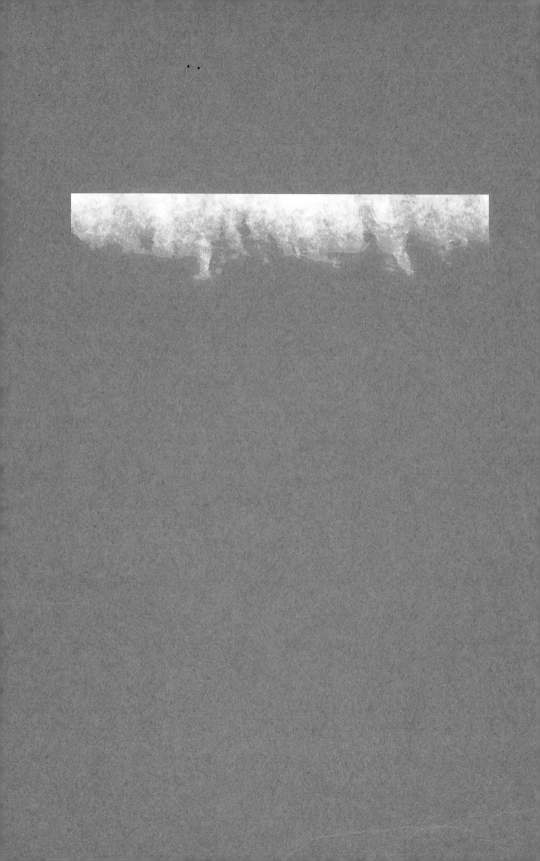